Memories of Absence

Memories of Absence

HOW MUSLIMS REMEMBER JEWS IN MOROCCO

Aomar Boum

STANFORD UNIVERSITY PRESS
STANFORD, CALIFORNIA

Stanford University Press
Stanford, California

Printed in the United States of America on acid-free, archival-quality paper

Library of Congress Cataloging-in-Publication Data

Boum, Aomar, author.
  Memories of absence : how Muslims remember Jews in Morocco / Aomar Boum.
     pages cm
  Includes bibliographical references and index.
  ISBN 978-0-8047-8699-7 (cloth : alk. paper)
  ISBN 978-0-8047-9523-4 (pbk. : alk. paper)
  1. Jews--Morocco--Public opinion. 2. Muslims--Morocco--Attitudes. 3. Collective
memory--Morocco. 4. Public opinion--Morocco. 5. Morocco--Ethnic relations--History.
I. Title.
  DS135.M8B69 2013
  964.00492'4--dc23   2013025713

  ISBN 978-0-8047-8851-9 (electronic)

Typeset by Bruce Lundquist in 9/15 Palatino

This book is dedicated to

Faraji, son of Lahcen; Mahira, daughter of Mohammed;
Norma Mendoza-Denton; and Majdouline Boum-Mendoza,

for their lifelong, unlimited support
and their unconditional love

Contents

Photographs follow page 76

Abbreviations

AIU	Alliance Israélite Universelle
CAM	Comité d'Action Marocaine
CCIM	Conseil des Communautés Israélites du Maroc
COM	Chaykh Omar Museum
ENH	École Normale Hebraïque
ENIO	École Normale Israélite Oriental
FJMCH	Foundation of Jewish Moroccan Cultural Heritage
FZF	French Zionist Federation
JDC	American Jewish Joint Distribution Committee
JMC	Jewish Museum of Casablanca
MN	Mouvement National
OSE	Oeuvre de Secours aux Enfants
PCM	Parti Communiste Morocain
PDA	Parti Démocratique Amazigh
PDI	Parti Démocratique de l'Indépendance
PNRR	Parti National pour la Réalisation des Réformes
PRN	Parti des Réformes Nationales
PUM	Parti de l'Unité Marocaine
SGP	Société de Géographie de Paris
UGSCM	Union Générale des Syndicats Confédérés du Maroc
UMT	Union Marocaine du Travail
UNEM	Union Nationale des Étudiants Marocains
UNFP	Union Nationale des Forces Populaires
USFP	Union Socialiste des Forces Populaires

Acknowledgments

Mostly written at Café Luce in Tucson, this book is the fruit of ten years of ethnographic and archival research, which took me to Morocco, France, and England. I am foremost thankful to my informants throughout southern Morocco for welcoming me inside their homes and granting me long hours of tedious interviews. Without the stories of these men and women, this book would have never seen light. I would like to express my appreciation to Ibrahim Nouhi, curator and owner of Chaykh Omar Museum, for allowing me to interview him over a period of three years and use his historical archives. I am also grateful to Mouloud and Lahoucine, my main ethnographic guides, for making my stay in Akka and its surrounding villages an easy experience.

I am indebted to the rigorous research oversight and advice of Thomas Park, whose mentorship still guides my scholarship and academic writing. Dr. Park has taught me how to think about social and cultural issues, and ask the right questions as an indigenous anthropologist and historian. Special thanks are owed to Daniel Schroeter, who guided me through the complex history of North African Judaism. Similarly, I owe a considerable debt to the late Michael E. Bonine, one of the best mentors I have had in my career. I wish he lived to see this manuscript in its final shape. I also acknowledge James Greenberg, Jane Hill, and Julia Clancy-Smith for their intellectual inspiration.

The University of Arizona has been generous in supporting my work, awarding me a Junior Faculty Leave to finish the manuscript. I am also grateful to my colleagues at the School of Middle Eastern and North African Studies, namely Scott Lucas, Yaseen Noorani, Leila Hudson, Adel Gamal, Maha Nassar, Amy Newhall, Kamran Talattof, and Samira Farwana. Edward Wright and Perry Gilmore deserve a special thank-you for their help. Outside the University of Arizona, many friends have always been there for advice. I am indebted especially to Sarah Stein, Bambi Schieffelin, Paul Silverstein, Oren Kosansky, Asli Igsiz, Frances Malino, Susan Slyomovics, Abdellatif Bencherifa, Robert Satloff, André Azoulay, Mohammed Kenbib, Jamaa Baida, Norman Stillman,

Sarah Levin, Susan Gilson Miller, Matti Bunzl, Doug Foley, Deborah Dwork, Dale Eickelman, Chouki El Hamel, Jonathan Entelis, Michael Brenner, Deborah Kapchan, the late Edmond Amran El Maleh, the late Simon Levy, Ethan Katz, Helene Sinnreich, Bruce Maddy-Weitzman, Asher Susser, Nils Bubandt, and Mark Graham.

I am also grateful to Kate Wahl, my editor at Stanford University Press, for her boundless support and clear instructions that shepherded me during every stage of the writing of the book. Thanks also to the staff at Stanford University Press, especially Frances Malcolm, for their help in the preparation of the book for publication. I also thank the reviewers for Stanford University Press for their constructive comments and suggestions. Anne Betteridge, Emily Gottreich, Thomas Park, and Norma Mendoza-Denton have contributed in different degrees to the final editing and improvement of the manuscript. Special thanks go to Luise Erdmann, my development editor, for making this book better.

Over the past six years, I presented different parts of the manuscript in the form of public lectures to students and colleagues in many academic institutions, and their feedback proved to be beneficial to rethinking and revising my final drafts. I thank the following institutions: UCLA, UC Berkeley, UC Davis, Portland State University, University of Maryland College Park, Columbia University, Lewis and Clark College, Wellesley College, Kent State University, Cornell University, University of Pennsylvania, Arizona State University, University of Arizona, Cambridge University, Duke University, University of North Carolina Chapel Hill, Université Tunis El Manar, University of Munich, Université Sorbonne, Youngstown State University, Yale University, and Al-Akhawayn University.

This book would not have been possible without the institutional support of many universities and foundations. The ethnographic and archival research for this work was partly funded by a Brandeis University–Tauber Institute Graduate Research Award, the CEMAT/TALM Fellowship for Maghribi Studies, the UCLA–Maurice Amado Foundation and the Memorial Foundation for Jewish Culture, and the United States Holocaust Memorial Museum Judith B. and Burton P. Resnick Fellowship.

Outside the academic family, I acknowledge the friendship and moral support of Ziad Fahmy, Abdessamad Fatmi, Mohammed Errihani, Jamal Faik, Mourad Mjahed, Nourreddine Bennani, and mostly Farzin Vejdani, for patiently listening, reading, and critiquing my work. I am thankful for the support of Rudy Mendoza-Denton, Ozlem Ayduk, Nezha Garimi, Kevin Funabashi, Barnet Pavao-Zuckerman, Mitchell Pavao-Zuckerman, Daniela Triadan, Dan McFatten, and Qing Zhang. Above all, I am grateful for the support of my extended family. I would like to acknowledge my brothers, Abdallah, Lahoucine, Mohamed, and Abderrahman; my sisters, Khadija, Kaltouma, Amina, and Zahra; and their respective families for their support throughout my schooling. Special thanks go to Abdeslam Ait-Tastift, my best friend in the world. My greatest acknowledgment is to my mother, Mahira; father, Faraji; wife, Norma; and daughter, Majdouline. Their wisdom, love, and sense of humor guide me.

At 12:45 P.M. on May 7, 2004, the temperature reached 115 degrees, breaking the previous day's record by two degrees. The mattress in my hotel room made it impossible to sleep. As I lay down on a wet sheet on the floor, I could still feel the heat radiating from the cement building. A dozen soldiers lined up across the hallway outside their rooms to take a cold shower in the only bathroom of the only hotel in the commune of Akka as they waited for the only bus heading north. The historical oasis of Akka, in the province of Tata in southern Morocco, is not far from the contested region of Western Sahara.

It had been a month since I had arrived in this remote region. I was one of the few customers who had stayed for more than a night in this five-room hotel. Located at the center of the administrative quarter of Akka, the hotel's dilapidated windows overlooked Tamdult, the long-gone center of trans-Saharan-trading caravans.[1] Throughout these hot days of May, sandstorms roared across the windswept eastern part of the neighboring Anti-Atlas Mountains. Specks of dust covered a folded worn-out blanket and a white plastic table in my room. Summer had already begun; the blazing heat and annoying sandstorms kept me from traveling that morning to the village of al-Qasba to interview a descendant of a Muslim judge about legal cases involving Jews and Muslims. I could not risk damaging my recording equipment, which was highly sensitive to dust.

My day usually started with an early breakfast in the hotel. After conducting one interview in the morning, generally in a villager's home, I walked back to my room unless someone forced me to stay for lunch. I tried to avoid lunching with my hosts because I wanted time to think about my interviews. A mid-day nap was a standard activity before leaving for late-afternoon interviews. When I could not sleep, I would join Omar, a Muslim in his mid-forties and the hotel's owner, for a cup of mint tea. That day, as it became difficult to close my eyes because of the heat, the stench, and the noise, I sought Omar's company. As I closed the squeaking door of my room on the second floor, the voice of

Jil-Jilala, a popular musical group from the 1970s, filled the hallway leading to the café downstairs. I sat on the stool by the counter as occasional strong winds drowned out the song. Yet a refrain continued to fill the air, as if the cassette had been stuck on this part of the song. As Omar ordered a ten-year-old busboy to clean a table that was attracting flies, a toothless man in his mid-fifties gulped down his hot mint tea and began humming the song's refrain:

> Oh, Arab! Oh, Muslim! Your state of affairs is painful.
> Zionists destroy the Mosque and you have given up.
> Oh, Arab! Oh, Muslim! When are you going to decide?
> Zionists destroy the Mosque, why are you still thinking?[2]

Like a number of musical groups of the 1970s and early 1980s, Jil-Jilala, along with Nass El-Ghiwane, Lamchaheb, and Essiham, produced songs about the Palestinian issue and the question of Jerusalem (al-Quds). These songs became national hits, reflecting the Moroccans' support for the Palestinians.

Yet, despite its dominating resonance, nobody seemed to pay attention to the song except the toothless man. Two soldiers slowly sipped their tea as they shared a Berber omelet. A group of children played games in the southern corner of the café. Outside the building, a demented man covered in rugs slept in the sun, not bothered by the heat. As one customer picked up a lemonade bottle from the counter, Omar turned around, served me a cup of tea, and interrupted the man's humming in a mocking manner:

"Since I came of age, the only story we have been hearing is the one of Zionists and Muslims! We have blamed everything on the French, Europeans, Christians, Jews, and Americans."

The toothless man abruptly stopped the Muslim and jokingly noted:

"You said that because you are Sharon! You think like Ariel Sharon! You are the only Jew left here in Akka. They left their trade for you!"

Throughout my stay in Akka, I overheard customers comparing Omar and Israel's former prime minister through funny, stereotypical comments about his short physique, hanging stomach, and broad shoulders. Omar had arrived in Akka in the 1980s, when a large Moroccan military regiment was stationed not far from the administrative center of the village to defend the eastern borders of Tata from the attacks of the Polisario's guerrilla. Tamdult, Omar's café and hotel, was the only place where stranded travelers could stay and eat. At the time, all the Jews had left Akka except the Sarraf family, which continued to play a major role in the economic life of the village. For instance, in the late 1970s, the Sarraf family worked with a Muslim descendant of a former slave from the neighboring village of Tizounine to build a modern oven to supply soldiers with bread.

As Omar grinned at the humorous statements of the man, who happened to be a descendant of the former *qaid* (tribal chief) of Akka, an adult in his mid-twenties shouted from a corner of the café as he smoked a cigarette:

"You are right, Hassan! Sharon [Omar] is probably the only man in Akka happy with the assassination of Ahmad Yassin, the leader of Hamas."

With a smirk on his face, Omar turned toward me and noted:

"Look, Aomar! Probably sixty years ago, before all the Jews left Akka for Israel, Hassan's parents were not only the neighbors of Jews but also their friends and trading partners. Now he blames the economic and political fall of his family on Jews and Israel."

Before Omar finished his statement, Ali, a regular customer in his late eighties, argued back in a faint but serious nostalgic tone that seemed to counter the laughter of the other customers:

"I wish Jews were still here. This was the largest Jewish settlement in the region. Jews from neighboring villages came here to pick up kosher meat. The day they left Akka, we lost the thriving religious and economic center Akka used to be. These kids never saw what we had; if they did, they would not be laughing."

I avoided expressions of approval or rejection to the drama staged before my eyes. I chose a neutral position and sat in silence, thinking about this performance of ritual insults and laughter whose main target was Omar. The conversation abruptly ended with the arrival of a creaky bus heading south. Hassan shouted:

"Sharon! Prepare more tea, the bus is stopping!"

Memories of Absence

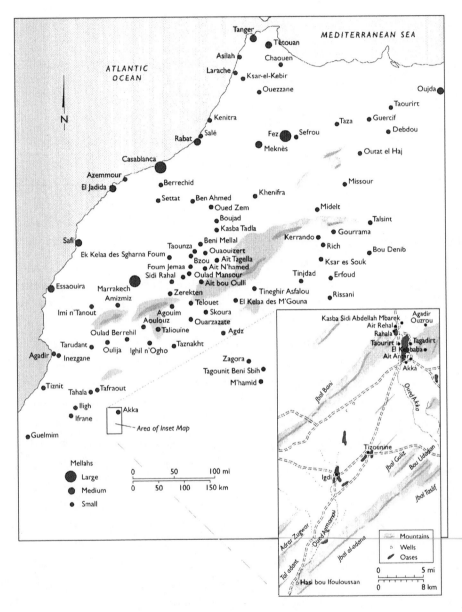

Jewish Communities of Colonial Morocco in 1953. *Inset*: Villages of Akka.

Introduction

Historically, Morocco had one of the largest and oldest populations of Jews in the Arab world, their presence stretching back to the pre-Islamic period.[1] At its peak before World War II, Morocco's Jewish community numbered about 240,000 (2.7 percent of the total population), living predominantly in urban centers in the French and Spanish colonial zones.[2] Called "people of the book" (*dhimmi*) by Muslims, the majority of Jews lived under the protection of the Moroccan king in return for submission and the payment of a tax known as *jizya*.[3] In areas outside the king's control, such as Akka, Berber chieftains ensured Jewish security.[4]

The Jews had ambivalent relations with their Muslim neighbors. Although Jewish communities resembled Muslim ones in language and custom, Jews faced occupational and social restrictions, such as in farming,[5] and were mainly artisans, peddlers, and merchants.[6] Rabbis and wealthy leaders who enjoyed special ties with Muslim authorities administered the Jewish community's internal social, legal, and religious affairs. Around 1862, the Alliance Israélite Universelle (AIU) built schools in the coastal cities and later in the hinterland, enabling many Jews to integrate into the wider world beyond Morocco.[7] Around the same time, however, political Zionism began to make inroads among the Jews of Morocco,[8] and a century later, in 1956 after Moroccan independence, Jews were affected by the new government's Arab-Islamic policies and a widely celebrated national Arabization program.[9] Zionist movements began to encourage Jews to move to Israel, and many people of Jewish descent left Morocco for Israel, Europe, and the Americas. Today, fewer than 3,000 Jews reside in Morocco, principally in major urban areas such as Casablanca and Rabat.

In the 1950s and 1960s, North African scholarship in general and Moroccan historiographical writing in particular had been mainly focused on issues of nationalism, pan-Arabism, and the Islamic character of North African societies.[10] Although a few scholars have begun to revisit and reexamine the histories and lives of ethnic and religious minorities in the region,[11] the place of religious minorities and of Jews in particular in this history has largely been ignored. Especially for native Muslim anthropologists, research on Middle Eastern Jewry and Judaism is still taboo. The reasons are obvious: scholars can be labeled (and stigmatized) as pro-Zionist just for conducting research on the Jews of the Arab world, and this labeling can have serious professional and personal consequences.

I am a native of a southeastern Moroccan oasis, perhaps a slightly uncommon native.[12] I was born and raised in Lamhamid, an oasis north of Akka at the foot of the Anti-Atlas Mountains. I left my village early to finish my primary, secondary, and, later, university studies. My parents are illiterate; my oldest brother was one of the first villagers to attend a secular public school, not only in my extended family but also in the whole province of Tata. My father is from the Haratine social group, which, unlike the maraboutic families (*shurfa*), do not claim descent from the Prophet Mohammed's family lineage,[13] and their purportedly inferior status limits their social mobility and economic improvement. Until independence, the Haratine were farmers working as day laborers mainly in lands owned by the *shurfa*. Very few owned property, which made the majority largely servants in the traditional subsistence oasis agriculture.[14] After independence, the Haratine and their descendants began to challenge both the inherited religious status and authority of the *shurfa* and their economic position by sending their children to modern schools.[15] It was through his attendance at these new secular schools that my brother was able to break away from the social hierarchies imposed on my father and other Haratine.[16] As a teacher with an independent income, my brother could sever any future ties of dependency on the political and economic system based on the religious authority of the *shurfa*.

Until I began studying the generational differences in Muslims' narratives and memories about their erstwhile Jewish neighbors, I had never ventured deep into the Sahara. As a native ethnographer, I had easy access to these Saharan communities. However, my personal ties to the region and my anthropological knowledge and vantage point were usually challenged because of my research topic. On numerous occasions, just being black earned me the label of a Falashi (Ethiopian) Jew. "The only thing you need is a Jewish yarmulke and you will be one of them. You would be mistaken for a Falashi even in Israel," one of my consultants remarked when he heard that I was studying Moroccan Jews. It was said in jest, but jokes bear bitter truths. In this part of Morocco, blacks and Jews have historically been relegated to a lower status in the community. Thus, members of the white clans sometimes invoke the appellation *Falashi* to remind blacks of their supposedly degrading origins. During my daily encounters, it was clear that the study of Jews by a local Muslim anthropologist remains a taboo in the minds of many of my interviewees. For instance, a Moroccan historian from the University of Mohammed V in Rabat who studied the Jews of southern communities faced the same negative public perception to the extent that throughout the south people recalled him as "Abdellah *'udayn*" (Abdellah the Jew, in Berber). The study of Jews living in Muslim societies was believed to be the task of Jewish researchers and Western scholars.

Despite the stigma, I looked at the history of Saharan Jewries by following their trading routes and examining their social and cultural customs.[17] I interviewed many Muslims about their memories of these communities, all of which disintegrated as the Jews left for Israel, starting in 1962. During these interviews, I realized that while international Muslim scholarship was generally silent about the role of Jews in North African history, this was not the case in Morocco itself. Until recently, research by Moroccan Muslims focused on histories of Jewish-Muslim relations before independence.[18] Moroccan scholars, largely historians, have begun to reflect on the history of Jews in Morocco after independence, and archival research remains their primary resource. Ethnographic research on Jewish communities by North African scholars is still rare.

Narratives about the French Protectorate are still ingrained in the southwestern Moroccan imagination.[19] The elders of the farthest Saharan oases remember French agents and their role in maintaining control in the region. Colonial memories are not outside the daily frame of reference of the older generation, and even of certain members of the younger generation. My ethnographic encounter with the people triggered some of those dormant community memories and views of the colonial officers, missionaries, and travelers who once visited the area disguised as Jews or Muslims.[20] Since 9/11, my study brought back the memories of foreign spies, lack of trust, and questions surrounding the production of colonial knowledge about the region. For some people, I was part of the Western tradition of knowledge. By comparing my work with those of European travelers such as Charles de Foucauld, I was cast as part of a continuing colonial legacy of knowledge. By studying the Jews of Morocco, I was thought by many informants to be in the process of writing another colonial ethnography on Moroccan Jewry.[21]

But what kind of "reconnaissance" should scholars of Moroccan Jews produce today? Should it be based on a colonial genealogy of knowledge or other sources of knowledge? Should I reject the claims of colonial narratives in their entirety, as some nationalist historians advocated?[22] De Foucauld's study of Moroccan society in the nineteenth century has as many strengths as it has flaws. My own ethnographic encounter corroborated information reported by de Foucauld more than a century earlier. Nevertheless, other sources could complement de Foucauld's study: legal manuscripts, personal Muslim narratives, and colonial as well as post-colonial Jewish and Muslim newspapers. In any post-colonial revision and reevaluation of Moroccan historiography, we have to accept that colonial knowledge is an interpretation of local reality. This interpretation, like any other, is open to deconstruction. It should be analyzed, critiqued, and appreciated as a phase of Moroccan history and not rejected because of its link with a colonial power. Following that line of thought, colonial narratives such as de Foucauld's should be used despite their attitudes toward Jews and Muslims because each narrative is told from the perspective of the moral and intellectual climate of both teller and century. While absolute truth may not be available to humankind, knowledge and deliberate ignorance are incompatible.

In many spontaneous group conversations, Muslims discuss Moroccan Jews today in terms of nostalgic memory,[23] gossip,[24] ritual insult,[25] and political ridicule.[26] While members of the older generation express nostalgic sadness about the absence of Jews from Morocco, younger subjects use humor, jokes, hearsay, and mockery to protest, ostracize, demonize, and resist Israelis and Jews in general, whom they see as their political and social enemies. Laughter and derision[27] serve as fuel for the perceptions, especially for those of the generation that have never met a Jew, that Jews are political spies and religious inferiors to Muslims.

Historical and Longitudinal Narratives

The key questions of this book are: Which factor is central in the formation of Muslim memories about absent Jews? Is it the long-circulated narratives of shared experiences between Muslims, like Ali, and Jews? Or do actual current events in the Middle East—in particular, the Arab-Israeli conflict—have greater weight in forming opinions, attitudes, and ideologies about Jews and their relationship to Muslims? This historical ethnography examines the narratives and memories of four successive Muslim generations about their former Jewish neighbors in marginal communities of the southeastern Moroccan hinterlands. Through a close reading of new sources such as travel narratives, legal manuscripts, newspapers, and interviews, I hope to shed light on the silenced and marginalized histories of these rural Jewish communities and their complex relations with Muslims.[28] Each generation in the ethnographic sample was equally divided along ethnic background (Arab and Berber). Although I was not refused access to women as interviewees, given the strong cultural restrictions surrounding male-female encounters, I decided to focus my study in the field only on male respondents. The hovering presence of male relatives during a few interviews with women was behind my decision. I felt these consultants were prevented from talking freely in the presence of their husbands or brothers.

The study included men from four generations (great-grandparents, grandparents, parents, and young adults), who were selected by a stratified,[29] purposive[30] sampling method according to the political period during which they came of age. The first category's great-grandparents came of age during the Moroccan Protectorate (1912–1956). The second category includes grandparents who witnessed the outcomes of the Vichy era (1940–1943) and the establishment of Israel (1948). The third group includes parents who experienced Moroccan independence (1956), the wars between Israel and the Arab countries (1967, 1973), and the increasing migration of Jews to Israel (1960). The fourth category's younger people may never have met Jews, but they have experienced them through the media, the Intifada (1987), the Oslo Agreement and its aftermath (1993), the al-Aqsa uprising (2000), and ongoing Middle Eastern events.

My main sample included eighty respondents, twenty from each age group; they ranged from their early twenties to late nineties. The respondents—from both Arab and Berber lineages—are also equally divided into two groups: *haratine* and *shurfa*. The Haratine are usually black descendants of either slaves brought from sub-Saharan Africa or the indigenous black population. They form the majority of the population of many villages in southeastern Morocco and practice farming, and they have generally been regarded as belonging to an inferior social stratum. The lighter-skinned *shurfa* are a mixture of Berbers from clans, such as ayt-Mribat, ayt-Sh'ayb, ayt-Rasmuk, and ayt-Habul, and migrant Bedouins, such as the Oulad Jallal clan. The ayt-Mribat, ayt-Sh'ayb, ayt-Rasmuk, and ayt-Habul historically controlled the political decisions of the region and spread their control over the villages in Akka.[31]

My data collection relied largely on open-ended questions, which led to long stories about interviewees' relations with Jews, their educational background, their dreams, and their aspirations for their children.[32] I spent hours with villagers at their farms and houses, streets and cafés, inside tents and under palm trees, around a cup of tea or sharing a spicy *tajine*, a southern dish made with vegetables, camel, or beef. These meetings sometimes grew into spontaneous focus groups in which members of three or four generations shared and debated their views on similar topics. To highlight these perspectives, I have reproduced portions of the narratives in this book because their words inform our understanding of the intrinsic connections and ruptures between various accounts.

To understand how Jews are perceived, I looked at both personal and collective memory across different generations in the contexts of colonial and post-colonial Moroccan politics.[33] Individuals, Tina Campt notes, "remember as members of groups—that is, through common points of reference, contexts, and associations. Memory is about individuals making the past meaningful, not so much for what it was but for how it is of use to us today."[34] In this case, memory is not solely about Muslims' stored beliefs about Jews; it also represents the continuous historical process of Jewish representation in Moroccan society, which changes across time and space.

There are methodological reasons why focusing on this remote Muslim community will allow us to gain a greater understanding of Saharan Jews (and those in Akka in particular). My focus on memory and change in attitudes requires an environment where different generations of subjects are not uniformly exposed to similar media likely to reinforce analogous views. The geographic remoteness of Akka and other Saharan communities limited the exposure of many of my interviewees, especially members of the older generations, to mainstream political, educational, and media influences. The fact that a few members of the older generation left the region for urban areas and that many of them were illiterate compared to their children and grandchildren provided variability in the sample. Finally, the long historical presence of Jews in different hamlets throughout southeastern Morocco and the visibility of this historical memory in this regional landscape make the process of remembering possible.

There are large variations among the different categories of respondents with regard to educational achievements. They vary not only in terms of the age groups of those interviewed but also in terms of their ethnic and language backgrounds. Recall that in each of the four cohorts there are twenty respondents, half Haratine and half *shurfa*. The great-grandparents showed very limited access to education. However, 15 percent of the respondents attended Qur'anic school. (All of those educated were *shurfa*.) All of the Haratine expressed their inability to get an education because they were forced to toil on the agricultural lands.

The grandparents' group not only showed an improvement in schooling but also reflected the beginning of the Haratine's access to education (30 percent of ten Haratine respondents attended Qur'anic school and 10 percent attended only primary school). The post-colonial government encouraged more people to enroll in schools and provided an avenue for the Haratine to break away from the social hierarchies imposed on them over the years. Although only 40 percent of the grandparents' group remained uneducated compared to 85 percent in the great-grandparents' category, the respondents agreed that had it not been for the lack of good infrastructure, more people might have attended school. Not all villagers in these remote areas were able to get to far-away schools, nor did they have the financial means to further their schooling.

The parents interviewed showed the first educational results of the independence era. Only 10 percent of these respondents never attended primary school. This is the first time that at least one respondent attended school all the way from the Qur'anic level to the secular university. Respondents ascribed this rise in school attendance to the accessibility to schooling in their rural districts. They no longer had to travel long distances to attend a primary school and then move to a neighboring city's boarding school to finish their secondary and high school education. Still, schooling expenses continued to be an extra burden on the households. Many parents chose to keep their children in the village instead of spending more money on their education. Many villagers, mostly Haratine, were eventually able to allow their children not only to attend but also to actually finish school because their relatives provided remittances after migrating to France and other European countries. In time the Haratine became some of the most highly educated people in the villages. In some villages, the first primary school teacher was of Haratine ancestry.

In the young adult category, 60 percent of the respondents had a university degree. Ninety-five percent had concurrently attended the Qur'anic and primary school; 80 percent pursued secondary education. Bureaucratic jobs require diplomas, and despite the high rate of unemployment among university graduates nationwide, the majority of the respondents still believe that education is the best means of social mobility. Forty percent of young adult respondents who had university training are Haratine. This shows that the level of education continues to increase among the minority than the majority after independence. According to Haddou, a Haratine descendant, "We had nothing. No lands. No shops. No business. The only way to improve our situation is to get a university degree and training to take care of our families. The *shurfa* do not want to study because they had land, water shares, and still own the majority of palm trees in the villages."

The educational achievement of the different groups in the current schooling system has also influenced the linguistic profiles of many respondents as well as their occupations. Looking at the correlation between the age groups and the number of languages spoken, we can distinguish between two categories of languages: native and colonial. Schooling, as may be expected, has encouraged the acquisition of foreign languages. Access to languages and the level of proficiency in them turned out to be a significant factor in the young participants' choice of university degree specialization. More than half of those interviewed had majored in geography, Arabic, history, law, and Islamic studies. The majority of them explained this choice by noting their desire to finish their degree in the field of Islamic studies rather than economics and mathematics, which require a fluency in French. Equally important, many students could not afford their college education, so they relied on the Ministry of Education's scholarship (US$500 a year). If they failed their annual exam, they would lose their financial support. A degree in Islamic studies relies on a prior knowledge of the Qur'an and the Hadith (the collection of the Prophet's sayings and deeds), so these students are generally able to finish their degrees in four years. Finally, access to education improved the respondents' ability to listen to different news channels, participate in the political system by joining a party, and therefore be able to move outside the village. The relationship between the age cohort and primary place of residence (urban vs. rural) reflected a higher mobility among the youngest cohort. This group and some members of the parents' cohort spent time in certain cities, such as Casablanca, Rabat, Marrakesh, Fez, Tangiers, and Agadir.

Few studies have considered modern Muslim generational attitudes toward Jews of Moroccan descent in Israel, the United States, France, Canada, and other parts of the world.[35] Anthropological research has focused largely on the Moroccan Jews themselves, as opposed to what Moroccan Muslims might think of Moroccan Jews. Furthermore, most of the studies that relied on Muslims focused on members of the older generations, who had nurtured personal contacts with their Jewish neighbors, leaving aside the attitudes of other Muslim cohorts. My work takes into account this methodological limitation to answer questions about the perceptions and both negative and positive attitudes of Muslim generations.

As the voices reveal, I suggest that there is a breakup at the level of transmission of knowledge to the extent that the very notion of Jews as indigenous Moroccans is alien to many interviewees. In the minds of many Moroccans, including some of Omar's customers, Ariel Sharon and other leaders have been joined with Moroccan Jews. In fact, in one newspaper article, "Our Jews: Are They Afraid?," Daniel, a Moroccan Jew from Casablanca, betrays his perception of a widespread attitude toward Jews: "I am not a killer of Palestinians, I was born in Morocco, I am a Moroccan and I have the right to live in peace."[36] This confusion between Moroccan Jews and Israel and Israeli policies has largely put Moroccan Jews today outside Morocco. The stories that follow describe the historical shifts in Muslim attitudes and perceptions toward Jews in local, national, and global contexts.

1

Writing the Periphery

COLONIAL NARRATIVES
OF MOROCCAN JEWISH HINTERLANDS

Global Links and Jewish Disguises

As a columnist and foreign correspondent working in the early twentieth century, Pierre van Paassen, a Dutch-American writer, worked for a number of newspapers, including the *Toronto Globe*, the *Atlanta Journal Constitution*, the *New York Evening World*, and the *Toronto Star*. He became one of the best-selling and most influential authors of his time. In addition to reporting on colonial issues in North Africa, including the slave trade, van Paassen investigated Middle Eastern issues and interviewed many key political figures in the region including the Grand Mufti of Jerusalem, Hajj Muhammad Amin al-Husayni (1895–1974) in 1929.[1] In 1933, accompanied by a British intelligence officer, van Paassen visited the Dome of the Rock disguised as an Arab *hajj* (pilgrim) to gather information during the Friday sermon about local views regarding the British Mandate and Muslim attitudes toward Jewish migration to Palestine.[2] Despite his wide-ranging activities as a journalist and writer, van Paassen gained fame for his reports on the relationship between Arabs and Jews within the British and French Middle Eastern colonies.

As a world-famous Unitarian Christian reporter, van Paassen was an ardent supporter of Zionism and a lobbyist mainly in the United States for the establishment of a Jewish state.[3] He accused the League of Nations and Britain—in particular—of betraying the Jewish People, especially after what befell European Jews in the Holocaust. Van Paassen prefaced *The Forgotten Ally* with a critique of the British Colonial Office in the Near East, highlighting Europe's failure to protect Jews and secure a country for the Jewish People in Palestine. Van Paassen stated that "as one who is aware and who feels with a sense of personal involvement Christianity's guilt in the Jewish people's woes and the constant deepening of their anguish, I could no longer be silent."[4] His political zeal for a Jewish state became reflected not only in his call for supporting European Jewries in the aftermath of the Holocaust, but also in facilitating Jewish *aliya* (immigration to Eretz-Israel) worldwide, even among the Jews of Africa.

On November 7, 1928, as the Paris-based foreign correspondent for the *New York Evening World*, van Paassen wrote an article about what he deemed a small and remote Jewish community in the heart of the African desert:

> Hostile tribes, disease, hunger, poverty and other vicissitudes had interfered with the ancestral project of reaching the Promised Land, and they had remained in the desert. But the Jews . . . never had abandoned hope altogether of continuing their interrupted migration some day and of ultimately residing in the land that "that flows with milk and honey."[5]

This passage was written about the Jewish society of Akka—the main ethnographic site of this book. Van Paassen based his story on an interview with René Leblond, whom he presumed to be the French consul of Akka, and who had descended on the outskirts of the Jewish settlement when his plane developed an engine problem and was forced to land. Leblond was collecting geographic and cartographic data for the colonial mapping of the southern Moroccan territories that the French military had yet to control. By 1928, Sémach, a Bulgarian teacher of the Alliance Israélite Universelle (AIU) in Iraq and Morocco, questioned the truthfulness of the story, alleging that there was no French consul at Akka and that Leblond did not show up in the registers of the French Foreign Ministry.[6] Yet, van Paassen's story about the presence of "a flourishing and tranquil Jewish community, numbering several thousand souls, in the heart of the African desert, surrounded on all sides by savage and semi-civilized Moor and Berber tribes,"[7] has become part of an authoritative and institutionalized historiographical narrative about the Jews of Akka in particular and Saharan Jewries in general, despite its unsubstantiated sources.[8]

Apart from a few notes about the history and culture of the small Jewish community of Akka, van Paassen simply skipped over many historical dates and events without providing detailed information. He noted that the last European visitor the Jews of Akka had seen was "an explorer in 1866" and that "since that day no traveler from Europe had been in their midst."[9] Contrary to this claim, the French traveler Charles de Foucauld visited Akka around 1882 with his guide, Mardochée Aby Serour, himself a native Jew from Akka.[10] I do not question here van Paassen's sources; Leblond, if such a name existed, could have been told of these events by the Jewish elders of Akka he claimed to have interviewed. The inaccuracy of these dates and the vagueness of events reflect the dilemma of reliability in oral sources that faced European travelers and later scholars of rural Jewish societies throughout the Middle East in general and Morocco in particular.[11]

As rural and Saharan Jews were "discovered" by European travelers and are now studied by Moroccan historians and anthropologists,[12] how should these historical and ethnographic accounts be assessed and analyzed? What are the biases and agendas of colonial and post-colonial narratives that frame the historical discourse about Saharan Jewries in particular and Middle Eastern Jews in general? What is the role of post-colonial national researchers in the re-writing of these rural marginal communities? If we use a combination of European travelers' accounts and local oral testimonies, how should we understand these sources despite their purported contradictions and likely inaccuracies?

In this chapter I grapple with these questions and reflect on the connections, silence, and amnesic gaps between the colonial and post-colonial historical narratives, as I wade through European travelers' accounts, post-colonial nationalist histories, Moroccan literature about Jews, and my own ethnographic experience as a native Moroccan Muslim anthropologist studying the Jews of my hometown and region. Through the chapter we will meet pro-Zionist Christians and Muslims, and deeply anti-Semitic government officials and colonial administrators, and learn the stories of alliance and betrayal in the common lives of my ethnographic subjects and their parallels in historical figures. The common practice of disguising oneself as a traveling Jew not only links the stories of van Paassen and the colonial administrator de Foucauld, but returns in my own ethnographic experience, as I become the object of a similar rumor while in the field. Before I discuss these issues, I begin with a short ethnographic narrative that contextualizes the Jewish community of Akka in the wider region of southeastern Morocco.

Jewish Society in Saharan Hinterlands

When I arrived in Akka in February 2004, I walked through the Jewish shops outside the *mellah* (Jewish neighborhood) not far from where the market of Tagadirt took place. I could not access any of the tiny shops lining the *mellah*'s entrance. It was obvious that these shops had not been open for business since the last time Jews left for Israel in 1962. A *suq* (market) without Jews, as the

Moroccan proverb goes, is like bread without salt. "When the Jews settled out-side Morocco," Ali, a ninety-year-old consultant, noted, "the market lost its salt." Masses of thickened red dirt collected around the shops' entrances leav-ing their small wooden doors to the mercy of termites. Between the late 1820s and 1880s, a number of European travelers such as Davidson and de Foucauld[13] described the markets of Sus region and the Anti-Atlas as central trading and resting posts in the western sub-Saharan trading routes. When I visited these once busy markets in the Saharan fringes, the Moroccan adage made sense to me, especially when Ali, my guide, stopped in the middle of the square where the weekly *suq* was once held and said:

> Look around you, the only thing left of Jews today is their deserted and decay-ing buildings; their shops are closed. Their houses are mostly unoccupied. The only reminder of their presence is their cemeteries. Their tombs remind us of a Jewish time and place. It is as if Tagadirt is a factory that closed, leaving thou-sands unemployed and without salaries. I wish Jews had never left. They added yeast to this economy.

According to Ali, without Jews, local markets could not grow or prosper. Hence, when Jews left for Israel, Akka as well as other rural and urban communities throughout Morocco suffered from the absence of the "salt" they had added to the local and regional economies. Ali's remark echoed many statements I heard from other members of his generation of great-grandparents, whose narratives and memories were replete with nostalgic moments about a Jewish time and place that was.

In the nineteenth century, Marrakesh, Essaouira, and to an extent Tarudant and Agadir, were major urban epicenters of the Saharan economy.[14] Jewish ped-dlers and merchants throughout the southern regions of Morocco exchanged their commercial articles as they traveled between these epicenters and chains of satellite rural communities throughout southern Morocco.[15] Southern Mo-rocco includes the Anti-Atlas, the Noun (region along the Atlantic Ocean), Oued Sus Valley, the southern slopes of the High Atlas, and southern Draa Valley, all stretched out before one can enter the Saharan interior. Throughout the Sus region, Jews lived among Berber and Arab communities; Jewish fami-lies resided in this area until their final exodus to Israel in 1962.

Early legends claim that these Jewish communities are some of the oldest in North Africa. The Jewish kingdoms of Ifrane (Oufran) and the Draa Valley date back to the pre-Islamic period.[16] The trading centers of Essaouira (Mogador), Agadir, and Tarudant had always been regarded as the urban capitals of the Jews of Sus, although Marrakesh was also a major urban destination of Jewish students and traders (Table 1).

In the southern Saharan hamlets, Jews lived among Muslim communities under the protection of tribal lords. As the French succeeded in their gradual pacification of the south, completed by 1933, a few Jews applied for French protégé-status for fear of losing local tribal support. The Jewish communities of the *bled* (hinterland) continued to fall under the protection of tribal lords and local individuals.[17] The French administrators left the political and economic management of the south in the hands of tribal *qaids*, known as the lords of the Atlas, specifically Si Abdelmalek M'Tougi, Si Taieb Goundafi, and Thami Glaoui.[18] The use of the tribal *qaids* was for the subjugation of the tribal dissidents. Therefore, Marshal Hubert Lyautey, the first resident-general in Morocco (1912–1925), and his followers opted for a policy of indirect rule in the lands under the management of these lords, deferring to local *qaids* on issues relating to local Jews. In Teluet, a village under the control of Thami Glaoui, Slouschz reported that the chieftain of Teluet would imprison members (including Jews) of tribes he had conflict with when they attempted to travel to Marrakesh for business until his feuds with the tribes were resolved. Slouschz claimed that during his travel through Teluet, "there were ten Jewish merchants from

Table 1 Jewish population in some areas of Sus, 1884–1951

Jewish Settlement	1884	1936	1947	1951
Tarudant	1,500	926	950	915
Tata [Tintazart]	70	40	-	-
Akka [Tagadirt]	60	129	163	118
Tamanart [Foum El Hassan]	100	4	2	-
Oued Noun [Guelmim]	200	24	73	93
Tiznit	-	357	425	461
Ammeln	-	181	171	171
Ifrane	-	122	129	141
Inezgane	-	68	331	396
Agadir	160	503	1,104	1,600

Askura who had been imprisoned because their Mussulman patrons had refused to recognize the authority of the Kaid of Teluet."[19]

Throughout southern Morocco, Jews were caught in these political changes,
remaining indispensable economic agents as well as marginal political players in
the social structures of these rural communities.[20] The traditional rural economy
was reliant on Jewish peddlers and artisans,[21] who provided important services
to the local agrarian Muslim society. As peddlers, metalworkers, and saddle-
makers, the Jews of Akka and other communities throughout the Anti-Atlas
played an active role in tribal economy, which depended on them as mediators
between the city and remote rural settlements.[22] In return for these valuable services, Jews were guaranteed the protection of local Muslims—though guaran-
tees were sometimes jeopardized by feuds between neighboring tribes.

Akka became an important satellite community in the trans-Saharan commercial chains in the nineteenth century.[23] It housed one of the most important
Jewish communities at the fringes of the Moroccan Sahara. Akka is a green valley of palm groves at the mouth of Oued Akka, a tributary of the Draa River. It
comprises the villages of Irahalan, Rahala, ayt-'Antar, Tagadirt, Taourirt, Agadir
Ouzrou, Qabbaba, and al-Qasba. An abundance of water (ten water sources)
has made it one of the major settlements of the Anti-Atlas that survive on intensive subsistence agriculture.[24] Situated about thirteen kilometers from the
ruins of the Islamic city of Tamdult,[25] Akka emerged as an entrepôt in western
Saharan trade following the fall of Tamdult in the fourteenth century. During
the nineteenth century, Akka and Tata (Tintazart) became among the most prosperous centers of the Moroccan south. According to de Foucauld, Akka was one
of the principal resting posts of the caravans toward Essaouira.[26] Gold, slaves,
leather, and fabric brought from the Sudan were traded in its markets.[27]

Jewish communities were largely concentrated in urban conglomerations of
the region of Sus, such as Agadir, Tiznit, and Tarudant, as well as pre-Saharan
remote settlements like Aguerd (Tamanart), Tahala, Tintazart, and Ouijjane. As
part of a colonial census of the Jewish population of Sus in 1936, Capitaine
de La Porte des Vaux argued that the Jewish population of Sus underwent
major transformations because of massive local and regional movements since
de Foucauld's *Reconnaissance au Maroc* in 1888.[28] De La Porte des Vaux asserted
that major economic changes during the nineteenth century at the level of mari-
time trade, in addition to the breakdown of Saharan trade routes, caused the

disappearance of certain Jewish settlements and the growth of non-traditional ones, such as Agadir.[29] Traditional Jewish settlements were located along key trade routes and protected by local chieftains. The economic struggles of Jews of pre-Saharan oases started after the diversion of caravan routes from Tindouf toward the coastal zone.[30] This trend forced many Jews to move toward urban conglomerations where they had better economic opportunities.

Politically, Akka was under the control of the ayt-Mribat tribe, headed by the ayt-Wirran faction, who settled in the region after the collapse of Tamanart. In the nineteenth century ayt-Wirran controlled most of the economic and political relations in Akka, Tamdult, Tizounine, Tamanart, and Icht. The local *qaid*s (chieftains) provided protection for the Jewish merchants and communities of the different settlements in Akka. Akka is also the home of the *zawiya* (religious brotherhood) of Muhammad ban Mbarak al-Akkawi, a disciple of al-Jazuli. His son, 'Abd Allah ban Mbarak al-Akkawi, the founder of the village of Agadir Ouzrou, played a major role in negotiating peaceful agreements between the different factions of Akka during the sixteenth century and was one of the main supporters of the Sa'dian Dynasty. His descendents gained a religious status for Muslims within the area and established trading partnerships with Jews.[31]

Given Akka's economic importance, Jewish merchants and artisans were allowed by ayt-Wirran to settle there during the nineteenth century. The protection of the *zawiya* of Akka and the *qaid*s of ayt-Mribat enabled Jews to maintain trading networks with Essaouira and the Sudan. Monteil in 1946 counted thirty-four families in Akka in comparison to the twelve families mentioned by de Foucauld in 1883.[32] These families were related to seven bloodlines: ayt-Didi (ayt-Twati); ayt-Ya'ish (ayt-Abisror); ayt-Shabbat; ayt-Dabda; ayt-Yahya (ayt-Sarraf); ayt-Illiwi; and ayt-Ibgi. The families came from Tuat, Tamdult, Tamanart, Debdou, Tarudant, and Tahala. Following the establishment of the first Jewish *mellah* in Irahalan, Jewish families moved to Taourirt and Tagadirt. Other local narratives by members of the great-grandparents cohort mentioned an ancient Jewish settlement in Agadir Ouzrou destroyed by flooding.

After independence in 1956, Akka became a regional administrative center linked to the commune of Guelmim, province of Agadir. On July 19, 1977, the province of Tata was established by the royal decree of 1-77-228 and the bill 2-77-605. The center of Akka and its villages were linked afterwards to the

province of Tata. During the most recent administrative changes in the king-
dom, Akka was turned into one of the main communes of Tata that oversees
other local and regional villages and administrative centers around it. Today,
only a few Muslim families have occupied these Jewish quarters (*mellahs*) despite the sixty years since Jews left for urban centers in Morocco and Israel. The
Jewish shrines and cemeteries of Akka are still visited by the descendents of
the Jews of Akka, who live mainly in Inezgane, Agadir, and Israel. Even with
the long Jewish absence from Akka and its surrounding villages, their memory
lives with many Muslims through the deserted quarter of Akka, the Jewish
cemeteries, and shrines.

Saharan Jews as Colonial Explorers: Mardochée Aby Serour

Mardochée Aby Serour, the fourth child of a Jewish jeweler by the name of Ya'ish
Aby Serour, was born in the late 1820s in Akka.[33] His ancestors, he claimed,
were originally from the Sahara. Before his father settled in Akka, he lived in
Mhamid El Ghozlan in the lower Draa Valley. In his article on the Daggatouns, a
tribe of Jewish origin in the Sahara, Mardochée traced his genealogy to Tamentit
and the Jews of Tuat. He reported:

> In our family our ancestors told their children, who taught us, that Tementit
> [Tuat] was once a capital of Judaism. . . . Between Tementit and El Hamméda
> there is still today descendents of Jews once expelled from Tementit, we call them
> Tementilins. They and the inhabitants of El Hamméda have conserved their tra-
> dition and their history. My father and his brothers and their father were born in
> El Hamméda and my father continuously narrated to us these events.[34]

Before 1492, the Jews of Tuat and Tamentit were a thriving community in
the Sahara.[35] Tuat Jewry ended when the renowned preacher Muhammad 'Abd
al-Karim al-Maghili issued a fatwa claiming that Jews had bribed the powerful
Muslim elite instead of paying the *jizya* (poll tax), thus voiding their status of
protection through subservience.[36] By introducing his fatwa against the Jews
of Tuat and other Saharan communities, al-Maghili limited Jewish movement
across the Sahara for centuries to come.[37] Saharan Jewish settlements were thus
concentrated in the northern fringes along the pre-Saharan margins from Libya

to Morocco, even though a few Jewish traders managed to cross the Sahara and settle in some of the southern oases.[38] In fact, at the legal advice of al-Maghili, and after the destruction of the Jewish community of Tamantit, the emperor of Songhay, Askiya Muhammad, forbade Jews to trade in Songhay.[39] In 1860, Aby Serour became one of the first recorded Jewish merchants to arrive to Timbuktu since al-Maghili's fatwa, going as far as establishing a community in the city despite resistance from Muslim merchants and scholars. In 1870, Aby Serour noted in a report to Beaumier, the French consul in Essaouira, that no Jew had ever ventured to travel south of the northern termini of the trans-Saharan trade since al-Maghili's fatwa.[40] This claim is supported by Leo Africanus' report that Askiya "is an inveterate enemy of the Jews. He does not wish any to live in his town. If he hears it said that a Barbary merchant frequents them, or does business with them, he confiscates his goods."[41]

In the late 1850s, Aby Serour, about thirty-two years old, went back to Akka after a long absence spent between Jerusalem, Damascus, and Algiers.[42] Yet, as an ordained rabbi, young Mardochée was too ambitious to settle down in Akka and teach children how to read the Torah and write Hebrew in the same synagogue where he was once taught. Instead, he got in touch with Salomon Ohayon, a Jewish merchant from Essaouira, and the two became associates in business.[43] By then, Akka was one of the most important western caravan entrepôts linking the Sudan with Marrakesh and Essaouira, although it was starting to lose its importance to the rising market of Tindouf.[44] As Aby Serour succeeded in his regional trading, his ambition grew and he thought about taking his own caravans to Timbuktu. No Jew had ever ventured to do so after the expulsion of the Jews of Tuat, Aby Serour would claim in his Judeo-Arabic letter to Beaumier.[45] In the autumn of 1858, accompanied by his younger brother, Isaac, Mardochée joined the regular large annual caravan heading to Timbuktu passing through Igdy, where the British doctor John Davidson was killed in 1837.[46] At Arouane, Aby Serour and his brother were held in captivity by the shaykh of the city, Sidi Ahmed Ould El Abied Ould Muhammad Ould El Rahal. He was able to convince the shaykh to release him; and in 1859, Mardochée was authorized by the shaykh to leave for Timbuktu. However, Aby Serour's trials were not over. Even though René Caillié[47] (alias 'Abd Allah) and Heinrich Barth[48] (alias 'Abd al-Karim) entered Timbuktu, in 1828 and 1850 respectively, it was because they disguised themselves as Muslims, dressed in Muslim garb, and prayed in Arabic.[49] Aby Serour did not attempt this strategy even though he knew that Jews were not welcomed in the city. Instead, when he arrived in Timbuktu he sought the help of the Moroccan traders, particularly Thaleb Muhammed ben Talmdoy. Fearing competition, the Moroccan merchants plotted against him instead and tried to bar him from trading in the city.[50]

Aby Serour relied on his knowledge of the *shari'a* to protect himself in Timbuktu. To counter the Moroccan merchants originally from Fez and Marrakesh, he made his case in front of the rulers of Timbuktu, using his knowledge of the Qur'an and the Prophet's tradition.[51] His arguments were accepted and he was allowed to settle in the city and pay the *jizya* as a Jew, as the Islamic law prescribed. In 1860, Isaac joined his brother in Timbuktu and they became competitors of the Muslim merchants from Morocco. In 1863, Aby Serour returned to Akka and traveled to Mogador (Essaouira), where he bought twenty-two camel loads of merchandise. His two brothers, Ysou and Abraham Aby Serour, and the two sons of Ysou (Aaroun and David), traveled with the caravan and joined the newly established Jewish community of Akka in Timbuktu. Concerned by the new Jewish competition, the Moroccan merchants tried to talk the local leaders into assigning the Jewish community to a separate quarter of the city. Mardochée, aware of the risk such seclusion would bring in times of hardship, nevertheless managed to disperse his family and co-religionists into different rented houses scattered about the city. In 1864, Mardochée went back to Akka and for the first time to Italy, where he bought fine textiles, merchandise highly sought in the Sudan. On his return to Timbuktu, he was accompanied by another group of five Jews from Akka, among them Isaac ben Mouchi, who later renounced Judaism and converted to Islam.

Mardochée suffered huge losses because of the insecurity of the caravan routes. For instance, one caravan to Timbuktu was pillaged, and another one heading to Essaouira with gold powder (*tibr*), ostrich feathers, and ivory suffered the same fate. Bad luck followed the rabbi trader afterwards: his brother Isaac died in 1867; Abraham suffered the same fate in 1870; his property was confiscated; and on his return from Timbuktu in 1870, he was attacked and robbed of his last fortune.[52] After his business had been ruined by the successive pillages of the Rguibat, Tajakant, and other Saharan tribes along the dangerous western trading route, Aby Serour left Akka with his wife to settle in Mogador. On his return from Timbuktu, his father had already died and his family refused to share their inheritance with him, forcing him to resettle in Algiers as a teacher in a local synagogue.

The story of Aby Serour dramatically demonstrates that the absence of extensive social networks limited Jewish settlements in the Saharan interior. Jews were unable, just as Goitein[53] and Levtzion[54] argued, to settle in the Saharan interior because of the absence of a strong client-patron relationship that guaranteed their protection in times of political change and economic upheavals. In the southern Moroccan fringes, and despite their marginal roles, Jews interacted with Muslims in many ways within rural settlements. When tribes fought each other, Jews were their economic mediators. Slouschz observed in the early twentieth century that "no one knows the country or its people better than they [Jews] do."[55] Their knowledge of local Arabic and Berber dialects also facilitated roles as economic mediators. In addition, the social status of Jews as *dhimmi* provided them with a special standing within the southern tribal Saharan settlements, which defined their position both as outsiders of the political system and as insiders of the marketplace.

In 1866, Beaumier heard about a newly established Moroccan Jewish community from Akka in Timbuktu and had been fascinated by the story ever since. France and other European colonial powers started to become interested in the conquest of Africa and established geographical societies to facilitate colonial exploration.[56] Despite the crushing defeat of France by the Prussian army, Aby Serour made the news in France in 1870. The *Bulletin de la Société de Géographie de Paris* (Bulletin of the Geographic Society of Paris), published Aby Serour's trading account in Timbuktu after its translation from Judeo-Arabic to French by Beaumier under the title "Premier établissement des Israélites à Timbouctou."[57] Beaumier started another campaign in favor of Aby Serour, urging the director of the Société de Géographie de Paris (SGP) and the AIU to put him on the board of their scientific mission in southern Morocco. This marked the beginning of Aby Serour's relationship with different players among the French colonial authorities and scientific organizations in Morocco, as well as the AIU.

Aby Serour was enlisted to serve France with his knowledge of southern Morocco and his experience in Timbuktu. Beaumier believed that, as a southern Moroccan Jew, Aby Serour could be the perfect agent for the French colonial enterprise in the region of Sus. In May 1873, Beaumier introduced Mardochée to Samuel Hirsch, the director of the AIU School in Tangiers, during his inspection of the school of Essaouira. Between 1870 and 1874, Beaumier sent letters to the AIU headquarter in Paris to ask that Aby Serour be hired as an agent in Morocco's southern *bled* (hinterlands). In April 1874, the AIU and the SGP funded Aby Serour's short trip to Paris for training in data collection. He was presented to Henri Duveyrier, the French Saharan explorer, who introduced him to the use of the compass, the barometer, and the thermometer. He was also familiarized with the basics of photography. French newspapers and newsletters published small biographies of Aby Serour. Many saw him as France's new explorer of the Sahara.[58]

On his return to Morocco, Mardochée instantly conducted scientific missions in the Sus region to collect plants and insects for the SGP. Duveyrier published the results of Aby Serour's mission to Djbel Tabayoudt in the *Bulletin* of the SGP in 1875.[59] In 1876, another article was published on Aby Serour's tour in Sus and his discovery of some prehistoric rock drawings.[60] In 1876, Mardochée's long time supporter, Beaumier, died. Mardochée's relationship with SGP ended shortly after because its officials lost faith in his ability to do scientific work.

However, before his return to Algiers, Aby Serour was asked by the AIU to send reports on the Jewish communities of the Sahara. The AIU saw some benefits in utilizing Aby Serour as a native Jew to gather information on the subject. Mardochée's knowledge of local dialects was seen as an advantage for the collection of statistics on the ancient Jewish populations. However, Mardochée's relationship with the AIU and the SGP ended in 1880. He went back to Algiers where he taught in a local Jewish school before his return to southern Morocco as the guide of the French explorer Charles de Foucauld.[61]

Saharan Jews, European Explorers, and the Colonial Project

Contrary to van Paassen's claim, de Foucauld visited Akka in 1882 and documented his journey throughout southern Morocco in his travel narrative *Reconnaissance au Maroc, 1882–1883*. One of the important themes of this work is its discussion of the ethics of disguised scientific exploration. The issue of overt and covert observation in the daily lives of ethnographic subjects has been at the core of European travel accounts, colonial ethnological studies, and modern anthropological fieldwork. Disguised observation rarely mattered as a moral and ethical issue in the endeavors of European travelers who journeyed and lived worldwide in some form of disguised identity or role. For instance, Caillié pioneered disguised geographic exploration in the Saharan interior. He was successful in his report on the state of southern Morocco and its Jews because of his approach to the exploration of the region. He spent many years learning Arabic, getting acquainted with the local customs, and studying Islam before his travels. In a Muslim disguise, Caillié began a tradition for Europeans that would be followed by Lenz[62] and others. He outlined a set of steps for future explorers of Morocco and the Sahara.[63] Lenz, an Austrian geologist and explorer from a German background, traveled in southern Morocco as an Arab under the name of Hakim Umar bin Ali in 1879.

De Foucauld was never concerned with the ethical position of the ethnographer in relationship with his subjects. In 1870, a fever of geographic exploration caught most of Europe and was funded mostly by the geographical societies of Paris, Berlin, London, Madrid, and Rome. In France, the SGP that was established on December 15, 1821, began to urge French exploration in the early 1870s, linking explorers to national interest. The SGP went as far as imploring the public to aid travelers in their expeditions, citing "the honor of France" as a motive. In May 1873, the SGP underlined three objectives of its program: national honor, scientific interests, and commercial prosperity.[64] As the economic interests of France in the African continent increased, the geographic exploration of the Sahara and the development of trade with its interior communities intrigued the leadership of French colonial authorities.

With de Foucauld, the situation was different. His knowledge of Morocco and of local customs was very meager, and his understanding of Islam was almost non-existent. MacCarthy, curator of the national library in Algiers, advised de Foucauld against taking an Arab disguise and counseled him to take off as a Jew. The Jews, MacCarthy claimed, were "rootless people who came from many lands and spoke many languages, all with a foreign accent. . . . Furthermore, the Jews were a small minority in Morocco; with centuries of abuse and persecution behind them, they would instinctively protect de Foucauld from Moslems, even though they saw through his masquerade."[65] These colonial interests highlight how little importance subjects' rights had in the policies of European geographic societies: the benefits of disguised explorations outweighed ethics. After all, European explorers were engaged in the *"mission civilisatrice"* of the dark African continent. In the name of economic exploration the European traveler was briefed and asked to hide his identity as an Arab and Muslim, dress like the native, learn the language, and discard any informed consent. Many travelers saw this as part of their profession and never questioned it. Others, like de Foucauld, were partly bothered by it and tried to justify it. In his introduction, de Foucauld laid out issues related to entrée to the field and rapport with the subjects to be studied. His choice of disguise as a rabbi from Palestine accompanied by Aby Serour underscores the issue of self-preservation that many Europeans faced in their journeys throughout the Islamic world as they sought to collect data for European societies. De Foucauld highlighted this dilemma in the following way:

> Could I travel as a European, or should I use a disguise? There was good reason to hesitate; on the one hand, I found repugnant the idea of passing off as something I was not; on the other hand, the principal explorers of Morocco, René Caillié, Rohlfs and Lenz, had always travelled in disguise and declared this precaution indispensable: this was also the opinion of many Moroccan Muslims I consulted before my departure. I reached the following compromise: I would leave in disguise; once on the road, if I felt my disguise necessary, I would maintain it; if not I had only to chuck it aside.[66]

It could be argued that de Foucauld's interest in pre-Saharan rural Morocco was not colonial in the literal sense—whether the French government had plans to colonize Morocco at the time of his trip or not. Unlike other travelers, de Foucauld struggled to get financial support for his expedition. He was not recognized until his safe return and the publication of his narrative. However, some men I interviewed in Akka and Tissint believed that "Christian travelers," including de Foucauld, were spies and agents of the French colonial administration in Algeria. Others ascribed the French entry to Morocco to their intelligence reports.

Before his departure to Morocco, de Foucauld was in close contact with the French military in Algiers. He contacted the division commander about undertaking an expedition to fill out the largely blank military maps of Morocco. His request for official funding was refused, however. During his trip in southeastern Morocco, he introduced himself in Essaouira as a former officer of the French army, and on the way back to Algeria he "made for the divisional headquarters of the French Army to reestablish himself as ex-cavalry officer and shed his masquerade as Rabbi Josef Aleman."[67] All these actions put a question mark on the relationship between the traveler/scientist/spy and the French military. De Foucauld's narrative had definitely benefited the French military in its subsequent conquest of southern Morocco: Lyautey used the *Reconnaissance au Maroc* as a "travel guide" when he landed in Morocco in 1912.[68] Carrouges claimed that there was a theory that viewed de Foucauld as an agent of the Deuxième Bureau (Intelligence Agency).[69] Although he became a hermit and led a solitary life in Tamanrasset, de Foucauld was still regarded as a spy in another disguise.[70]

Throughout his journey, de Foucauld was a guest of members of southern Jewries. He stayed with families and spent nights in their synagogues. He ate their food and was introduced to Morocco through them. He even dressed like them. De Foucauld chose to travel throughout southern Morocco as a Jew:

> There are two religions in Morocco. I had to be a member of one of them. Would I be Muslim or Jew? Should I put on the turban or the black cap? . . . I was alarmed by a disguise that, far from aiding my studies, could in fact hinder me; I cast my eyes on the Israelite costume. It seemed to me that this latter, by degrading me, would allow me to pass unnoticed, and give me more freedom.[71]

De Foucauld knew that he could be a target at any time during his journey in the Moroccan interior. He understood Moroccans' extreme intolerance towards Christians:

> Five-sixths of Morocco is . . . fully closed to Christians; they can enter it only through ruse and at risk of their lives. This extreme intolerance is not caused by religious fanaticism, and has its source in another common sense to all the natives; for them, a European traveling in their country can only be an emissary to recognize it; he comes to explore the land for an invasion, he is a spy. You kill [him] as such, rather than as infidel.[72]

In Algiers, de Foucauld became aware of the perils European travelers encountered in the Moroccan interior. At the height of European explorations during the nineteenth century, Morocco was still inaccessible. Algeria, Senegal, and Tunisia were already under French control and European powers had their eyes set on Morocco, "the Sick Man of the West."[73] Europeans managed to explore parts of southern Morocco as well as arrive in Timbuktu, although some met their deaths at the hands of tribal lords.

A close look at the narrative of de Foucauld demonstrates that he had very little respect for his guide and the Jews of Morocco in general. In his acknowledgment, he discussed the sympathy and friendships he had developed during his journey into the Moroccan interior. It is very telling to notice the absence of the word "Jew" and even the name of his guide from the list of people he thanked. In his quasi-military report, which aimed at a complete "reconnaissance" of southern Morocco, de Foucauld chose not to acknowledge his guide and the assistance provided by other Jews throughout Morocco. In October 1887, while writing his much awaited narrative in Paris, he talked about the lingering positive memories of the people who had helped, protected, and encouraged him in his voyage. These people, de Foucauld stressed, were French and Moroccan, Christian and Muslim.[74] De Foucauld might have been excused for not mentioning his Jewish guide if he did not add the following qualifiers: "They were Christian, they were Muslim." Why did he eliminate from the acknowledgments the names of Jews such as Aby Serour (his guide), Jacob Danan (*mellah* of Tétouan), Samuel Ben Simhoun (Fez), Bou Douma (Taza), David Aoulil (Sefrou), Mousi Aloun (Bejaad), Mousi Ammer (Tikirt), Abraham Ben Oukhkha (Taznakht), and Nessim Aby Serour (Tintazart, Tata)? Why did de Foucauld, after all the help provided by Mardochée and his co-religionists, deride them in *Reconnaissance au Maroc* and have negative attitudes towards them?

Some biographical elements in de Foucauld's life shed light on his ambivalent stance towards Mardochée and the Jews of Morocco in general. At Saint-Cyr and Saumur, de Foucauld was deeply entrenched in an anti-Semitic culture that developed in the French army after the 1870 defeat by the Germans. Although this anti-Semitic culture would reach its apogée in 1892 with the Dreyfus Affair,[75] de Foucauld had already been influenced by anti-Semitic sentiment in the army. He was a close friend of Antoine de Vallombrosa, Marquis de Morès, who was famous for his anti-Semitic campaign in Algeria at the end of the nineteenth century, before the Touareg killed him in 1886.[76] De Morès played a major role in spreading anti-Semitic discourse among French settlers in Algeria by claiming that Saharan Jews conspired with Britain to conquer the African desert. De Foucauld unwillingly traveled as a Jew. In Morocco, he experienced the

reality of being a "persecuted" minority, which he never thought, as French no-
bility, he would have to face. For instance, in Tlemcen, just before he crossed to
Morocco, de Foucauld, disguised as "Rabbi Aleman," was sitting on the ground
in the company of Mardochée, eating bread and olives. All of a sudden, a group
of soldiers of the Fourth Chasseurs d'Afrique came out of the officers' club.
De Foucauld recognized all of them. One looked at the two "Jewish" men and
pointed to de Foucauld in a derogatory manner, comparing him to a monkey.
Nevertheless, instead of sympathizing with Mardochée and the other Jews of
Morocco, de Foucauld, in many passages in his narrative, reinforced the same
anti-Semitic ideas and prejudices he himself had faced as a "disguised Jew."

My own consultants from the great-grandparents' generation remember stories about the presence and traces of both de Foucauld and Aby Serour. Regarding the relationship between Jews and colonialism, my consultants claimed that
Christians relied on Jews in their reconnoitering journeys of southern Morocco.
Hsain, a great-grandfather from Tissint, noted how "Jews and Christians are enemies of Muslim societies: Christian and Jewish minorities throughout the Muslim world played a key role in facilitating European colonialism." According
to a conversation with Hajj Muhammad Thami, a great-grandfather in his late
nineties, de Foucauld and Aby Serour stayed with the rabbi of the Jewish community of Taznakht, Abraham Ben Ouakhkha. He added that Ben Ouakhkha
probably did not know that Mardochée and de Foucauld were collecting data
for France's future conquest of southern Morocco:

> I was told that in the late nineteenth century two Jewish rabbis arrived to Taznakht
> and stayed with rabbi Ben Ouakhkha. Ben Ouakhkha himself told Moshe, the
> only Jewish jeweler in the hamlet of Lamhamid, during one of his monthly visits
> to the village. In those days, Lamhamid and other hamlets did not have a large
> [enough] Jewish community to have its own rabbi. Therefore its Jewish peddlers
> and artisans had to wait for the rabbi of Taznakht to slaughter animals or perform
> certain ritual according to their law. I was told that Mardochée and de Foucauld
> visited Jewish communities of Akka, Tissint, and Tata. Later we heard from some
> villagers in the dates market of Tissint that they were French spies.

In French colonial historical literature, Aby Serour and de Foucauld are
widely remembered as two different yet intertwined French colonial "celeb-

rities."[77] Their stories, separate and combined, were widely narrated by the colonial institutions as part of the French success in accessing the risky and unexplored Moroccan Saharan interior. They both produced copious writings on topics of interest to the French colonial authorities, and were both affiliated with the SGP. Yet, the relationship between Mardochée and de Foucauld was also widely discussed because of the role of Mardochée as a native Moroccan Jew in producing one of the most celebrated and quoted colonial ethnographic works on the Moroccan Saharan interior. Although Mardochée was not credited for his effort in the Saharan exploration, at least when the book was published, he was recognized as central to the project. Both men played a key role in laying the cornerstones for a historical legacy that was alternately contested and praised. Both men were celebrated for their role in documenting the history of the Saharan Jewish communities and rejected for their colonial connections.

In their stories, I find similarities and echoes of my own. In this historical and historiographical context, my ethnographic study was also mistrusted by some subjects who contended that Israel and America sent me back to my native region to collect legal documents about the property Jews sold to Muslims before their migration. Like de Foucauld and Aby Serour, I was construed as paving the ground for a "Jewish colonial return," and not only in the minds of the older generations. Kaddour, a twenty-three-year-old undergraduate student at Ibn Zohr University in Agadir, and a member of the youngest generation, questioned my identity as a native: "You cannot be a Muslim from here. In my mind you are a Jew. Allah's words are clear about this: Jews and Christians will never be satisfied with Muslims until they follow their religion. Only Jews study Jews. You are a Jew. You are no different from de Foucauld and his Jewish spy." In this context, and despite my being native to the region, people were suspicious of my ethnographic study to the extent of arousing on some occasions the same apprehension the names of de Foucauld and his Jewish guide continue to stir in certain minds.

Outside the *Mellah*

MARKET, LAW, AND
MUSLIM-JEWISH ENCOUNTERS

A Necessary Friendship

In his cement block house at the center of the administrative quarter of Akka, I interviewed Hajj Najm Lahrash, one of the richest notables (*a'yan*) of the community and the son-in-law of the former judge of Akka, al-Hashimi al-Bannani al-Fassi. We talked about his partnerships with Jews before they left for Israel in 1962, their relationships with Muslims, and their social and religious life. Lahrash agreed that religious differences and boundaries separated Muslims and Jews. However, he stressed friendly Jewish-Muslim encounters and commercial relationships. Holding a cigarette in one hand and a piece of bread in the other, he commented as he struggled to keep a fly away from his eyes:

> We needed Jews for our economic survival; they depended on us for their personal security. We had to coexist to endure the desert. We had to agree on a fenceless space and a legal framework that organized our relationship. The market and the *shari'a* made this interdependence not only possible but also sustainable.

Lahrash contended that the market was a transitional space where religious, tribal, and ethnic differences were allowed and tolerated. At the same time, different legal repertoires provided a framework to help these relationships work and to protect Jews as well as Muslims from political and social transgressions. He enumerated many examples of this relationship:

> On the eve of the French Protectorate, Yusuf Sarraf bought a field in the village of Rahala by way of pledge [*rahn*].[1] After a period of time, the Muslim wanted back his plot. In return Yusuf the Jewish creditor demanded his money. Nevertheless, the Muslim claimed back his land without paying back his loan, breaking his legal pledge to the Jew. The Jew sought his Muslim protector's help in the neighboring village of al-Qabbaba. That same day the Muslim mounted his

white horse and headed to Rahala where he asked his fellow Muslim to pay back his Jewish protégé. In fear, the Muslim went to his house, brought the sum of money, and paid back Yusuf. This is the way justice [*'adl*] used to be implemented with regard to Jews.

Lahrash's recollection is supported by thousands of legal documents still found in family collections throughout southeastern Morocco. In his work on the history of Tafilalt, Mezzine unearthed many documents of the social histories of marginal pre-Saharan communities.[2] Mezzine is one of the few local historians of the nationalist historiographical school after independence to combine local manuscripts and oral history in the social history of Tafilalt. Although he acknowledged the works of al-Mukhtar al-Susi and Muhammad Dawud as pioneers of Moroccan regional histories,[3] I argue that from a historiographical perspective, Mezzine's Western academic training combined with his familiarity with the region allowed him to go beyond hegemonic colonial and post-colonial narratives and historiographical paradigms to decipher the complexities of private documents in local, regional, and national contexts.

My work on the Jews of Akka and Sus partly builds on legal manuscripts that I collected from families around the oasis of Akka. These legal papers show a plurality of intricate and overlapping forms of jurisdiction, such as *'urf* (customary law) and *shari'a* law, that together offered a social, political, and economic space for Jews in southern Morocco to negotiate their social relations and economic needs, as well as to address legal grievances with Muslims. These legal spaces in and beyond which Jews could move constitute *juridical fields* in Bourdieu's sense.[4] Despite the legal and social regulations that confined Jewish movements within this largely Muslim social and legal pre-Saharan space, Jews managed to break from these confinements by using Islamic, customary, and later Western legal systems for public matters, and rabbinical law in family and communal dealings. This ability to deal with issues that comprised social and economic hazards for Jews in Akka was also facilitated by what I call the *transference of legal concepts* from customary law to *shari'a* and vice versa. This movement of legal ideas helped the Jewish minority adapt to the different interpretations of each legal system, where sometimes a legal ruling based on the *shari'a* was annulled or just ignored because the Jewish and Muslim litigants reached a settlement (*sulh*) without needing the judge (*qadi*) or the tribal council (*jma'a*).

In her study of speakers of Nahuatl, a central Mexican Uto-Aztecan language, Hill identifies what she calls the syncretic project in linguistic production based on a wide range of semiotic material. Speakers mix different linguistic styles to manipulate hegemonic metalinguistic structures.[5] In a similar way I claim that southern Moroccan Jews used what I call *legal syncretism* to manipulate the restrictions of the social and political system in pre-Saharan Morocco. While Jews needed the protection of Muslims, they were able to benefit from the multiplicity of legal systems, which allowed them to escape many social restrictions. I argue that in Akka, the Jew could pick and choose based on factors that served his interest in the marketplace, guaranteed his safety as he peddled in the hamlets and markets, and protected his property and money in the *mellah*. He could either reach a settlement through the presence of his Muslim protector, present his case before a Muslim judge and write down the ruling in case of future problems, ask for the legal protection of the tribal council and benefit from the rights that customary law gave him, or (after the French colonization) just ask for the legal protection of the French, British, or other European consulate.[6]

Breaking with the Colonial Past:
Local Archives and Regional Histories

Almost nine months after I began my fieldwork, Ibrahim, the owner of the Chaykh Omar Museum, introduced me to Idir, a descendant of a renowned religious and political figure in Akka. Idir invited me to neighboring Tizounine, one of the important slave markets in the western trans-Saharan trade route, to check a large cache of manuscripts in one of the abandoned houses that his great-grandfather had owned in the late nineteenth century. The large wooden box contained documents of family credits to Berber and Arab tribes across the Sahara as well as *commenda* (a form of commercial partnership in which financial and human resources are combined for trading purposes) and trade partnerships with Jewish families as far away as Tindouf and Essaouira. Many of these documents describe tribal and family relationships during the years of famine that struck the region in the late nineteenth century and the first quarter of the twentieth century.

When we arrived at our destination, we unlocked the wooden door but could not enter the house, which was in the oldest part of Tizounine. The ceiling of the hallway leading into the courtyard had fallen and was blocking the door; that was still in good shape, although an army of termites had munched through its frame. After almost two hours, just before dusk, we managed to get inside the house, where artifacts from Timbuktu littered the corners. The whole place was falling apart. Old and broken pottery was scattered everywhere. A few small baskets lay on the ground, ravaged by termites that left them without bottoms. My eyes were scanning for the box of manuscripts. In a dark room in the north part of the building, we finally found a huge wooden box about a meter and a half long and two meters high. I thought I had found my *khazina* (treasure trove). As we lifted its heavy top, we saw only a handful of documents stuck at its bottom. Since it was getting dark inside the windowless room, we sent for a pair of candles at the nearby shop. Lighting the room, we saw hundreds of paper fragments dispersed all over the place. My heart ached when I realized that the documents had been vandalized and left to the destructive powers of the natural elements and the extreme heat and cold.

Despite a few attempts by some national scholars to look at local and family manuscripts,[7] this vignette illustrates a frequent indifference to the local and regional archives that could shed a new perspective on regional histories. Before March–September 2004, I was able to collect thousands of manuscripts on southern tribal relations, histories of the Sahara, Saharan Jewry, and social, economic, and political relations throughout the Anti-Atlas region. Many documents were folded, so it was difficult to photocopy them without damaging them. They came in many forms and shapes written on paper as well as wood. Some were stored in reeds, while others were folded into bundles in wooden boxes and palm-leaf baskets to protect them from termites. Despite cases of loss such as the one described above, I was still able to preserve many, some of which I reproduce in this book, by putting a piece of glass on the document before photographing it with a digital camera. I also made copies of each collection for the owner.

After independence, Muhammad Dawud's *tarikh titwan* (History of Tetouan) and al-Mukhtar al-Susi's *al-Ma'sul* opened a new nationalist historiographical school, building on traditional Moroccan documentation (*al-masadar al-maghribiya al-qadima*).[8] By the early 1950s, this movement not only critiqued French and European histories of the Maghrib, but also called on Moroccan historians to deconstruct their premises and sources. The decolonization of the history of the

Maghrib would take place at the level of the source. The chronicle, genealogy, hagiography, and legal manuscript were the foci of historical revision and rereading.[9] At the same time, a new relationship between scholarship and Moroccan nationalist ideologies replaced French colonial policy and its historical production. However, apart from the traditional movement led by Muhammad Dawud and al-Mukhtar al-Susi, writing after 1956 largely responded to and interacted with new European methods and theories. The influence of European and American anthropologists and historians stimulated an increased interest in the study of local and regional histories and minority groups.[10] Ahmad Tawfiq,[11] Rahma Bourqia,[12] Abderrahmane El Moudden,[13] Mohammed Kenbib,[14] Jamaa Baïda,[15] and Aomar 'Afa,[16] to name a few, produced groundbreaking works on the relationship between the Makhzan (central government) and its subjects and provinces by shedding light on new local archives and juxtaposing them with colonial documentation and historical analysis.

It is in this environment that this study of the regional history of southern Moroccan Jewry marks a major shift in the national historiography. Its focus on the Anti-Atlas, and Akka in particular, provides the basis for rethinking the central issues and questions about the historiography of the pre-Sahara through a combination of local archives and oral accounts. It aims to displace the colonial ethnographies from the center and insert the local population's voice and perspective.[17] I argue that European ethnographers and travelers have looked at Tafilalt primarily through their French and Western historical gaze, making little effort to consult and excavate the mines of documents that the native people still hold in private family libraries. This work thus resonates with al-Manuni's critique of French historiography in its failure to consult Arabic sources.

It is in this context that I reason for a new approach to the study of Saharan Jewry by looking at family archives as sources of historiographical writing. Although al-Mukhtar al-Susi was one of the early historians to collect and discuss the importance of local manuscripts in rethinking the history of Sus, he and other nationalist leaders paid little attention to marginal groups such as Jews and Haratine.[18] Like Mezzine and al-Manuni, I hope to focus the historian's lens on marginal groups (in my case, southern Jewry) and highlight their historical presence through legal texts and discourses. Before I turn to these documents and analyze the legal context of Jewish-Muslim encounters, I want to describe Jewish-Muslim encounters in the marketplace.

Dendritic Markets: Jewish Peddlers on the Move

Although Jews and Muslims interacted in many ways in villages throughout southern Morocco, Jewish-Muslim relations were strongest in the marketplace, so much so that one respondent from the great-grandparent generation noted: "When the Jews left Akka, it was like a company of one thousand workers that went bankrupt. Akka is still waiting for its Jews to prosper again." In the nineteenth and early twentieth centuries, Jews in Akka and other hamlets were important actors in trade relations in the settlements of Iligh, Marrakesh, Essaouira, Guelmim, Tindouf, and other interior and sub-Saharan African communities. Jewish mercantile networks in the Saharan communities were based on dendritic market structures.[19] These regional places were secondary to the epicenters of Marrakesh and Essaouira. Smith has argued that these peripheral markets existed because of a combination of their functional characteristics for local populations and external peddlers in addition to the convenience of merchants.[20] The Jewish peddlers controlled commercial activities, and the Muslim population showed a low participation in trade. Jewish predominance in trade was partly reflected in movements around branching weekly markets attached to regional centers.[21] As itinerant traders (*'atara*), the Jews periodically loaded their goods on mules and made long rounds of the tribal settlements and weekly rural markets. Hsina, a grandfather from Rahala, noted:

> Jews never stayed in their homes for more than a week except during religious holidays. With the exception of the rabbi, they went out [*kharju*] for weeks, sometimes months. They would load sacks of donkeys and mules full of textiles, spices, shoes, and other articles and wander around nearby Arab and Berber villages and towns; they would barter and exchange these commodities for maize, old clothes, jewelry, eggs, wheat, dates, ostrich feathers, and barley. They went as far as Marrakesh and Essaouira.

These markets were located in what has been known in the historical literature as *bled siba*[22] (land of dissidence), where weekly markets were forms of tribal meetings. The most important aspect of the market was its neutrality. Individual groups and separate ethnic entities came together in a space where nobody had political or moral authority. In this public arena, political differences were set aside and intertribal discussions and friendships took place.

Such a binding system guaranteed a safe trading network and protected the Jewish outsider, who served as a mediator among the different tribal forces. Traders, mostly Jewish, attended markets that can be divided into two categories: small dendritic markets like that of Akka and large core markets as in Essaouira. The nature of the market system is defined by the size of the transaction and the people that attend it on a weekly basis.[23] Low-level market systems, to use Smith's terminology, are generally held in the territory of a tribe or at the boundaries of two or three tribes. Large or higher-level market systems are usually held in strategic locations of major significance to a number of tribes.[24] Spatially, the markets are dendritic in nature because they are in the middle of many confederations or tribal lands serving local populations, visiting nomads, and itinerant Jewish peddlers. What is considered the sacred nature of the market is sometimes corroborated by the existence of a shrine of a local marabout (*sayyid*) in or at the periphery of the marketplace, which provides refuge for people in case of blood feuds. It is morally wrong to steal, kill, or put the life of people in jeopardy in a marketplace.

The Jews were embedded in a feudal hierarchy where they paid tribute and other forms of material compensation to Muslim patrons in exchange for protection. Hess described this system of protection: "Every Moroccan has 'his own Jew.' Sometimes he has two. Therefore he is always certain of his economic profit."[25] Nevertheless, although this political situation might tell a story of economic and social exploitation, the relations that Jews ended up fostering with Muslim patrons through trading alliances translated into complex and ambivalent networks of friendship, protection, and interdependence. I argue that Jews used their social "pariahhood," mobilized their personal networks (*m'arfa*), and called upon their *dhimmi* legal status to shape different legal jurisdictions to their own benefit.

John Davidson was one of the early European travelers to venture into the southern fringes of the Moroccan south. *Notes Taken During Travels in Africa* is a posthumous narrative published by Davidson's brother and based on his notes, which were recovered in Tafilalt. The chronicle provided many details about the different social and economic characteristics of Sus, as well as the geographical and ecological features of the area. Davidson's story is also one of the early eyewitness accounts of the Jewish communities in this southern part of Morocco, which was forbidden to Europeans. In one of the letters addressed to the duke of Sussex, Davidson described the legal position of these communities:

> The Jews of Atlas are far superior, both physically and morally, to their breth-
> ren residing among the Moors. Their families are numerous, and each of these
> is under the immediate protection of a Berber (the aboriginal inhabitants of
> North Africa), patron, or master. They have, however, their own sheikh, a Jew,
> to whose jurisdiction all matters are referred. Differing from the Jews residing
> among the Moors, who are punished by the Mussulman laws, they are not in the
> same state of debasement or servitude; their case [is] one of patron and client,
> and all enjoy equal privileges, and the Berber is bound to take up the cause of
> the Jew upon all emergencies.[26]

Davidson not only clearly distinguished between two systems of jurisdiction (tribal Berber and Moorish Arab), but also described how differently both
systems treated their Jewish communities. He recognized that the Jews in the
Anti-Atlas relied on special personal bonds, where the Muslim was the protecting patron and the Jew the protected client. The Jews relied on the Muslims to
convey their goods over long distances. In the customary law of Anti-Atlas,
Jews were given God's protection (*Aman Allah*) because it is wrong to turn
away people who ask for protection. Edward Westermarck pointed out:

> The *'ar* [shame] is of great boon to strangers, especially in those parts of the coun-
> try where the Government has no power. Among the Berbers, if a person wants
> to settle down in a strange tribe, he makes an 'ar-sacrifice outside the house or
> tent of a native, who then becomes his protector, or at the entrance of the mosque
> of the village, in which case he becomes the protégé of the whole village.[27]

The legal status of the Jew in Akka and other Anti-Atlas communities was regulated through the concept of protection (*himaya*). In customary law, Jews were regarded as marginal strangers to the tribe; tribal chieftains treated them through
what is called primary and secondary protection. When a Jewish stranger (or
Muslim expelled from his tribe) sought the tribe's protection, the process of
being granted tribal safety was called primary protection. Once Jews or other
strangers were granted permission to reside among the tribe, they needed a

secondary protection from a family in the village who would be their protector in return for certain gifts. This friendly relationship between the Jew and the Muslim was generally established by the ritual slaughter (*dhabiha*) of a sheep by the Jew before a Berber or Arab patron of power. The patron had to have influence in the community to assure his client's protection. The patronage and clientage were generally hereditary. Despite the legal and social limitations, tribal councils granted the Jewish communities the right to manage their own internal affairs. The personal status of Jews was regulated and governed by rabbinical law. In the aftermath of the French conquest, this system was kept intact, and Jews were given the freedom to regulate their legal affairs in such issues as divorce, the status of women, inheritance, and marriage.[28] This body of rules was derived from the Torah and the Talmud and interpreted by individual rabbis.

Local Manuscripts and the History of the Jews of Akka

A southern Moroccan proverb reads: "What leaves the head does not leave the paper." This saying translates the daily concern of the population about their private ownership (*milk*) and the importance of preserving their legal records and documentation. The '*aqd* (legal document) was critical to accountability; written documents were one of the few available legal sources used by plaintiffs to prove their rights over property.[29] In times of war, Hajj Najm Lahrash reported, oasis dwellers left their papers with friends. In order to protect their capital and resources, Jews occasionally registered their belongings as labor partnerships,[30] contractual partnerships,[31] financial partnerships,[32] proprietary partnerships,[33] and credit partnerships[34] with their Muslim neighbors.

When a legal case involved a Jew and a Muslim, Muslim courts or judges had jurisdiction over the rabbinical courts. The judges generally applied *shari'a* law. Legal procedures were sometimes influenced by the king's representatives, called *qaid*s, who tended to settle cases in an arbitrary way. Under this system of both customary and *shari'a* law, Jews theoretically had the same rights as Muslims, given the importance and the necessity of testimony in Islamic courts. However, they needed a Muslim witness for their testimony to be legal. In fact, Jews, despite this legal obstacle, were able to get a fair settlement.

After the French Protectorate in 1912, *shari'a* courts were slightly reformed. The colonial authorities made a distinction between four systems of justice (see Table 2). Although Chouraqui held that the Makhzan civil court system,[35]

Table 2 Court systems available for Jews in Southern Morocco

Type of Court	Jurisdiction
Civil and commercial courts[1]	Cases involving Muslims and Jews
Shari'a courts[2]	Religious litigation among Muslims
Customary law *'urf* courts[3]	Tribal areas
Rabbinical courts[4]	Religious cases involving only Jews

1. *Al-mahakim al-madaniya wa al-tijariya*
2. *Al-mahakim al-shar'iyya*
3. *Al-mahakim al-'urfiya*
4. *Al-mahakim al-yahudiya*

supposedly secular, was unfair to Moroccan Jews, the documents that I collected tell a different story, at least in terms of Islamic jurisprudence dealing with cases involving the People of the Book (*ahl al-dhimma*). Chouraqui noted, and rightly so, that the Makhzan system retained an Islamic character and that France did not take the opportunity to purge it of its Islamic characteristics. There was an exception in the tribal areas, where France tried to make a distinction between tribal customary law and Islamic jurisdiction.[36] The documents I collected suggest that the system, despite its Islamic nature, was more complex than has been previously thought. The legal cases that I encountered, dating from before the colonial era, during the French Protectorate, and after independence, demonstrate that Muslim judges were generally following legal procedures outlined by *shari'a* law and that Jews used this system by negotiating these legal fields as long as the cultural, social, and political environment allowed it.

Legal Syncretism:
The Jews of Akka Between 'urf and shari'a Law

In North Africa, and in Morocco in particular, the Maliki school of Islamic jurisprudence has given *'urf* a key role in the issuing of *fatwa* (legal ruling). Like the Hanafi school, Maliki scholars regard *'urf* as an *asl* (original source) of jurisprudence when there is no definitive legal text. In Maliki law, *mufti*s take into account the concept of public interest (*istislah* or *istihsan* in Hanafi law). The public interest (*maslaha* or *manfa'a*) is the cornerstone of Maliki law in legal reference (*istidlal*). Ibn Malik maintains that using *'urf* when it does not contradict *shari'a* can be the basis of a legal opinion and should not be put aside by the jurist, especially when it is relevant to the general public interest. Maliki law is concerned with the place of *'urf* and its dynamic relationship to *shari'a*. That is why al-Maqarri argued that custom in Maliki law is like the conditional (*shart*), because it restricts the absolute and makes the general more specific.[37] Over time, tribes came to write down these regulations and legal conditions on tablets. The customary law was written down and preserved on boards and planks known as *l-luh* or *l-lawh*, in reference to the penal codes drawn on wooden boards.

In the southern fringes of the desert, along the Anti-Atlas Mountains, Berber and Arab tribes have preserved, despite Islamization, their traditional system of jurisdiction, locally known (depending on the tribal confederation) as *luh, lawh, qanun, izerf,* or *azzarf*. Literally, the term *lawh* means the inscribed tablet used by children in the Qur'anic school for memorizing the Holy Book. In the Anti-Atlas region, the term *lawh* translates into the Berber word *izerf*. *Izerf* is the collection of tribal penal codes recorded in *lawh* specifying the clauses (*bunud*) of the penal law that organize retribution when an infraction takes place. Every time a tribal rule was broken, tribal notables checked the clauses of the *lawh* for the right retribution. In the Sus region, these tablets specified the nature of each infraction. If a crime was committed, a monetary fine was usually paid; sometimes, if it was a serious crime, the person was banished from the community forever.

Although practices differed from region to region, it was clear that customary law was stronger in rural mountainous and tribal areas than in urban centers. This legal system was highly respected throughout the *bled* (hinterland), where environmental and social factors demanded such legal codification. The tribe's *izerf*—a tribal legal system that is usually juxtaposed to the Islamic law—dealt mainly with the penal legal code and outlined the fines for each crime. Each tribe had its own *izerf*, although it was sometimes copied from another tribe.[38] The *izerf* is also written in a way that translates tribal control not only over its territory but also over the behavior of its members. In this way, the customary law (*'urf*) has always been seen—especially by the legal scholars (*'ulama'*) of the central government—as a system of law outside the king's control and, therefore, of the *shari'a*. Nevertheless, Al-'Uthmani argued that the *'urf* among the Jazula of the Sus region did not contradict the Islamic religion.[39]

Customary law was widely practiced among the southern Berber tribes of Sus and the Bani region. It gave these tribes a form of independence from the central government that allowed them to avoid paying government taxes. Many kings were aware of this, and they tried to buy off these tribes through incentives. Others used powerful lords in these tribes to gather taxes and maintain their allegiance to the central government. In July 1882, during his *harka* (military expedition) to Sus, Sultan Mawlay al-Hasan I wrote to the pasha of Meknès:

> These tribes have demanded that we maintain their practice and acknowledge their customs. They already possess old *dahirs* from our former generals and Muslim sultans. We acknowledged at the site their customs and we renewed their *dahirs* [decrees].[40]

Mawlay al-Hasan I thought that the customs of Sus were legal because the older community of Muslim leaders (*al-salaf*) found that they did not contradict the Islamic law, *shari'a*. Therefore, he supported using the same system with the condition that scholars, local notables, and leaders would not transgress what had been acknowledged by Islamic jurisprudence. On the eve of the French Protectorate, the legality of the tribal *'urf* would be confirmed by the *dahir* of September 11, 1914. However, the French government went beyond recognizing the *'urf*, proposing that it have the same status as the *shari'a*. Therefore, early in the protectorate, the French introduced a legal division between the regions inhabited by mainly tribal Berbers and the cities, where most of the Arab populations lived.[41] The French colonial government also initially refused to establish *shari'a* courts in the tribal regions it conquered. Tribal customs tended to contradict the *shari'a* in some legal cases.

Given the tribe's emphasis on the protection of the stranger and the extension of its responsibility to Jews and other foreigners in danger, there was a need to regulate it. Accordingly, every *lawh* specified who could and how they should host a stranger. The following legal clauses are examples of customary traditions that governed Jews and other strangers. I found these references in some manuscripts of customary law I collected around Akka and the Sus region:

> He who brings to the village a *dhimmi* is fined twenty *mithqal*.
>
> He who harms a guest of the tribe or another tribe is fined five *mithqal*.
>
> The *'ar* of the Jews and the artisans belong to the tribe.

The Jew is treated as the *'ar* of the tribal council [*al-jama'a*]. He is a guest stranger to be protected. He is like a poor man who does not have the power to insult or fight back.

The *dhimmi* can seek refuge in the tribe when he is hosted by *al-shurafa', al-murabitun,* or other village notables.

The testimony of Haratine and Jews is not valid inside the village.

When a *dhimmi* offers a *dhabiha* to someone in the village and obtains his protection, nobody else in the village can be the protector of the Jew.

Who destroys a legal document containing the laws of the tribe pays ten *mithqal*.

Who contests the validity of a binding contract has to orally testify with five witnesses.

When someone is caught writing a legal document and claims that it is the writing of the local *faqih*, he will be summoned in front of them; if they acknowledge that it is their writing, then so be it, and if they did not, he pays a fine of twenty *mithqal*.

These legal clauses emphasize two main points. The first is that economic interest as well as political reasoning drove their writing. Strangers, namely Jews, were always seen as potential friends or collaborators because of their commercial activities. Village notables who controlled the tribe's general affairs made sure that other people from different clans could not have access to the privileges that could be gained by hosting or protecting a stranger. Second, in order to maintain their economic hold, the notables needed to legitimize contacts with Jews. Although writing framed social relations in legal terms, it was not accessible to everybody; literacy was confined to certain families who ended up controlling not only the very process of writing through the local judge(s) but also the attendant economic relations.[42]

The Local Qadi

A Susi proverb goes: "The judge listens to both parties; and the *qaid* listens to the witnesses." It communicates the complexity of the jurisprudence given the number of actors involved in every legal action. Although rules and regulations controlled social, political, and economic transactions, personal networks[43] were largely responsible for how a plaintiff's complaints were justly solved. Therefore, even though customary law and *shari'a* regulated the way the tribal council and judges should tackle legal cases, these matters occasionally tended to be settled on the basis of personal connections. Nevertheless, there was a certain respect for the law as it was laid out in the *'urf* and the *shari'a*. In Akka, the judges held their meetings in their homes, the local *zawiyya* (religious brotherhood), the weekly market, or after Friday congregational prayer in different villages. They had been trained under the patronage of Muslim scholars in Sus or in the traditional centers of Islamic scholarship, Fez and Marrakesh.[44] It is useful to consider the point al-Mukhtar al-Susi made about the state of affairs of Islamic scholarship. He argued that the majority of Muslim judges in the region were trained locally, although to a large extent under the advice of judges trained in urban centers. He wrote about the families of judges in the different corners of Sus and also listed Islamic schools and their locations, funding, and the scholars and judges they trained.[45]

In Akka, I noticed that the social capital of being a judge was kept and transferred within certain families, namely, descendants of *shurfa* and Murabitun. Generally, the tribal council appointed these judges based on their reputation and scholarship. Judges were also confirmed through official letters from the sultan. The selection of judges either through the tribal council or the official nomination of the central government continued until the French control of southern Morocco. One of the oldest courts in Akka was known as *mahkamat al-zawiyya*, where Abu Bakr ban Muhammad al-Tamanarti served as a judge.

The important question that arises is when and how judges' rulings and customary law were applied, toward both Muslims and Jews. The Spanish traveler Badia Y Leyblich (known by the pseudonym Ali Bey) suggested that in Morocco, Jews got little benefit from justice under Muslim rule. He noted:

> The Jews of Morocco are in the most abject state of slavery; but at Tangier it is remarkable that they live intermingled with the Moors, without having any separate quarter, which is the case in all other places where the Mahometan religion prevails. This distinction occasions perpetual disagreements; it excites disputes, in which, if the Jew is wrong, the Moor takes his own satisfaction; and if the Jew is right, he lodges a complaint with the judge, who always decides in favour of the Mussulman.[46]

Manuscripts collected in family archives throughout southern Morocco give a different perspective from the ones outlined by many European travelers, as seen in the narrative at the beginning of this chapter. Lahrash discussed with me the importance of the Muslim protection of Jews. He also stressed how the Jews used documents as legal proof to protect themselves. According to some elders, the Jews were very careful to document every piece of land or credit they bought from or lent to Muslims.

Case Studies: Qadis and Akkan Jews

In order to demonstrate the concept of legal syncretism and the ability of the Jews of Akka to survive their social, political, and religious limitations, I present eleven cases from family archives to show how the Jews relied on the ruling of local judges to protect their property and capital. I collected the material from Akkan individuals, such as al-Hajj al-Najm Lahrash and Oubaha Muhammad, whose documents were handed down through their families. These cases[47] highlight the nature of the social, political, and legal relationships between Muslims and Jews outside the *mellah*. They deal with mortgages (cases IV, VI, VII, VIII, and IX), water (case III), economic partnership (case I), sale (case II), loans (cases X, XI), and rent (case V). Unlike the colonial archives, they have been excluded from the historiographical narratives of southern Morocco. I offer them as context for the ethnographic narratives of great-grandparents and grandparents. The texts, which I translated from classical Arabic in their entirety, are reproduced here. I then follow with an analysis of these records.

Case I

Praise to Allah alone, [. . .]. The litigants arrived for legal proceedings [*majlis al-shar'*] at the court of the judge of Akka: the plaintiff Dawid ban Yusuf from the Jews of Tagadirt and the defendant Ahmad ban Husa ban al-'Abd the representative of the inheritors of Balqasam ban Muhammad Ahmad from Tagadirt [. . .]. The plaintiff answered that the referred above, I mean Balqasam the above-mentioned, while alive [*fi hayatih*] took from the mentioned plaintiff Dawid ban Yusuf *sab'at 'alaf riyal* [seven thousand riyal] and with the numbers [*wa bi al-ramz*] 7,000 like this as a credit. He traded with it and shared the profit. After this he [Dawid] received from Balqasam from the mentioned capital [*ra's al-mal*] three thousand

and three hundred. No instead, three thousands and seven hundred, 3700 *riyal*.[48] And there remained in the hands of Balqasam the above-mentioned three thousand and three hundred from his capital. He (Dawid) left this amount with him (Balqasam) until they clarified how much profit he earned from this. Instead [*bal*] Balqasam kept the described amount of money simply planning to give back the capital little by little because he could not pay it all at once. And when Balqasam fell sick and remained bedridden, his wife Fatim bint Ahmad [. . .] from qasr al-Rahalin of Akka went to pay a visit for her husband to Balqasam the above-mentioned and she met the brother of plaintiff Makhluf ban Yusuf and he asked her where she was heading and she told him the story of Balqasam's sickness and the seriousness of his state. Makhluf went to his brother the above-mentioned plaintiff and informed him. Then Dawid accompanied Si al-Bashir ban Yahya to Balqasam who was not able to speak and who did not care where he was at the time. He [Dawid] stayed there until Si al-Bashir ban Yahya wrote down for Dawid all that he had lent to Balqasam. Now the defendant asks what is the position of the Islamic law [*shar'*] in what the *dhimmi* Dawid wrote in the hour (I mean the hour when he was dying). On the date of 8 *shawal* of the year 1376/9 May 1957. The slave of Allah Ahmad ban al-Madani al-Wakhshashi and [. . .]. Judge's seal. (From Ibrahim Nouhi Archives)

Case II

Praise Be to God, and His prayers on His Beloved Prophet. With Allah's power and might, the *dhimmi*s al-Hazzan Dawid ban Yusuf and his partner Ishaq ban 'Amran bought from their seller Hmad Abra Abu Shayat Lamrabti al-Warrani all four units of measure [*dhira'*] 124 of land in Dr'a River [*wadi dar'a*]. The purchased land is neighboring their [the *dhimmi*s'] land as it is stated and described in the title deeds that they own and which they presented. The sale was valid, authorized, complete, and free from ignorance and harm, the full price ['*idatuha wa nihayatuha*] nine *riyal hasani*[49] coarse/worn *dirham*s of the mint of the period, received by the seller from the *dhimmi*s. The receipt was complete and without denial and harm. This is what the above-mentioned Hmad testified to and it was written in the year 1344 [1925–26] [. . .]. The slave of Allah Ahmad ban al-Hasham al-Wakhshashi. Judge's seal. (From Hmad Ouhamam Archives)

Case III

Praise to Allah with all due Praise, and prayers on His Beloved Prophet. To get to the point [*wa ba'd*] al-Murabit al-Sayyid Muhammad ban Ahmad 'Uhamam from Hisn al-Hajar ascertained that he received in addition [*bi wajhi al-ziyada*] six *riyal qirta*[50] from the *dhimmi* Bardkhin ban Hab of Yahud Akka Hisnat bani Shu'ayb in exchange for one turn of his share of water from Tishshit spring ['*ayn* Tishshit] during the nightly turn of the family of 'Uhamam. This was written in their presence on the 15 *shawal* of the year 1350/23 February 1932. The slave of Allah [. . .] and the slave of Allah Ahmad ban al-Madani al-Wakhshashi. Judge's seal. (From Ibrahim Nouhi Archives)

Case IV

Praise to Allah alone [. . .]. The plaintiff Muhammad ban Ibrahim ban Balla al-Tizunini attended the *majlis shar'* (legal proceedings) of the court of the judge of Akka and claimed that the defendant Dawid ban Yusuf of Tagadirt in Akka put his hands illegally upon [*tarama lahu*] half of a house at the qsar of Tizunin which is bordered in the directions of the east [*qibla*] by [name], of the south by the shops of the market, and of the west by [name]. The plaintiff Muhammad ban Ibrahim asked the defendant Dawid ban Yusuf to take his hands off the house [. . .] that he has been using over nine years and he has up to now refused. Until now the plaintiff asks that the defendant gives him back the other half of the house especially because he has not produced any reason [*sabab*] why he does not want to do so. The decision [of the *qadi*] will be rendered following the defendant's response. This was written on the date of 21 *rajab* of the year 1376 [21 February 1957] [. . .] [unrecognizable seal]. Judge's seal. (From al-Najm Lahrash Archives)

Case V

Praise to Allah Alone, It was witnessed to me that al-Husayn ban Salam Agamman Amraybat from Idda Bshit al-Warrani received in addition the entire thirty *riyal* Hasani from the hands of the *dhimmi* Ishaq ban 'Amran. The first party added that through access by the second party to the land [*turab*] of his wife [name], meaning the land of Hamma ban S'id 'Udawud [. . .]. He [the *dhimmi*] will be paid along with receiving the original sum someday [. . .]. The weak slave of Allah 'Ali ban 'Abd Allah Abahtuk from the village [*rabwa*]. Allah's kindness upon him. *Amin!* Judge's seal. (From Ibrahim Nouhi Archives)

Case VI

Praise to Allah with all due Praise, It was witnessed that 'Alla Barra Uhmad Gannu from Hisn al-Hajar owed [*thabata 'ala dhimmatihi wa malihi*] a measure [*sa'*][51] and a half of wheat equivalent to the capital [*ra's al-mal*] of a *dirham*[52] to the *dhimmi* Ya'qub ban Ishaq ban Yahya and the period of credit [*ajal*] ends in May. This was written in the month of Ramadan of the year 1323/1905. The weak slave of Allah al-Husayn ban l-'Abd al-Jilali al-'Antari. Judge's seal. (From Hassi Ouqandou Archives)

Case VII

Praise to Allah with all due Praise, and prayers and blessings on His Beloved Prophet. It was ascertained that 'Ali ban Hmad 'Alla ban Ganna from the *rabwa* [hill] of Akka [Tagadirt] owed [*bi dhimmatihi wa malihi*] to the plaintiff the *dhimmi* Dawid ban Yusuf ban Ishaq ban 'Imran, Jews of al-Hisna, *sa'ayn* [two measures] of barley equivalent to [*aslu*] two *dirhams* and the period of credit ended in May and he is not free from his obligations [*la-yubara'u dhimmatuhu*] until he pays. This was written during the month of Ramadan of the year 1322/1904. The weak slave of Allah Muhammad ban Muhammad from the *rabwa* of Akka. God's Grace to him. Judge's seal. (From Ibrahim Nouhi Archives)

Case VIII

Praise to Allah with all due Praise, and prayers on His Beloved Prophet. Mohammed Ajbir came to me and witnessed that he owes a small teapot and it is also ascertained that he mortgaged this year's date harvest from the field [name] to the owner of the capital, the *dhimmi* Makhluf ban Yusuf. The deadline is until he returns back from travel without conditions or dispute. Otherwise he pays fines when the deadline is surpassed. This was written at the beginning of *shawal* of the year 1322/December 1904. The weak slave of Allah al-Husayn ban Muhammad ban 'abd Allah ban Ayyub al-Jilali al-'Antari. God's Grace to him. Judge's seal. (From al-Jaafari Archives)

Case IX

Praise to Allah with all due Praise, It was witnessed to me by Shtumr the daughter of Muhammad Uballa, and the wife of the late Hmad ban Ahmad Uballa of Hisnat [village] bani Shu'ayb that by operating on behalf of her sons she received [bi-wajhi al-ziyada] all of the four riyal Hasani from the dhimmi al-Hazan Dawid ban Yusuf ibn Dawid Yahud al-mallah below the mentioned Hisna and this is in addition to [ziyadatan] what he got from her field [faddan] known as Taskdit located in the land [turab] of the al-Haratin spring ['ayn] a true loan [ziyadatan ṣahihatan] to be paid all at once on the day of the redemption. This was written in the middle of the month of Allah jumada al-'ula of the year 1323/July 1905. The weak slave of Allah al-Khadhir ban Muhammad ban 'Abd al-Rahman from the Hisna of banu Shu'ayb Allah's kindness upon him. Amin! Judge's seal. (From Ibrahim Nouhi Archives)

Case X

Praise to Allah with all due praise, and prayers on His Beloved Prophet. Our beloved [. . .] friend Yusuf ban 'Ali al-Murabti peace on you and Praise to Allah for his blessings. [. . .] It is not unknown to you that the deadline of our credit to you is over and has expired a long time since. You have not sent me the articles you owe me. And now if you send me what is mine that would be what is expected of you on receipt of this message. If you fail to do so, we will add up the interest [lantris] upon you starting from the day you get our letter. I will write about your case to the Sultan God Bless him, he will write to your governor and order and force you to pay back [my due]. I wrote this letter to caution you and to respect our friendly relationship. Therefore if you do not send me back my merchandise, you will be called by the Makhzan and you will be paying all the expenses of the sakhkhar [servant] of his Highness and the wages of the al-raqqasa {mailman] and other expenses and you will be paying all these from your own personal money as well as my own credit to you. We informed you and we are not to be blamed after this. Salam. On the 15 rajab of the year 1310/February 2nd 1893. Merchant Rubil al-Malih from Essaouira. (From Ibrahim Nouhi Archives)

Case XI

Praise to Allah with all due Praise, Our brother in Allah and our friend Yusuf ban 'Ali al-Murabit al-Tizunini. Allah's peace and prayers on you and his Allah blessings [. . .]. What happened to you after all this period? One year has passed and the deadline is over and you have not paid me back my dirhams. This is not the right path. Shame ['ar] on you and I am upset. I wrote to your brother, (God

Bless him) to inform since he represents the sultan in the region. I have lost everything that I spent on you; if we do not settle I will add it and you have to pay me back. *Salam*. On the 20 Hijja of the year 1310/July 5 1893. Merchant Rubil al-Malih from Essaouira. (From Ibrahim Nouhi Archives)

Case I is an example of what is usually referred to in Islamic law as *qirad* or *commenda*. Although commenda is a form of partnership, it is different from a regular partnership (*sharika*). In a commenda, only the capital provider bears the risks in case of capital loss, while both parties of the *sharika* share the loss. Udovitch had defined commenda:

> An arrangement in which an investor or group of investors entrusts capital or merchandise to an agent-manager, who is to trade with it and then return to the investor(s) the principal and a previously agreed-upon share of the profits. As a reward for his labor, the agent receives the remaining share of the profits. Any loss resulting from the exigencies of travel or from an unsuccessful business venture is borne exclusively by the investor(s); the agent is in no way liable for a loss of this nature, losing only his expended time and effort.[53]

The commenda brings together two elements: credit and partnership.[54] While one party invests and risks capital, another invests and risks time and energy. The partnership does not entail any form of liability to the investor in case of the loss of the business. When a business makes a profit, the borrower gives back the invested capital and a share of the profit. In the Islamic tradition, the Prophet Mohammed engaged in a commenda with his wife-to-be, Khadija, in which she provided the capital and he invested his time and expertise. The issue in Case I is a commenda between a *dhimmi* and a Muslim.

Ibn Qayyim al-Jawziyya wrote that the Prophet had a partnership with the Jews of Khaybar in the Medina. Given this precedent, and although some jurists viewed it as reprehensible (*makruh*), it is widely agreed among the different schools that a Muslim can have a partnership with a *dhimmi* as long as he controls the trade. The reason for this was that *dhimmi*s practice usury and deal in alcohol and pork.[55] Udovitch called the economic partnership between a Muslim and a *dhimmi* an interdenominational commenda. He held that the views of Muslim law on this form of collaboration are not unequivocal.[56] The main bone of contention remains the religious identity of the agent. Muslim jurists argued that a *dhimmi* who oversaw a partnership with a Muslim might engage in practices such as selling pork and alcohol that would invalidate the contract.

In the commenda in my sample, the Muslim (Balqasam ban Muhammad Ahmad, from Tagadirt) was the agent of the commenda. Although Malik Ibn Anas looked down on a commenda between a Muslim and a *dhimmi*, even if the condition of the Muslim as the agent of partnership was met, this commenda was legal. The issue, however, concerned the Muslim's commercial activities and accounting. One of the requirements of the commenda is that the agent keep fairly detailed accounts of his transactions and separate his personal expenses from the provisions of the commenda unless it was stated otherwise. In this case, the Muslim agent supposedly used the commenda for his personal expenses. When the Jew found out that he was on his deathbed, he raced to his house with a Muslim friend to document that his partner still owed him 3,300 *riyal*s. Because the Jew did not write down the contract of the commenda, he ran the risk of losing his money. The central issue was therefore the following: Did the judge accept what the Jew's friend had written down while the other Muslim was on his deathbed? The response of Dawid ban Yusuf shows his understanding of the cultural and religious importance of the written document. The defendant questioned the validity of the document since it was written while the agent was dying and might not have been at his full mental capacity.

Case II is an example of a free and clear sale of land. The judge left no room for speculation that the sale was incomplete by writing that "the sale was valid, authorized, complete and free from ignorance and harm." Since these conditions were all met and the price was paid in full, nobody could contest this deed in the future. This document informs us about another level of social relationship between Muslims and Jews: the fact that Jews not only gave credit but also were allowed to buy, own, and sell property. Goitein described similar transactions throughout the Mediterranean based on the Geniza papers.[57]

Case III gives us a clear idea of a normal case of a *rahn*. The borrower here was al-Murabit al-Sayyid Muhammad ban Ahmad 'Uhamam from Hisn al-Hajar (Agadir Uzru), and the lender was the *dhimmi* Bardkhin ban Hab of *yahud* Akka Hisnat banu Shu'ayb (Tagadirt). The contract stated that the borrower received in addition (*zada*, or *ziyadatan*) six *riyal qirta* from the *dhimmi*. The phrase "in addition" (*bi wajhi al-ziyyada*) is a critical legal and technical word and essential to the whole transaction. It assumes that there was a contract prior to this one, which it replaced. To understand this concept, I asked the grandson of Muhammad ban Ahmad 'Uhamam from Hisn al-Hajar, who provided me with the following story behind this document, although he could not locate other documents that were drafted before and after this case. He explained:

> In those days, people needed money or seeds to invest in their lands. Let us take this document, for example: my ancestor Muhammad ban Hmad 'Uhamam owned many fields in Akka and a lot of water shares in the different springs of the oasis. During the period of drought, he ran short of money. Because of his status in the community and his ownership, he could borrow money by way of *rahn* [pledge] from Jewish or Muslim merchants. What I suspect here is that my grandfather has already borrowed an amount earlier from the same person; because he was not able to pay on time, he allowed the Jew to use a nightly turn of his water share of the spring of Tishshit, but only one. The fact that he allowed him to use only one turn of water shows that he thought that he would be able to give the Jew his six *riyal qirta* after the next payment deadline. My family used to have a lot of land and water, so they could manage to pay back their credit [*dayn*] or mortgage [*rahn*]. There were many poor families who had to mortgage their property for years until they ended up selling it to the Jewish or the Muslim creditor.[58]

The *rahn* (pledge) was an important economic strategy that merchants used to gain profit. Park described this pattern in the region of Essaouira between the 1930s and the 1950s. He wrote:

> The transactions dealing with rural property that are most significant are sales/purchases and mortgage [*rahn*]. All those interviewed in Essaouira maintained that a mortgage would only be entered into in an emergency. In Morocco, a rahn usually involved a contract which specified that the owner of a piece of land agreed, in return for a sum of money or quantity of grain to (a) grant the lender the usufruct [legal right to use and enjoy profits of something belonging to someone else] of that piece of land for a given number of years and (b) return the same quantity of money or grain to the lender at the expiration of that period. On successful conclusion of this contract, the owner would recuperate but

if he was unable to fulfill his obligation to repay the amount borrowed, he could sell the land or, as was usual, take out a second or further mortgage (at more disadvantageous terms). In the latter case, the lender got further usufruct of the land for a similar or longer period in return for lending an additional smaller sum. A series of mortgages almost inevitably led to the loss of the land.[59]

A *rahn* transaction is a legal (*shar'i*) economic operation from an Islamic perspective because, in theory, both parties involved share risk, unlike a regular example of usury, in which a party lends money in return for an increase. Therefore, what looks like interest is pure profit from an Islamic point of view, because there is an element of shared and contractual risk for both parties. Nevertheless, this kind of transaction has some elements of exploitation whereby the lender benefits from the hardships of the borrower, especially during times of droughts or hunger.

Although some historians limit this activity to Jewish lenders in southern Morocco, many Muslim families also practiced *rahn*, in both rural and urban areas. Akka is mainly an agricultural community where water and land are basic assets. By taking these resources away from the most vulnerable households of the community, pressures were put on these families during the period before World War II. Park described this phenomenon in a detailed analysis of the ledgers of the judge of the Khemis Meskala region of Essaouira Province from 1931 to 1956.[60] He summarized property transactions in this region through a graph showing that 3,186 sales and 325 mortgages were generated between 1931 and 1956. Park postulated that, given the number of registered sales versus mortgages (*rahn*), Jewish merchants were particularly concerned with having a legal document that would protect them in the case of a future problem.

Case IV deals with a legal complaint regarding the ownership of a section of a house. During my stay in southern Morocco, I was informed on multiple occasions that Jewish traders and artisans either rented local Muslim places or made *rahn* with their owners. Many actually rented rooms in Muslim households. Many *fatwas* gave the Muslim community permission to allow Jews or Christians to live with Muslims in the same house (*dar*) or some neighborhoods (*darb*). Al-Wansharisi gave an example of a case where "a tributary (Jew or Christian) can rent or buy the floor of a house whose ground floor is used by a Moslem."[61] Given that the *shari'a* ruling regarding the *dhimmi*'s rent (*kira'*) or purchase (*sharya*) of a Muslim's building is seen as a legal transaction from an Islamic perspective, Case IV is basically about whether Dawid ban Yusuf had proof that supported his refusal to hand over to the Muslim creditor the house that he had occupied for more than nine years. Although the document does not offer any solution, two main assumptions can be deduced. The judge might rule in favor of the *dhimmi* if he produced enough documents to support that he either bought it or had a *rahn* on it and that the Muslim did not fulfill his obligation to recover the house. The judge might also accept the Muslim's testimony (*shahada*) and rule in favor of the Muslim, especially if the Muslim could also argue that the Jew was engaging in immoral activity such as the sale of alcohol.

Case V is an example of a long-term lease of land (*turab*). The most interesting idea in this contract is that, unlike the sequential *rahn* in Case III, where the lender got the legal right to use and enjoy the profit of the land through a series of mortgages, this case was a final mortgage (*rahn*) until the Muslim repaid the amount borrowed (thirty *riyal hasani*). The land in question might cost the first amount of money lent to the Muslim in addition to the thirty *riyal hasani*; therefore the lender saw that any addition would amount to a loss. Henceforth, he stopped the transaction at this level and specified that he would use the land unless the amount was paid back someday.

Cases VI, VII, VIII, and IX show another kind of *rahn*. Families used this *rahn* to survive natural calamities. The plague, locusts, and famine not only represented a serious threat to households but also threatened the leadership of many kings, as political chaos usually reigned after famines. According to Park and Boum:

> The plague was regularly introduced into Morocco by returning pilgrims arriving by boat in northern ports and consequently targeted urban areas, the north, and the coastal plains most prominently. Locusts usually originated in the Sahel and flew north, so they usually devastated the south more than the north. Famines often followed the plague because the population losses ruined people's abilities to bring in the harvest with calamitous results for the following year. War, excessive taxation, and weak sultans, who had no reserves set aside to help out the population, also weakened the ability of the population to resist natural calamities.[62]

During the famine period, rebellions erupted, and the central government (Makhzan) usually responded by sending regular military expeditions (*harka*) to collect taxes and to subdue the rebellious tribes.[63] These cases are only four instances of the thousands of *rahn* of lands, water shares, palm trees, and other kinds of property that families were forced to pledge as collateral to survive drought and locusts' devastations. At the beginning of the twentieth century, southern Morocco was hit by two major droughts (1902–3 and 1906) and two devastating plagues of locusts (1901 and 1907–10), which led to massive crop losses.[64] These natural calamities forced the population to mortgage their land in return for a small measure of barley and wheat, mainly for consumption—as we see in Cases VI and VII. Sometimes an annual harvest of dates was sold in exchange for a utensil, as seen in Case VIII. Finally, families in desperate economic situations had to mortgage part of their harvest to cover the cost of food they borrowed in times of famine, as in Case IX.

The last two, Cases X and XI, are unique and different in nature and content, also linking us to some preexisting accounts of the families involved. They provide another example of commercial transactions in the region as well as a different type of lender: a Jew of the sultan (*tajir assultan*). Both cases describe the complaint of a Jewish merchant named Reuben El Maleh against Yusuf ban 'Ali al-Murabti, a Muslim merchant of Akka who happened to be the brother of the sultan's governor in the region. Reuben El Maleh was one of the privileged merchants associated with the sultan at the end of the nineteenth century. This relationship gave a number of Jewish families in Essaouira (Corcos, Afriat, Macnin, and El Maleh) the authority to become wholesalers and shippers of products between Timbuktu and Europe.[65] A small number of Muslim and Jewish merchants became part of a group called Tujjar al-Sultan. Schroeter commented:

> The ties of interdependency between merchants and Sultan were reinforced by a particular kind of fiscal relationship. The tajir traded on interest-free loans from the Palace. Out of his profits, derived from commerce, the tajir repaid the Sultan in monthly installments. The proscriptions regarding interest on loans in Islamic law prevented the Sultan from making direct profits from royal advances. Indirectly, however, the *Makhzan* was operating like a bank, investing in a tajir who was usually already a man of considerable means. By promoting the merchant's

business enterprises, the makhzan could expect to gain substantial returns from custom duties paid by the tajir to the government agents at the port.[66]

However, the government's commercial and political authority was largely challenged when the European protection (*himaya*) of many Moroccan Jewish and Muslim merchants began after the Spanish invasion of northern Morocco in 1860.[67] The El Maleh family was an example of the traditional Jewish merchant of Essaouira, who benefited from the sultan's protection before becoming a protégé of foreign Jewish organizations and European consulates. According to Schroeter, the El Malehs dominated the local Jewish organization for more than eighty years,[68] the result of their social positions in the community as rabbis and *dayyans* [judges]. "Elmaleh's position as leader of the community," Schroeter argued, "therefore, was rooted in his personal charisma. His religious functions and commercial activities legitimized his authority. For the Elmaleh family, piety and commerce went hand-in-glove."[69] El Maleh owned many places in the *mellah* of Essaouira through ownership and mortgage. Schroeter, one of the few scholars who has written extensively on the history of the family, asserted that much of the profit of the El Malehs came from their property investment in Essaouira.

Reuben El Maleh, who died in 1925, was the son of Joseph El Maleh. He became responsible for his father's business in the early 1880s when Joseph started traveling to England and other parts of Europe. In 1886, Joseph died in London, and Reuben took over the business, becoming one of the main shippers of Essaouira, not only to Europe but also to the local and regional merchants, peddlers, and retailers of the interior south. The family of ayt-Mribat was one of his business partners. Yusuf ban 'Ali al-Murabit al-Mribti al-Tizununi was the brother of the *qaid* of Akka. He was in charge of family business. In the 1890s, a period of drought and famine affected his trade. The situation was exacerbated by the uncertain political climate, which threatened the caravan trade between Akka and Timbuktu, where Yusuf sold most of the products he obtained on credit from the merchants of Essaouira, including Reuben. One of the interesting points in both cases is the tone of the letters. Neither was a typical document written by a judge or a notary. They were personal letters of complaint sent directly to Yusuf al-Tizununi by Reuben. The letters highlight three major points. First, Reuben stressed his relationship with the Palace to make his point to the

Muslim merchant that he should pay him as soon as possible. Second, Reuben called on the *qaid* of Akka (the merchant's brother) to intervene in order to accelerate his payment. Third, Reuben threatened to take the case to the sultan if he was not paid back his dues, which would put more expenses on Yusuf, including the dues of *sakhar*,[70] *raqqas*,[71] and even *lantris*.[72]

These letters confirm my argument of the importance of credit as social capital. While Jewish lenders in Akka were careful not to break their relationship with their Muslim debtors, Reuben's status as a merchant of the sultan and an outsider to the village explains his interest in the payment of the credit instead of maintaining a social relationship with Yusuf. Reuben was a rich outsider merchant whose commercial transaction with Yusuf was not crucial; in fact, the more quickly he received his credit, the better he would feel, since he was not making any profit if his merchandise remained in the hands of Yusuf for a long period.

Mezzine, Tawfiq, and al-Manuni, among others, have provided a regional historiographical model that combined oral history and archival documents they collected from families in different regions of Morocco. During my ethnographic study, I used an approach pioneered by Mezzine in Tafilalt to study the Jews of Akka through legal documents. My focus on private collections allowed me to look at the history of these Jews through *'urf* and *shari'a*, which informed my interviews about Muslims' memories of their former Jewish neighbors. In Akka, Jews were able to move among many legal systems, giving them the flexibility to transcend the restrictions of the Islamic and tribal legal and social structures. As weak and protected merchants and peddlers, Jews benefited from the rights that customary and Islamic laws gave them outside the *mellah*. Accordingly, they were able to mix their strategic efforts through what I term *legal syncretism*. In the Jewish quarters, as I describe in the next chapter, Jews were legally independent, as rabbis interpreted and controlled the internal religious and social relations before the arrival of the Alliance Israélite Universelle and the introduction of secular education.

3

Inside the *Mellah*

EDUCATION AND THE CREATION
OF A SAHARAN JEWISH CENTER

Men with History

Sitting in a circle under a shady but dying palm tree by the only road between Ouarzazate and Akka, a group of old men dressed in colorful blue, white, and yellow *jellaba*s chatted about local economic issues and environmental challenges. As Abdallah, Abdarahman, Mbarak, and I joined them, a barefoot child tucked his shaved head under one of the men's shoulders as he tried to save himself from the torture of a fly. At another point in the circle, a man in his late nineties leaned against the adobe wall of a shop as he put a white lotion on deep cuts on his coarse left heel while a large pack of flies swarmed over his hand without disturbing him. On the other side of the road, a group of children and teenagers crowded the only café in the oasis—Café des Amis—to watch a championship soccer game between Spain's biggest rivals, Barcelona and Real Madrid. The men's conversation was occasionally interrupted by loud screams of celebration or frustration from the fans of each team. As the sun began its descent behind the rocky Anti-Atlas Mountains, some women headed to the farming plots, part of their daily ritual, to harvest alfalfa for sheep and cows. Swarms of locusts followed the women as they walked through the thick fields. In the far distance, a water-pumping machine could be heard. In the last few decades, the villagers have relied on modern technology to water their fields and dying palm trees.

On the other side of the village, silhouettes of men and women stood on the roofs, waiting for sunset before breaking the fast. Just before the daily Ramadan *iftar* (breakfast), old villagers met late every afternoon before sunset and shared their thoughts about their daily activities, the American invasion of Iraq, and the war on terrorism, as well as the Palestinian and Israeli conflict. However, the lingering drought and the alarming waves of locusts dominated their discussions. As we sat down, the single daily bus heading to the city of Tata made its casual stop to let out some villagers coming back from Marrakesh. Groups of children of all ages suddenly rushed out of the café and ran toward the bus to help the travelers carry their loads of packages. There was a moment of silence as the old men turned their heads toward the bus to satisfy their curiosity for the news of the day.

Wearing a white *jellaba*, Hajj Muhammad ben al-Kabir was the center of the conversation. His face did not show any signs of a man in his early nineties, though it was clear that he had a hearing problem. I noticed that when the men spoke, they tended to raise their voices to accommodate his handicap. As if this was not enough, he leaned toward every speaker, holding his broken glasses from the middle. Hajj Muhammad was one of the few members of the great-grandparents generation who could talk about an event and give its date, time, and every detail you could possibly want to know. His memory had earned him the label "historian of the village." On several occasions I asked my father about certain events in the history of the surrounding communities. When he did not know the answers, he usually advised me to contact Hajj Muhammad. He noted without hesitation, "I do not have the history ['*ana ma'andish tarikh*]. Hajj Muhammad knows everything. He will give you the history in detail [*ghadi ya'tik tarikh b-tadqiq*]."

As I meticulously studied his sun-darkened face, coarse hands, and wrinkled forehead, Hajj Muhammad interrupted the brief moment of silence as the men looked at the bus. He proceeded in a long soliloquy as if he were talking to himself without losing sight of 'Ata, a villager who was over a hundred and who nodded as if he wanted to assure Hajj Muhammad that he approved his views:

> Did you remember ['*qalt*], 'Ata? Just twenty years ago, you cannot see the groves through the palm trees. Today everything is gone. The water is gone! The people are gone! Even the Jews are gone! We are left here to this scorching heat that killed everything and the locusts that destroyed what remained of the palm trees. Even our youth does not want to work anymore. Of course, they see people like Aomar with American jeans and backpacks and they all want to leave. What a shame! We lost everything! Even our children refuse to obey us! They all want to be rich. So they are joining the thousands of Moroccans who get killed in the waters of the Mediterranean every day just because they want to get a piece of the Europeans' [*nsara*] rosy world!

Hajj Muhammad made these comments with a grin on his face. For him, other great-grandparents, men and women, these conversations are not simply moments of socialization and entertainment but nostalgic recollections of histories as well. In their narratives, great-grandparents recall both the mundane details of ordinary days and the extraordinary events that marked their lives.[1] These stories, whether accurate or not, reveal the beliefs, concerns, and attitudes of each generation.[2] For Hajj Muhammad, the past represented glory while the present stood for loss. Jews were an integral part of this glorious past. In approaching the study of Jewish-Muslim relationships through stories told by Hajj Muhammad and other Muslims, I believe that they tell us about the events in the lives of these Muslims as well as the critical attitudes that govern the worldview of each group.

This ethnographic journey begins with Hajj Muhammad as someone who knows local history and who also represents the generation of the great-grandparents. His stories reflect different aspects of the colonial narrative of de Foucauld and Aby Serour. For six months I tried to interview Hajj Muhammad, to no avail. Every time I returned from Akka, he was either on a short trip to a friend in a nearby village or visiting his children in Casablanca. My brother advised me to plan on spending some weeks of the holy month of Ramadan in the village if I would like to meet him, since he usually spent the month there. Mbarak, my brother's friend and one of my younger consultants, was close to Hajj Muhammad. During the winter, when he returned from the fields, he kept Hajj Muhammad's company and listened to his long and entertaining stories. I joined him on one of these visits. The moment Hajj Muhammad referred to Jews, Mbarak purposely gave me an opening by asking, in a dramatically innocent manner, if he remembered the Jews of the village:

"Do you know if Jews lived here?"

Boujama, a villager who knew many Jews in Zagora, interrupted before Hajj Muhammad could answer Mbarak's question: "Of course, there were Jews in the center of Foum Zguid. They were even here in Lamhamid, our village. They rented houses and rooms from the tribesmen. You see that building by the acacia tree? That is where Shlomo had a stall and repaired shoes."

Boujama also boasted of having Jewish friends in Israel; he reconnected with them every summer when they came back for religious holidays to celebrate the anniversary of the death of the town's rabbis, known as *hillula*.[3]

Since I returned to my home of Lamhamid in January 2004, I had been traveling back and forth to Akka, which made the villagers curious. News traveled in the community as well as to surrounding villages that I was investigating the history of the Jews of this region. Occasionally, without intending to, I got into long conversations about the Jewish families that had lived in the different communities. People wanted to share with me what they remembered about their Jewish neighbors, friends, and business partners. At times, the conversations became repetitive. Hence, although I already knew Boujama's piece of information, I nodded my head as if this were the first time I came across this information, not wanting to interrupt the flow of conversation. As if his historical authority had been challenged and his memory questioned, Hajj Muhammad challenged everyone to name Jewish peddlers and families that had lived in Lamhamid. The discussion became a contest of memory: "Who has the history of the Jews of Foum Zguid?" he asked with a self-satisfied expression on his face. Some produced the name of Moshe. Others recalled names such as Meir and Hazan Sham'un. However, nobody could satisfy the requirements of the man who mastered the history of the region. After triumphantly listing the names of the families, their children, the rabbis who came to slaughter the sheep for them, and the dates they settled in the region, he proceeded in a confident way:

In the past, there were no buses. There were mules and donkeys. Jews rode them and brought us information as well as goods. Without them, it would have been very hard to know what goes on in other places because we were most of the time fighting each other. No one could harm them because just like women they were *hurma* [untouchable]. They could travel from here to Akka or Taznakht and nobody could touch them. There was an agreement that the Muslims in each village should not touch the Jews of other Muslims. Each tribe has its Jews. They were Taznakhti, Alougoumi, Foum Zguidi, Tissinti, and Akkawi Jews. Therefore, they peddled without major risks but sometimes were harmed.

Every village in the Anti-Atlas Mountains had its Jews. Akka, one of the farthest settlements in this region, housed one of the oldest and largest Jewish communities. Unlike their interactions with Muslims outside the *mellah*, Jewish life in the *mellah* was largely governed by rabbis who stressed traditional and religious customs in the synagogue, in the Jewish neighborhood, and in each household. Unlike the spaces outside the *mellah*, one consultant from the great-grandparents cohort described how "inside the *mellah* the Jew was king. Muslims never intervened in their marriage, circumcision, prayers, and their personal relations." In the eyes of many great-grandfathers and grandfathers, the *mellah* was a private space where Jews were free to practice their religion, educate their children, raise families, and build their community.

The Jews of Akka: Family, Community, and Religion

In 1948, about 20,000 Jews lived in the villages around the Atlas Mountains of Morocco.[4] Residing in Berber and Arab tribal communities,[5] the Jews lived in separate neighborhoods within the *ksur* (walled villages) of the mountains and on their slopes.[6] Some villages held no more than a few dozen families. Others housed between 100 and 600 individuals. Most of these people had little contact with areas outside the region. Unlike the Jewish communities of Tangiers, Casablanca, and Essaouira, these mountain enclaves remained essentially closed to any European influence.

Today, throughout these pre-Saharan marginal communities, occupied and deserted Jewish neighborhoods are still sites of memory, where Muslims' memories of encounters with Jews are "moulded into the material and physical structures of the domestic space."[7] There were two types of Jewish settlements in the Moroccan *bled* (hinterlands). In one, Jewish peddlers and itinerant merchants rented homes from Muslims in small Berber and Muslim communities in order to store their merchandise and sometimes to live for a few days if not weeks. These communities connected satellite markets linking Marrakesh and Essaouira with Timbuktu and other trading entrepôts throughout the Sahara. This type of settlement had usually less than the ten men required for a *minyan* (quorum) to fulfill the commandments to recite prayers. In the other, many villages and hamlets such as Akka, Taznakht, Tamanart, and Iligh had large Jewish settlements. Many great-grandparents claimed that the Jews established their neighborhoods throughout Berber and Arab hamlets after Muslim chieftains and tribal councils granted them protection and land to settle. For instance, Ibrahim, the owner of the Jewish museum of Akka, noted that the Jewish neighborhood of Tagadirt was bequeathed by the *shurfa* of ayt-Sh'yab as a lifetime pledge (*rahn*) that gave Jews the usufruct of the land but maintained Muslim ownership. Ibrahim described the situation:

> Centuries ago, the political establishment in the village of Tagadirt needed to expand its political power and strengthen its economic resources vis-à-vis other regional powers such as Tamanart, Tarudant, and Iligh. They invited the Jews of neighboring Errahala to resettle in their village by providing land and allowing the Jews to transfer property in the neighborhood to their future children. In a few years, the *mellah* of Tagadirt became the center of Jewish life throughout Akka; Jewish families moved there and to other areas in southern Morocco, especially after they were allowed to build houses of worship and expand them if they needed to.

Land ownership and especially the right to build houses of worship had been at the center of Jewish concern throughout the Sahara.[8] Tribal Berber and Arab leadership usually satisfied the Jews' religious needs. Sometimes Muslim scholars objected to the new synagogues or the expansion of old ones. This usually ended with the relocation of the Jewish community to more hospitable villages. Hsina, one of the few literate members of the great-grandparents cohort, commented:

> Islam required sultans to protect Jewish rights to life and worship. This was the basic principle of Islamic law as long as they paid the *jizya* and did not wage war against us. In my lifetime when Jews were here we never attacked their *sla* [synagogue]. Jews were religious people, and if you imposed laws against their religious practice they left. I know that many Jews who settled in Akka came from villages that limited their rights.

This vignette portrays the constant internal Jewish migration throughout southern Morocco that was conditioned by what I call *traditional risk*. Beck's work on risk society assumes that traditional societies did not have the concept of risk because systematic methods of dealing with social and political insecurities were introduced by modernity.[9] Looking at the patterns of Jewish migrations in southern Morocco,[10] I believe that economic risk and political insecurity stand at the core of the constant movement of the southern Moroccan Jewry.

Traditional Jewish communities were risk societies because they were "preoc-cupied with the future (and also with safety), which generates the notion of risk."[11] The rise in the number of Jewish families in Akka in the late nineteenth century shows that the Jews encountered less political and social antagonism at the same time that they benefited from religious, political, and legal protection.

Unlike the Jewish quarters in some cities,[12] the *mellah*s of the southern hamlets such as Guelmim and Akka were part of the walled *ksar*. The physical closeness between Muslim and Jewish households reinforced social and cul-tural warmth despite their religious differences. Nevertheless, the Jews' rela-tive isolation from the daily affairs of the Muslims permitted them to live as prescribed by Jewish law. Social life was conducted in accordance with the pre-scription of rabbis (locally called *rebbi*), whereby the seventh day of the week (Shabbat) was reserved for prayer.[13] Religion played a major role in dictating the procedures surrounding marriage, circumcision, death, and other festivals and cycles of life.

The synagogue was once the center of Jewish life in Akka. In the late nine-teenth century, there were three Jewish houses of worship: two in Tagadirt and one in neighboring Taourirt. Today, like many Jewish synagogues in southern Morocco, they are piles of dirt. The biggest synagogue in Tagadirt survived rain and time, although its ceiling fell in the mid-1990s, leaving two standing pillars still intact. The scale of this place of worship is a testimony to the size of the community compared to that of other satellite Jewish settlements in the region. I visited it with Moha, a *haratine* in his mid-eighties, and although we had a hard time opening the door because of a pile of dirt, we were able to get through a small covered hallway that led to the open interior. The corners of the run-down building still bore the smoke of the oil lamps that once lit this place. A pair of cooing pigeons nested on the crumbling *bimah* (raised platform of the synagogue). Piles of discarded vegetable matter, butchered fowl, and a small dead rabbit were scattered around the synagogue. I started taking pictures of the building as Moha commented:

You know Jews are not like us. They have three prayers: morning [*shaharit*], af-ternoon [*minha*], and evening [*ma'ariv*]. Unlike us, they wore a black and some-times red cord [*tefillin*] around their left hands, their heads, and started shaking their head up and down. We respected and listened to our imam; they listened to their rabbi. You see this bench, this is where the rabbi used to sit and discuss social and religious Jewish matters. If they fight, the rabbi is their arbitrator. In the 1940s, I used to take manure from the house of Rabbi Youssef to the fields. I saw on many occasions Rabbi Youssef mediating between husbands, wives, and other fighting parties.

To many members of the great-grandparents generation, the rabbinic authority was at the center of Jewish society. The Jews upheld the common belief in the authoritative body of the Hebrew Scripture (the Old Testament) and the Talmud. They also revered their rabbis as carriers of this common law. Thus, the rabbis administered *Bar Mitzva*, served as *dayyan* (rabbinical judge) as well as *shohet* (one who slaughtered animals based on rabbinical law), taught children in the *sla*, and led prayers. The imprint of the rabbinical law was everywhere inside the *mellah*, and good behavior was judged by language and actions. Rabbis made sure that children learned the difference between permissible and illicit behaviors, and consistently reminded their fathers to follow religious codes. This edifice of prescriptions governed every aspect of Jewish life in the synagogue, street, and home.

On many occasions those interviewed pointed out the striking similarities between Jewish and Muslim societies in terms of the religious dominance of men. They claimed that women were largely illiterate, and it was not until the arrival of the AIU that Jewish women made their official appearance at school. In Akka, men were in charge of the conservation, the transmission, and the interpretation of written tradition.[14] Abdel Aziz claimed:

[Women] cooked, bore and raised children and took care of their husbands. The synagogue and *sla* [traditional school] were outside their reach. They were not supposed to touch sacred texts because they menstruated. To be in the house of God, their rabbi said, they needed to be clean, which they were not. Because men were responsible for them, they prayed for their salvation and the salvation of their children.

Outside the synagogue, the rabbi's imprint was reflected in ritual, family, food, and personal relations. He blessed couples, performed circumcisions, slaughtered animals, and served as judge and scribe. He was the nerve center of Jewish life in Akka. As with Muslim judges and scholars, the position of rabbis was transferred from father to son. The males of the Sarraf family, for instance, held the position of the rabbi of Akka for many years within the late nineteenth and early twentieth centuries. Unlike the situation in Muslim communities, indigenous rabbis were able to monopolize the position of leadership, with the community entrenching hereditary succession and political dominance in the region. Unlike in urban Jewish communities, and even after the arrival of the AIU, a secular leadership never emerged in the *mellah* despite the changes that the community started to see at the everyday levels of dressing and way of life in the early 1950s. Faraji, a descendant of the *shurfa* of ayt-Rasmuk, highlighted this:

> In the 1950s, before Mohammed V was exiled, a man dressed in European clothes arrived with books, children's clothes and convinced the Serraf family to open a local French school outside the *mellah* by the children's cemetery. There was resistance but the community later accepted it. Soon their kids, including girls, began to wear Western clothes and take off their yarmulke [*shashia*] and baggy trousers [*sarwal*]. Local Jews introduced everything new to Akka: the first mill, the first bicycle, and the first truck. Jews understood change; Muslims did not.

In Akka, the rabbi and the elders of the community understood that any change at the educational level meant future transformations in family structures. Traditional households reinforced the rabbi's authority by socializing children and women according to religious laws and teachings. Like Muslim families, several generations lived under one roof, with married couples and their parents and sometimes grandparents sharing a house (*dar*). Each married couple occupied a single room in a mud-brick house that usually had two stories and few windows looking out to the main street of the quarter. During my conversation with Lahcen, a Haratine grandfather, he commented how "home privacy was sacred to Jews like to Muslims. Their women were asked to remain home and respect their religious laws." Said noted that Jews, like Muslims, married at an early age. There were girls who married at the age of twelve, and cousin marriage was very common. Marriages between close relations as well as polygamy were similarities between Muslims and Jews in Akka. In Akka,

I found out about one case of Jewish polygamy because of the inability of a couple to bear children. The wife encouraged her husband to take another wife and after years of marriage, he remained childless. Women belonged to their husbands. Like Muslim women, Jews' mothers, daughters, and wives were rarely seen outside without veiling or cover.

While men occupied public places such as benches outside homes in the main street of the *mellah*, the synagogue, the market, or shops outside the *mellah*, the movement of women was limited to interior spaces. Moha, a *haratine* with whom I visited the Tagadirt synagogue, noted that "in certain cases some women stepped outside their homes to enter their husband's household. There was no difference between them and us." Within the *mellah*, however, veiled women left their homes to exchange visits with other Jewish families in the event of birth, marriage, death, bar mitzvah, or sickness. These visits were a social obligation: women had to share with other women moments of joy and death. When someone died, the men took care of the religious preparation of the body while women mourned outside the home of the deceased in vigils that could last a week. Driss, a farmer from the grandparents' group, maintained that before the Sabbath women from each household took turns to sweep the floor. Asked about meetings between Muslim and Jewish women, many elders claimed that although such encounters took place, they were not the norm.

Traditional beliefs began to change as the community's exposure to the outside world intensified. By the early 1930s, France had extended its colonial grip to the southern pre-Saharan communities, accelerating the region's introduction to new social and cultural styles. At the center of these changes was religious education. In the following section, I highlight the educational transformation of Akka and other communities at the beginning of the modernization period and the later migration of rural Jewish communities to urban centers and Israel.

The Alliance Israélite Universelle and Social Change

In the course of my research, I collected a number of stories about Jewish and Muslim perspectives and experiences regarding education.[15] I was partly interested in how differences in educational background across generations influenced and transformed the Muslims' memories of the Jews. I was struck by my Muslim consultants' emphasis on the differences between Jews and Muslims in their response to the introduction of modern French and Jewish schooling. Haddi, a farmer in his late seventies, commented:

> When the French built the primary school in my oasis, we were asked by our religious authorities to stay away from this polytheistic institution and encouraged to attend Qur'anic schools only. On the contrary, Jews, although they were reticent at the beginning, ended up sending their children to both traditional religious and French schools. They studied French, Hebrew, and Arabic. They were able to attend French schools and became teachers and doctors. Just last year, I met one of them in the village during his visit to their neighborhood—he now works as a doctor in France.

Many of my Muslim and Jewish consultants noted that the Jews strongly believed in their traditional education and saw the synagogue as an important part of their daily lives. Mas'ud Sarraf, a fifty-six-year-old Jew from Akka, said:

> The synagogue and *sla* [traditional school] were the most important social institutions for the Jews of the *bled*. The synagogue fulfilled its service function as the house of worship. The *sla* ensured that children could read and write and respect their traditions, elders, and the moral structures of the community.

Sarraf, a descendant of a family of rabbis in Akka, emphasized the importance of education in these traditional communities. Education was closely linked to the synagogue, where Jewish boys were tutored by the rabbis. Therefore, similar to what Goitein discovered in his research on Yemeni Jews, education in southern Morocco communities was "carried out *within* the synagogue, *by* the synagogue and *for* the synagogue."[16] This emphasis on religious education started to decrease in the late 1940s, and the Jews became open to modern education for their children in the early 1950s. My Muslim respondents stressed that the Jews had a more positive attitude toward French schools in the region compared to the Muslims, who stressed the importance of Qur'anic education.[17] According to another Muslim grandfather:

> Before the French arrival in the southern region, villagers sent their children to the mosque to learn the Qur'an. . . . Only a handful of families could train

scholars who later became judges and respected men in the region. They could read and write; they were nominated by the sultans of Morocco as our judges. As for Jews, they had their own schools too and we never went to school together until the French arrived. Many of them were like us; only some of them could further their schooling in Marrakesh. Nevertheless, after the Alliance arrived they became much more interested in sending their children to the modern schools instead of the synagogue.

The openness of the Jews to the AIU schools was the result of the economic and political crises following World War II and the awareness of the Jewish elders and parents of the importance of a modern education to improve the condition of their children. For this reason, by the late 1940s, the AIU administration succeeded in setting up schools throughout southern Morocco without strong resistance. The AIU leaders managed to obtain the permission and moral blessing, as well as financial support, of the rabbis and parents.

While the AIU gained ground in coastal towns, Marrakesh, the capital of the south, resisted the implementation of its educational programs. In the early 1900s, Aubin made this observation about the Jews of Marrakesh:

In the Maghreb [Marrakesh] the orthodoxy of the Jews is as strict and conservative as of the Mohammedans. Religious forms are observed with the most fanatical ardour. . . . This uncompromising religious attitude makes the Moroccan Jews as suspicious of Christians as they are of the Jews of other countries. The foreigner is looked upon, in the Mellahs as in the Medinas, with no kindly eye, and is forbidden to enter the synagogue, as he is forbidden to enter the mosque.[18]

In her study of the historical patterns of Jewish-Muslim relations in Marrakesh, Gottreich noted that the mistrust of these Jewish communities toward outsiders (including Jewish outsiders) "helps explain the great difficulty experienced by the A.I.U. in gaining a foothold in the southern capital."[19] De Périgny described Jewish education in the *mellah* of Marrakesh as based solely on the rote memorization of Torah. He reported that rabbis

gave their lessons in sellahs, squalid rooms near the synagogues, sometimes in a wicked corner of the house. In most of these sellahs, children were placed there for the simple reason of not interfering with their parents and learning to stay quiet. It was a pathetic spectacle that these poor little beings barely dressed in a shirt, wallowing in soil contaminated with garbage, face smeared with dust and glanders, while the larger ones, grouped around a schoolmaster dirty and stupid, mumbled their way with one nasal voice through verses from the Bible by engaging in a continual waddle of the head and chest.[20]

European travelers and Jews continued to arrive in Marrakesh in the early part of the twentieth century and provided accounts of education in the *mellah* as backward and in need of reform. In his visit to Marrakesh, Slouschz discussed the state of education in its *mellah*:

> There are no proper synagogues in Morocco, and no Talmud Torahs that merit the name. The Kitab (*heder*), or schools, are in dirty, sordid rooms, where the master and the children are all seated on mats, in the midst of indescribable dirt. The Talmud is taught in a Yeshibah under renowned Rabbi Azar, but there are very few true scholars in Morocco, although there are gathered here the Jewish youths from all parts of the Atlas for instruction in the Law.[21]

Despite the opposition to any outside presence, Jewish and non-Jewish, the AIU was able to establish its first school in Marrakesh in 1900 under the director Moïse Levy. European travelers believed that French education was the only way to improve the wretched condition of the Jews of Marrakesh and the surrounding region. In 1916, Slouschz wrote: "The only glimmer of light in this wretched life of the Mellah is brought by the schools of the Alliance and their present director, M. Danon, who has done much to ameliorate social and hygienic conditions."[22]

Before the French arrived, there was no central Jewish educational system. Education was run through the local synagogue and supervised by the rabbi.[23] Before the establishment of the AIU schools, when Jewish children finished their rudimentary education in the *heder*, those who excelled and were financially able were sent to the regional *yeshiva*, where they finished their training to become rabbis. The *mellah* of Marrakesh housed one of these regional *yeshivot* attended by rural Jews from the High Atlas, Anti-Atlas, and Sus regions. Mardochée Aby Serour, de Foucauld's traveling companion, pursued his education in Marrakesh before he went to Jerusalem. In all the villages, Jewish parents sent their boys at an early age to memorize the religious texts as part of their socialization. Parents also did their best to send their male children to religious schools in Marrakesh to further their studies and prepare them for becoming rabbis. Women had no access to education, although they were taught the Jewish dietary laws and how to maintain the proper religious atmosphere to celebrate the Sabbath and other religious traditions.

The AIU and the Jews of Morocco's Southern Bled

Less than half a century after the death of Aby Serour, Elias Harrus grew up in southern Morocco by the time the French Protectorate started implementing its own educational policies. He was born on September 19, 1919, in Beni Mellal, a major Jewish settlement in the Middle Atlas Mountains. He also started his educational career in the local synagogue with the same success that Aby Serour demonstrated in his early years. Aby Serour's education was entirely traditional, taking him from the local *sla* to the *yeshiva* and ending in the highest rabbinical schools of Jerusalem. However Harrus benefited from the modern programs introduced by the French as they extended their power over Morocco. He attended the French primary school, which opened in Beni Mellal around 1919, before the AIU opened its own school in his town.[24]

Unlike Aby Serour, Harrus pursued his education not in a regional *yeshiva* but in the AIU school in Casablanca. This was made possible through a scholarship that paid for his living expenses with a Jewish family. His success in school earned him another scholarship, to the École Normale Israélite Orientale (ENIO) in Paris, to train as a teacher. He was also introduced to the techniques of pedagogy. By 1939, he had finished his training and returned to Beni Mellal for a short visit. The outbreak of World War II forced him to begin his career as a teacher in a primary school in Marrakesh. After the war, Harrus became the director of the AIU's École Professionnelle Agricole (Professional Agricultural School). At the same time, the AIU expanded its schools in the rural regions south of Marrakesh.[25] As a representative of the AIU in Marrakesh, Harrus devoted many years of his life to developing a system of schools in the Atlas Mountains and remote southern villages, and he emerged as one of the leading figures in expanding the Alliance's educational mission to rural southern Morocco. In 1942, he became the director of the AIU School in Demnat, one of the largest Jewish communities east of Marrakesh. This was also when he began photographing villagers, with no intention other than the pleasure of recording a special moment; he had no thoughts about documenting this as a way of life, which would disappear just around the corner.[26] Due to his own Atlas origins, he photographed Jewish villagers as if they were members of his own family.[27] His personal contact with these communities, his understanding of their traditions, and his own upbringing and awareness of their religious sensitivities made it possible for the AIU to expand its schools to Morocco's southern hinterland. The community's agreement to the building of each school was an important step for Harrus before any project took place.

On January 27, 1952, Harrus sent a letter to the delegate of the AIU in Casablanca reporting the opening of the AIU school in Guelmim,[28] a city at the southwestern end of the region of Sus. It was one of the major caravan stops before entering the Saharan interior. Many Jewish merchants and artisans lived in Guelmim[29]; they prospered because of their location in the trans-Saharan trading routes.[30] Harrus's report outlined the hiring of the teacher, the renting of the location, the enrollment of the students, and the relationships between the AIU delegation in Casablanca, the Jewish community, and the French colonial authorities.

In every school, the recruitment of the teacher was one of the top priorities of the AIU delegate in Casablanca. For the school in Guelmim, Harrus chose Mr. Harrosch, the son of a wealthy family from Marrakesh.[31] Although Harrosch failed the first section of his high school final exam, he had a broad knowledge of Hebrew and Talmudic studies. The community was extremely satisfied and pleased with his knowledge when he offered to lead the Sabbath morning prayer in the absence of the rabbi. Harrus also organized a training period in pedagogy for Harrosch with Marelli at the Sarfaty school, with the agreement of the inspector of primary education in Marrakesh. Harrus also taught Harrosch how to deal with formal letter-writing, accounting, and inventory and gave him practical advice about the school's activities.

Throughout the southern villages, teachers played a major role in the success of the AIU educational system. In 1976, Haïm Zafrani told Michael Laskier:

> It was not the policy of the Alliance in Paris that mattered in the bled. It was the policy of the school director who aided the communities in every way possible.

His influence in these communities resulted in the rise of prestige for the Alliance and its credibility. The director did everything: he taught courses, fed the children, at times he even taught them a trade.[32]

The teachers were trained at the École Normale Israélite Orientale (ENIO) and the École Normale Hebraïque (ENH). The ENIO, founded in 1867, brought to Paris the best students of the AIU networks of schools throughout the Middle East and North Africa and trained them to go back and "introduce young Jewish children to Western culture."[33] The ENH, created in 1946 in Casablanca, prepared trained teachers for traditional Jewish studies and modern secular education. Stanley Abramovitch noted:

> The École Normale Hebraïque changed the image of the Hebrew teacher in the AIU from that of *heder* product to one of a qualified young man who not only spoke Hebrew correctly but also knew the Bible, Mishnah, Talmud and History. The ENH taught its students how to prepare lessons and the art of teaching.[34]

In addition to Harrus, Vitalis Eskenazi, Haïm Zafrani, Cohba Lévy, and Alfred Goldenberg played a major role in applying the ENIO educational policies to southern Morocco. The AIU also hired rabbis to teach Hebrew. In 1960, Reuben Tajouri, the head of the AIU in Morocco, died and was replaced by Elias Harrus and Haïm Zafrani. Their challenge was to define the role of the AIU mission in independent Morocco.[35] The teaching of Arabic was enforced as a requirement of the new independent state. For instance, in Akka, given the fact that the AIU was not able to find an Arabic teacher, the local imam, al-Hafyan Hmad Ouhamou, was hired to teach Arabic.

In the countryside, the program in the AIU schools was a six-year track that culminated in a French primary school certificate. Students interested in pursuing their secondary education moved to Marrakesh or Casablanca and studied history, drawing, physical training, science, arithmetic, French language, and French reading, among other subjects. In order not to alienate the community, the Alliance curriculum included biblical history and Hebrew. Rabbis were hired to teach Hebrew. After independence, some schools started teaching Arabic. Teachers were provided with books and other material through the central office of the AIU in Casablanca.[36] They were asked to follow the guidelines for each subject strictly. In the meantime, the AIU delegate sent supervisors to each school periodically to check and grade the teachers' performance.

When Harrus decided to open the AIU school in Guelmim, he contacted the representative of the Jewish community about the location of the school.[37] In general, to save money, the AIU rented houses from both Muslims and Jews for its schools in southern Morocco. For instance, Harrus rented the house of the qaid of Tinghir.[38] In Guelmim, the site of the school was owned by Meyer Ohana, the son of Chalom Ohana, the leader of the Jewish community. Guelmim was largely composed of the extended family of Ohana, which moved from the neighboring community of Oufran after the French took over the south.

In many cases, Harrus was obliged to modify certain sections of the rented houses to accommodate the needs of the school and the teachers.[39] The mud-brick houses in Guelmim and Akka included five rooms and a spacious court-yard. Given that the number of students was too large for the rooms, Harrus decided to use the open courtyard as the classroom.[40] A teacher's table, a black-board, and twelve benches were arranged in the courtyard. The house included room for boarding the teacher as well. Recreation usually took place in an area outside the house in the main street of the neighborhood.

In addition to hiring the teacher and finding the school's location, one of the most challenging tasks that Harrus faced was the enrollment of students. Before the AIU arrived in Akka, male Jewish children attended the French pri-mary school along with Muslims until 1952, when Akka's AIU school was built. Unlike urban areas, where the AIU set up separate schools for boys and girls, the schools of the bled were mixed. These coeducational schools did not face any resistance, with a few exceptions. In Akka, for instance, a few elders op-posed the education of Jewish girls.[41] Laskier contended that since the majority of the Jewish communities of the bled "numbered only several hundred souls, the number of pupils was naturally smaller and therefore, the need for exten-sive educational facilities such as secondary and vocational schools, was not deemed as crucial as in the large towns."[42] The challenge was to satisfy the needs of every member of the community. For instance, in his description of his encounter with the community of Tinghir, Harrus wrote: "The welcome we had received from the community was very moving. Each individual accord-ing to his means, but all with one heart, wanted to celebrate this solemn event. Abenhaim the old rabbi came to talk with us."[43]

A preliminary consultation with the rabbis and the elders of the community was always the first step in the establishment of any school in the *bled*. In an interview with Sarah Levin in 1999, Emile Sebban, the director of the ENH, described how these meetings typically took place:

> We arrive in the morning with his car in a little village and Mr. Harrus asks to see the chief of the Jewish community, and he asks to bring together a dozen members of the community, those in charge. . . . So, he had this very humane way of entering into contact with people. . . . And it was then that he'd negotiate with them for the school. He would explain what an Alliance school was, and how it would serve them.[44]

After the initial meeting, Harrus started the process of enrollment. Parents were usually asked to bring their children to a public place. In Tinghir, the children were brought to the market.[45] The census of every child in the community would then be carried out. Parents usually attended the inventory process to make sure that their children were not left out, for they were aware that only a limited number of places in the classroom were available.

Before making a final decision, students were distributed by age and gender. When two or three Jewish communities were close enough to have one school to serve their needs, the census took into account the town of every child. For instance, in Tinghir, the closeness of the *mellah* of Asfalou led Harrus to open some seats for the children of this settlement. The inventory of the children, whose ages ranged from five to thirteen years old, was fifty-one boys and forty girls.[46] However, the room could hold only fifty students. Harrus decided to enroll thirty-nine boys and twenty-one girls, allowing each bench to seat more than three children.

In Guelmim, Harrus took a census of the children: twenty-seven pupils (thirteen boys and fourteen girls) between the ages of six and ten.[47] He also visited the neighboring *mellah* of Oufrane to convince its children to join the Guelmim school, where a number of seats were still open. Members of the community offered to put up some children. Ten children from Oufrane were added to the school (nine boys and one girl). In Akka, the school started with thirty-four students. In 1956, the report of Charles Bitton, the director of the school, to the inspector of primary education of Marrakesh noted that twenty-five students attended the school (seventeen boys and eight girls).[48] Five children moved to different areas in Morocco and three left for Israel before finishing their primary education certificate.

By 1956, Zionist movements began to encourage Jews to immigrate to Israel in light of the growing popularity of Gamal Abdel Nasser and pan-Arab ideology; so the Jews began to leave Morocco for Israel and Europe. The directors and teachers of the AIU schools in the *bled* became aware of the possibility of this migration.[49] On May 28, 1956, Charles Bitton reported to the AIU delegate in Casablanca that the number of students in the next academic year would increase to thirty or thirty-five students unless the "Jews of Akka leave for Israel."[50]

Despite the openness of many Jewish parents to the AIU schools in the *bled*, some were suspicious of the activities of the AIU. All the families were not prepared to abandon their customs, which the teachers challenged as superstitions. Many were opposed to the education of girls and were against the mixed school. Harrus and the AIU required the local rabbis to allow the girls to attend schools instead of supporting the tradition of child marriage.[51] Alfred Goldenberg, the founder and director of the school of Demnat, noted that the school faced strong opposition in enrolling girls because parents saw their roles as wives, child-bearers, and housekeepers.[52] The AIU teachers saw that part of their job was not only to educate these rural Jewish children but also to refute some of their old traditions. Although rabbinic support helped curb this tradition in some communities, it failed in others, sometimes even putting the AIU's work at risk.[53]

After World War II, the American Jewish Joint Distribution Committee (JDC) began to play a major role in subsidizing food, clothes, equipment, and medical support for the children in southern Morocco. The Oeuvre de Secours aux Enfants (OSE), an organization based in Paris, joined the AIU and the JDC to expand their medical and educational support to these communities. The Holocaust played a major role in enlisting the support of international Jewish agencies, such as the JDC, in attenuating the suffering of Jews throughout the world. The JDC, for instance, began subsidizing the canteen in Akka after the war. In addition, it also offered hygiene advice to families due to the high rate of trachoma and tuberculosis among the Jews of Akka. In the 1950s, the National Council of Jewish Women became interested in the welfare of the children of southern Morocco, sending packages of clothes from offices in Springfield (Ohio), Chicago (Illinois), Tacoma (Washington), and New York.[54]

In the late 1940s, the AIU spread its network of schools throughout different hamlets in Morocco's southern hinterland. The late arrival of the AIU schools to this area signaled a geographic shift in the AIU's policies that were supported by other international Jewish agencies, namely the JDC. Education was viewed as a necessary tool for the modernization of these forgotten communities. However, by the time the schools opened in southern Morocco, these Jews had started to move to Israel. Nevertheless, the teachers and school directors focused on the education of the Jews who remained in the *bled*. Many believed that schooling was the best preparation of these Jewish communities for emigration. It was not until the early 1960s that a new AIU (now called Ittihad-Maroc) closed most of the schools in the southern hinterland.

The AIU school was not able to affect a large number of children positively, despite its outreach and considerable approval in southern Morocco. Many factors hindered the AIU's mission. The late arrival of these schools and the shortage of funds, as well as the inability of many communities to support the schools, were part of the reason. In addition, rural communities were introduced to new educational systems at a later stage than urban ones in the modern history of Moroccan Jews. The movement from the *heder* to the AIU school required fundamental cultural and religious changes that a transformation of ten to fifteen years could not achieve. The growing exposure of the Jews of Akka to modern social changes among the urban Jews of Essaouira and Marrakesh accelerated the weakening of the traditional structures in the Jewish quarters. In addition, with Moroccan independence and the establishment of Israel, new political institutions limited the power of the rabbis and introduced drastic cultural changes to these communities.

The anthropologist on the trails of Jewish peddlers of the Anti-Atlas Mountains.

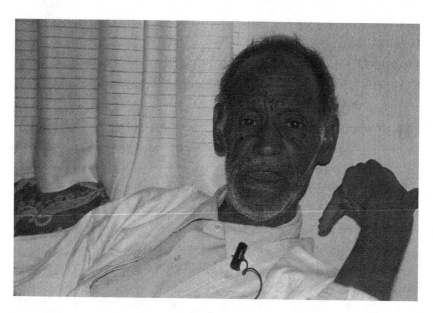

At the house of Hajj Najm Lahrash, discussing Jewish-Muslim partnerships.

A portrait of Soudani, a descendant of a family of slaves and former economic partner of the Sarraf family in Akka.

Closed Jewish shops outside the *mellah* of Tagadirt, Akka.

The building that housed the Shari'a Court of Akka during the colonial period.

The ruins of the main synagogue of Tagadirt, Akka.

The *mellah* of Taourit, Akka.

A portrait of Sh'yabi, a great-grandfather from the village of Tagadirt, Akka.

A portrait of al-Hashimi al-Bannani al-Fassi, the main judge of the Shari'a Court of Akka during the colonial and post-colonial period. Hajj Najm Lahrash family collection.

Ibrahim Nouhi inside Chaykh Omar Museum of Akka.

At the house of Ouquandou, inspecting his manuscript cache at the administrative center of Akka.

A portrait of Joubib Hana, one of the first girls from the Jewish community of Akka to attend the Alliance school before she emigrated to Israel.
© Chaykh Omar Museum of Akka.

A portrait of Sarraf Abraham, Tagadirt. © Chaykh Omar Museum of Akka.

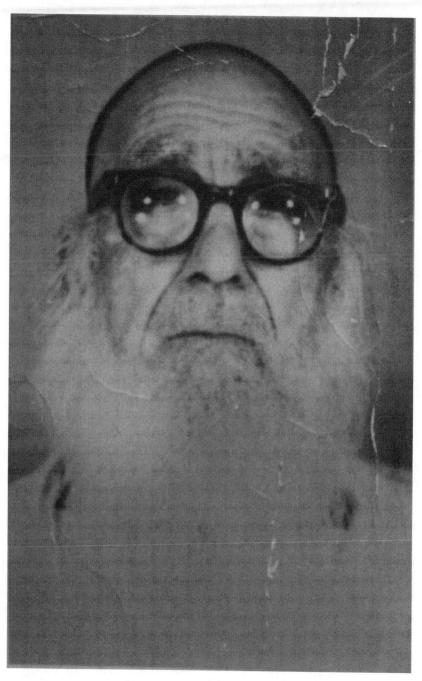

A portrait of Rabbi Yusuf Sarraf. © Chaykh Omar Museum of Akka.

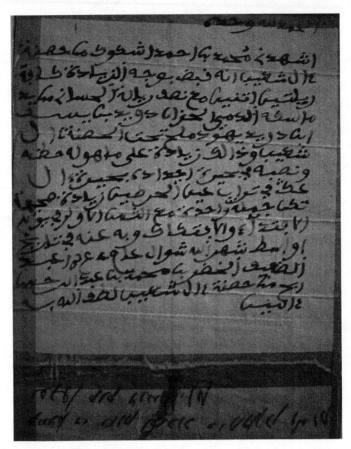

Facsimile of a legal document from the Museum of Chaykh Omar in Akka.

A new wall built around the oldest Jewish cemetery of Tagadirt, Akka.

4 "Little Jerusalems" Without Jews

MUSLIM MEMORIES OF JEWISH ANXIETIES AND EMIGRATION

News from Europe

Abbas, as a former soldier of the French Foreign Legion, fought for France during the Indochina War (1950–1953) before sustaining a serious leg injury. After his military release he settled in Casablanca. In the early 1990s, his health condition worsened and forced him to return to his hometown in southern Morocco. In the summer of 2004, we met in the village of Tissint, north of Akka, not far from the house where Charles de Foucauld stayed for months during his reconnoitering travel mission. Abbas welcomed me in the large mud-brick compound belonging to his oldest son. The building overlooked the salty Tissint River. A military medal hung on the wall of the living room, and a large, cracked, black and white picture of King Mohammed V overshadowed every article in the sparsely furnished room. To many members of the great-grand-parents and grandparents generations, Mohammed V remained a legendary figure. His pictures filled many households as if he were still alive, although it is now his grandchild King Mohammed VI, a son of King Hassan II (who died in 1999), who is the new Alaouite dynastic ruler of the country.

Abbas expressed pride in the Moroccan participation in the French Foreign Legion and in all the soldiers that fought for France in World Wars I and II.[1] While his great-grandchild sat on his skinny legs, he caressed a string of prayer beads. Sporadically, he loudly invoked the name of Allah when he wheezed, making short pauses between sentences and sometimes words to catch a breath. He seemed to be suffering from asthma, yet he never complained, and a wide smile dominated his face. Abbas began our conversation by showing me an album of pictures of himself with a local Jewish merchant, his partner in the late 1950s. Then he proceeded to tell me about his experience in World War II and the plight of Jews in Europe and North Africa:

"News traveled among Jewish communities that Germans were rounding up Jews and sending them to camps to be burnt. We heard that Hitler wanted to kill every Jew in Europe and later destroy every Jewish community in the world."

"How did you hear about this and who told you?" I asked.

"From Moshe, my Jewish partner. In 1940, he told me that Germans defeated France and began to send French Jews to Jewish death camps. He looked worried and scared because he was told that Germans and Italians would ask France to capture every Jew in the Maghreb and send them to France."

"What was the source of his information?" I interrupted.

He reported that the Jews in Moroccan cities were hearing rumors that the French authorities in Rabat were planning to ask Sultan Mohammed V to implement a set of policies against Jews. They were afraid that French colons had already started discriminating against their Jewish brothers.

"Did the French apply these anti-Jewish policies? Did the king accept them?" I asked.

"I don't know. To my knowledge no Jew in Tissint or other neighboring hamlet was taken or killed by the French. Business continued as usual. However, a Jewish merchant from Essaouira came to Akka for some business with the local government representative around 1943 and told me that Jewish doctors, bankers, teachers, and lawyers were restricted from doing their work in many cities throughout Morocco. Here, French soldiers and military personnel treated Jews and Muslims all the same. Jews and Muslims were asked to provide free labor [corvée] to clear roads. The cities were different because many nationalists had positive feelings toward Germany and did not like British and French colonial policies in Palestine and the rest of the Islamic world."

"Were local Jews aware of what was happening in Palestine?" I interrupted again.

"Yes! Yes! You have to know, son, Mecca to us is like Jerusalem to them. We share with them Palestine. But they prayed all the time for Jerusalem. When I began interacting with them and established strong personal relations with Jews in Akka, they used to tell me that Akka is their little Jerusalem and that it will always be their home, but the Promised Land is Palestine. I did not understand that until they left."

Like Abbas, great-grandparents and grandparents offered their perspectives on the migration of the rural Moroccan Jewry to Palestine in the context of national and global political and economic anxieties. My aim in this chapter is to show that a local perspective of history is at the root of rural Jewish migration from Akka and other communities in southern Morocco. I believe that the Zionists appealed to an already existing historical narrative of belonging to Eretz-Israel among southern Moroccan Jewry. In fact, although the economic factors and political stresses were strong factors in this migration, the success of Zionism in building support for this exodus to Israel can be explained largely by its emphasis on a local interpretation of Jewish history based on the belief in *aliya* (immigration to Eretz-Israel).[2] At the same time, I acknowledge that while Zionism used traditional messianic symbols that resonated with the rural Jews, the rural Jews had some agency in deciding to emigrate when the opportunity arose largely because of their particular view of history, which I will outline below. In general, my argument has three objectives: (1) it helps to explain why so many rural Jews from southern Morocco left for Israel in the second half of the twentieth century; (2) it provides a critique of the failure of early Moroccan nationalism to include Jews after independence; and (3) it clarifies the role of Zionism in Jewish migration.

It is worth noting that the migration of rural Jews to Israel started earlier, even before Moroccan independence, and the chronology of departure varied from place to place. In Akka, a southwestern oasis in the southern fringes of Morocco, some Muslim respondents attributed the Jews' exodus to their desire to die in Eretz-Israel; others claimed that the late King Hassan II gave in to the pressures of European and American Zionist organizations.[3] Many blamed the underground Zionist movement for their loss; only a few faulted the nationalist independence leadership for its failure to fully assimilate all Moroccan Jews through an inclusive vision of an independent modern state that would recognize that their religious rights extended beyond the political boundaries of Morocco. This political and legal exclusion, great-grandparents and grandparents maintained, led to a great fear among Jewish communities about their future in the independent Moroccan nation, causing them to choose exile after the strengthening of Arab Nasserite nationalism and the emergence of Islamism in Morocco.

Southern Moroccan Jewry and the Choice of Emigration

In March 2004, I met Ibrahim Nouhi, a Muslim and a former member of the Armée de Libération du Sud, which fought the French in southern Morocco.[4]

I had long meetings with Ibrahim over a period of nine months, in which he outlined the history of pre-Saharan Jewish communities, their political dependence on tribal chieftains, their social and economic relations with their Muslim neighbors, and their reasons for migration. In fact, Ibrahim became a central consultant for my study, given the historical relationship between his family and the Jews of the community. During an early interview, Ibrahim noted:

"Jews left for many reasons, economic, political, personal, and religious. But many left because we failed as nationalists to incorporate them even though we claim the contrary. It is true that struggles over power between the king and other political leaders had probably forced the government to strike a deal which facilitated Moroccan Jewish migration in return for economic and military incentives."

"So do you blame nationalist forces for this departure?" I asked.

"No! I do not blame anybody! I just think that we, as a nation, lost a very dynamic social group, which could have contributed to our young nation-state.

"But as a Moroccan, I was definitely accustomed to hearing that Jews left because the opportunity of return had been presented to them.

"That is not always true. I, as a soldier in the Southern Army of Liberation, worked with many Jews from the south. They never thought about leaving for Israel despite the fact that they viewed the land of Palestine as a sacred place, which they dreamt of visiting. Many of them saw Morocco as their country. When we were fighting the French around Akka, they provided their trucks, which they themselves drove to the battlefield. They made sandals, trousers, and even shaved the heads of soldiers! Did we acknowledge that after independence? No! I had to fight to get them recognized from the Ministry in Charge of the Affairs of Former Resistance Fighters for their contribution. We did a poor job in enlisting them in post-independence nation building. The Zionists succeeded where we failed."

Ibrahim incorporates many historical, social, and economic themes in Jewish-Muslim relations in the pre-Saharan environment. In the context of these, I want to explore a central question that has been partly ignored in the literature on the Jewish communities of the southern oases:[5] Why did the leadership of the nationalist independence movement fail to convince the rural Jewish population to stay in Morocco while the Zionist movement managed to encourage rural Jewries to leave southern rural communities in the early 1960s?[6]

In his study of the encounter between rural Jews and Zionism in the High Atlas, Tsur argued that the rise of nationalist sentiments among Jews of the High Atlas villages "had nothing to do with religion or religious feelings. . . . Religious feelings, if they played any role in the turn of these Jews to nationalism, were secondary."[7] He said that the success of Zionism to enlist rural Jewry is part of what Gellner referred to as diaspora nationalism,[8] which tends to develop among people of "originally foreign status, scattered, and lacking their own agrarian stratum."[9] Tsur largely saw the Jewish attraction to Zionism as an instance of a competition over economic opportunities with members of the dominant society; he posited that Moroccan and Zionist movements competed in the early 1950s over the membership of the rural population from the Atlas pre-industrial hinterland.[10] Tsur's study was based on the communities of the High Atlas, the hinterland of Marrakesh. My ethnographic study of Akka bears some similarities to Tsur's. In the Saharan fringes, Jews were caught in the middle of two imagined centers (Moroccan and Israeli nationalism) competing for inclusion in the project of nation-state building.[11] Both Israel and Morocco perceived the rural Jewish populations as theirs.

In Zionist historiography, diasporic communities have been conceived as part of a model of symbolic relations between the homeland and exile that assumes an ultimate return to Eretz-Israel. This assumption has been widely rejected in the recent literature of homeland-diaspora relationships. Boyarin and Boyarin rejected the perception of Jewish exile (galut) as negative.[12] Unlike Zionist thinkers, they called for a theoretical model for studying the diaspora outside the framework of national self-determination.[13] In their view, the Jewish diaspora has been successful in the "exercise and preservation of cultural power separate from the coercive power of the state."[14] Gilman provides a different perspective by shifting the theoretical discourse of homeland-diaspora from the concept of center and periphery to the model of the frontier.[15] This alternative model goes beyond the Israel-as-core versus diaspora-as-periphery model developed by Zionist historians.[16] This rejection of diasporic center is also part of Levy's study of Moroccan Jews in Casablanca during the 1990s. In his interviews with elderly Jews, Levy uses what he calls "the solar system model" of homeland-diaspora relationships to demonstrate how Jews "see their place in Casablanca not only as part of a global Jewish diaspora, but also as a homeland for a Moroccan Jewish diaspora."[17]

By focusing on Jewish and Muslim perspectives and in light of the homeland-diaspora theoretical debates of Boyarin and Boyarin, Gilman, and Levy, my plan is to show how Eretz-Israel and Akka, as two different geographic locations, are part of a Jewish frontier with complex meanings for the Jews of Akka, especially those who remained in Morocco. At the same time, I want to explore the perspectives of nationalists and Zionists by placing these vignettes in historical frameworks. I draw much of my historical data from Jewish and Muslim newspapers between the 1920s and 1960s. In light of this theoretical framework, my perspective is closer to that of Levy. I argue that Zionists appealed to an existing, deep historical narrative of return among southern Moroccan Jews. In order to demonstrate this, it is important to take a linear historical approach to underline this history of belonging that encouraged southern Jews to move to Israel. Zionism did not construct a sense of imagined community among these rural Jews. Instead, it relied on an existing religious feeling of membership in a diasporic community forced to settle in Morocco.

Socio-Politico-Economic Challenges

In the mid-1930s, Zionists started promoting Jewish immigration at the same time that some educated Moroccan Jews joined Arab nationalists in calling Zionism a "threat" to Moroccan Jewry and Judaism as well as to the historical Jewish-Muslim symbiosis interaction. The call for building strong Jewish-Muslim relations was launched in the publication of *L'Union Marocaine*, a Jewish newspaper that reported on the daily issues of the communities. It was established by Elie Nataf, the former principal of the AIU school and the secretary of the Jewish community of Casablanca. A number of local, regional, and international political developments would lead *L'Avenir Illustré*, a Jewish newspaper founded by Jonathan Thursz (1895–1976), to change its political position and emphasize *aliya* to Zion. These developments included the growth of Moroccan Arab nationalism, the rise of the Third Reich, and the centrality of the Palestinian issue in pan-Arab ideology.[18] Following these events, the political discourse of *L'Avenir Illustré* highlights the religious-messianic side of Zionism instead of the assimilation and integration of Moroccan Jews in Morocco's political and economic structures after independence.

In their encounter with the Jews of the Saharan fringe, Zionists referred to the symbolism of the "First Diaspora" as a central religious belief for rural Jews. The reference to messianic expectations and the vision of land redemption is what helped the Zionists motivate these Jewish communities to leave Morocco. Based on my interviews with many Muslims in southern Morocco, I concur with the conclusions drawn by Tsur where he distinguishes between messianic and modern Zionism. For Tsur, "Modern Zionism is based on the idea of a return to the land of the ancestors. Traditional Judaism includes the belief in the redemption of Israel, which may assume a concrete political meaning. Religion then supplies modern Zionism with a preindustrial quasi-national counterpart to its basic theme."[19]

Hobsbawm refers to the use of mythological referents embedded in historical contexts by hegemonic entities and states to harness support for national consciousness as "invented tradition," where historical references are "funds of knowledge" used selectively by the nation.[20] I suggest that the Zionists in southern Morocco, unlike the Moroccan nationalist leaders led by King Mohammed V and the Istiqlal party, successfully used the religious reference of Eretz-Israel to link Moroccan Judaism to a global and collective Jewish identity. Unlike the Zionist activists, the Moroccan nationalists called on Moroccan Jews to join the national liberation movement. In August 1933, Muhammed al-Kholti, a moderate nationalist leader, wrote a piece called "The Jews and Us" in L'Action du Peuple, stressing the citizenship of Moroccan Jews. Muslim nationalists also invited Moroccan Jews to contribute to their newspapers.[21] Al-Kholti stressed an entente between Muslims and Jews and criticized the "harmful" effects of Zionism on the positive relationship between Moroccan Jews and Muslims. On March 2, 1934, he singled out Zionism as a factor of disorder in Morocco and bade Moroccan Jews to unite with Muslims.[22] He responded to Zionist writing in L'Avenir Illustré: "Do not be mistaken fellow Jews, Morocco is for Moroccans, that is for us Muslims and for you Jews. It is our duty to collaborate together to defend our homeland. Say it once and for all that you have one homeland (not the Promised Land, but the land where you are now)."[23]

While Zionists began constructing the identity of rural Jews as focusing on the ultimate return to the Promised Land, Moroccan nationalists failed to capitalize on the contributions of many southern Moroccan Jews during the liberation movement to enhance a feeling of belonging to a new Moroccan state. In the 1950s, according to Ibrahim, the owner of the museum of Akka whom I discuss in the next chapter, Zionist literature became relatively widespread among rural Jewry. In addition, local Muslims felt that the AIU schools of the early 1950s enhanced a modern Zionist feeling in many southern rural hamlets. The rising poverty among these Jews and limited trading activity increased their drive to migrate despite their receiving aid from the American Joint Distribution Committee starting in the mid-1940s. In addition, as the war ended amid continuing economic struggles, plans to include these communities in the post-independence nation building were absent, especially in the context of anti-Jewish sentiments caused by the rising Nasserite ideology in Morocco, the discourse of the Istiqlal newspaper, and the political consequences of the 1967 war. The Arab defeat in 1967 led to a rise of anti-Jewish feeling among the Muslims. Despite the efforts of the national Moroccan Arab and Jewish leaderships led by 'Allal al-Fassi[24] to guarantee the security of Jews in the new Moroccan nation-state, the Moroccan commitment to the Palestinian cause and its membership in the Arab League[25] made Jewish emigration inevitable, especially as Israel's military engagements in the Middle East escalated the feeling of insecurity among many Jews. By the late 1960s, Jewish hamlets throughout the south were emptied of their population.

The Jews of Akka and Messianic Zionism

Throughout southern Morocco, Jews lived as neighbors of Arab and Berber communities. Many legends among these Muslim populations relate how, during Solomon's reign, Jewish merchants arrived in the Anti-Atlas.[26] According to Schroeter:

> Traditions on the arrival of Jewish settlers range in time from the deportation of the ten tribes of Israel by the Assyrians in the eighth century BCE to the conquest of Jerusalem and the destruction of the First temple in 587 BCE. The first Jewish settlers of Ifrane in the Anti-Atlas—reputedly the oldest continuously existing Jewish community in Morocco, where Jews lived until the 1960s—are traditionally thought to descend from refugees fleeing Palestine at the time of the destruction of the Temple (587 BCE). Crossing Egypt, they eventually reached the Anti-Atlas region in 361 BCE.[27]

The Jewish migration from Palestine and other regions of the Roman Empire continued after the destruction of the second temple in 70 CE. The arrival of these Jews triggered a massive conversion of the indigenous Berber populations to Judaism, creating a "Judaized Berber" community until the rise of Islam in North Africa.[28] The attribution of the ancient origin of these Jewish communities to the "First Diaspora" highlights a symbolic link between them and the ancient land of Israel and gives legitimacy to their rootedness in Moroccan soil.[29] Local narratives describe legends of Jewish rabbis arriving from Palestine who died on their way to the Saharan Jewish communities and were buried around these settlements in many parts of the Anti-Atlas. Shrines still stand in their honor and draw substantive tourism.

In the 1950s, a reporter named Attilio Gaudio accompanied a small military unit of the Armée de Libération Nationale to the pre-Saharan edges of southwestern Morocco. Gaudio was interested in documenting the Saharan war launched by the southern legion of the Armée de Libération against the French and Spanish colonial armies. Akka was the main military camp for the southern Moroccan Armée de Libération. Before his trip to the Draa Valley, a rabbi in Salé informed Gaudio about an ancient Jewish community that had lived in the oasis of Akka for almost two millennia. Gaudio described the *mellah* of Akka and his meeting with the chief rabbi of the community, Rabbi Youssef (the father of Masoud Sarraf, one of my interviewees in Agadir). Gaudio spent a night in the *mellah*, and at dinner the rabbi described the origin of the community and its connection with Eretz-Israel:

You see, he told me, we are the oldest Jews in the South. Long and hard was the way of our forefathers fleeing Palestine fallen to Nabuchodonosor. They were the only ones to avoid captivity in Babylon. They were of the tribe of Ephraim. Our fathers have relived, even more dreadfully, the suffering endured by the people of Israel in the Sinai, as they trudged towards the Promised Land. For tens of years they were nomad and miserable, overwhelmed by thirst in the desert, assailed and pursued across the Sahara by native savages. When the ocean stopped them from going forward, they settled in the caves.

Some centuries later, a Jewish city was born. They called it: "Little Jerusalem" for they had built it in the image of the lost city (this city is today's Ifrane, in the Moroccan South). They set in the new Synagogue the sacred objects and the laws of the Talmud, that they had saved from the destruction of the temple of Solomon. On parchment rolls, the rabbis wrote the births and deaths, so that the community would always be sure of the authenticity of its origins.

But one day, more than three centuries ago, a Berber king entered Ifrane, set it on fire and burned alive all Jews who were within. The synagogue was pillaged and razed to the ground. And yet again, only a few Jews could escape the massacre, take some rolls of laws and civil records and find refuge here, in the oasis of Draa. Our dead and our martyrs are left up there, next to Ifrane, abandoned in the wind-swept rubble. But if you go, you will see old broken flagstones engraved with words. These inscriptions are two thousand years old.[30]

This story refers to the widespread legend of the martyrs of Oufran (Ifrane), which probably stemmed from the massacres perpetuated by the Berber Bu Ihlas. In Essaouira and elsewhere, there were Jews who claimed descent from the families of the martyrs. My encounter with the remaining Jews of Akka (and the Muslims who worked with them) revealed that these Jewish communities saw themselves as descendants of Jews who had arrived from Palestine and of Berber tribes who had converted to Judaism.[31] Accordingly, southern Moroccan rural Jewry was a part of the wider Jewish world while rooted among the local Berber population. This historical connection rested on a messianic and religious concept of a return to Eretz-Israel.[32]

Despite the isolation of southeastern Morocco, Saharan Jewry, such as the people of Akka, maintained contact with their co-religionists in the Mediterranean region, for both trading purposes and religious reasons, as the communities kept their links of communication through the rabbis who traveled between Morocco and Palestine. Occasionally, rabbis from Jerusalem paid short visits to these areas. At the same time, local Jews left for Jerusalem to gain religious knowledge. For example, and as I showed earlier, Rabbi Mardochée Aby Serour, who was born in southern Morocco to a native family from Akka, traveled between Morocco and Ottoman Palestine.[33]

Before discussing the competition between Moroccan nationalists and Zionists over these Saharan Jewish communities, it is helpful to understand the early histories of the migration of these communities toward Palestine in the context of general Mediterranean history in order to see how the Zionist groups used these historical narratives to encourage these Jewish communities to leave their native villages.

By the sixteenth century, Moroccan Jewish communities constituted a colony of Maghrabim (*ma'aravim*) in Jerusalem, Hebron, Tiberias, and Safed. Fund-raising operations for rabbinical academies (*yeshivot*) in the Holy Land were organized in Morocco, and the remote diaspora communities annually received emissaries (*shlihim*) from the academies. These pilgrims collected funds in the urban centers and traveled in the villages of the countryside; many died on the road, leading to the emergence of tombs and shrines for the veneration of rabbi-emissaries.[34] These shrines were a major characteristic of worship in Moroccan Judaism. The shrines of saints such as Rabbi Ya'aqov Abu-Hatsera, Rabbi David u-Moshe, Rabbi Amran Ben-Diwan, and Rabbi David Ben-Baruch became important pilgrimage sites for Moroccan Jews.[35]

In the early 1770s, rural Jews throughout Morocco increased their contact with colonies throughout Palestine. Rabbis in search of knowledge represented the main immigrants. However, the age, number, social background, and economic situation of immigrants would change for different reasons. The increase in number was also partly due to persecution. During the rule of Sultan Yazid (1790–1792), there was a rise of religious intolerance toward Jews. In addition, the famine of 1776–1882 added to the plight of the Jewish communities, which began to be linked to the French of colonial Algeria.[36] Bar Asher ascribed the beginning of the Jewish return to the Holy Land to external ideological and socio-economic factors. They include "improved communications with Jews already in the Land, who were well represented by former agents (*Shelichim*) pressing Maghrebian Jewry to emigrate, and the increasing popularity of Lurianic Kabbalah which emphasized themes supportive of *aliyah*."[37] By the mid-nineteenth century, the trend of pilgrimage to Jerusalem had grown. This increase also had to do with improved transportation and increased security. During the colonial rivalries between Britain and France and the efforts of the French to expand their presence and ties to the Holy Land, many rural Jews came under French protection, including Aby Serour, who applied for French citizenship before his return to southern Morocco. The French occupation of Algeria increased the process of the colonial protection of local urban and rural Jews. Furthermore, Sultan Moulay 'Abd al-Rahman, who reigned between 1822 and 1859, became concerned by the loss of the revenues generated from the collection of the *jizya* as Jews continued to leave either for Algeria or Jerusalem via Marseilles. In 1846, Moulay 'Abd al-Rahman cautioned the governor of Tangier, Bouselham Ibn 'Ali Aztot:

> Wealthy Jews, May God curse them, have been increasing the trips [abroad] of their children claiming that they are going [on a pilgrimage] to Jerusalem. But they are not returning. Consequently Islam is harmed in two ways: first, in the diminishing [revenue from] *jizya*, and second, they are becoming reconnoiters, directing the enemy to the weak spots of the Muslims. On receiving this letter, prevent all of them from traveling from the ports of Larache and Tangier. Be indefatigable in your efforts with them. May God destroy them.[38]

This official attitude toward Jewish migration to Palestine, especially with the expansion of French and other European protection to the local Jews, spread throughout the south as some Jews also benefited from French and British protection through their affiliation with the Jews from Essaouira. In July 2004, I interviewed Ismail, a Muslim grandfather from Tagadirt village, in the presence of his grandchild. Ismail contended:

> The French are the source of our problem with the Jews. They convinced them to leave Akka to make us beg for their support and succeeded. You know in those days Jews had money. We farmed. The French knew that and convinced them to change, to go to school and leave the *bled* for the city. Then after that they facilitated their migration to Palestine. The French were the cause of our problem with the Jews.

As Ismail outlined his version of the causes of rural Jewish migration, Aziz, his grandchild, shook his head in denial and waited for his grandfather to finish his point before he said:

> Jews had been waiting for this moment to leave. The French never facilitated this. Jews used the French. They are untrustworthy. It is their nature. Look at their history. The French did not like us. But Jews did not like us either. After Hitler was defeated, they forced France and the Americans to help all the Jews of the world migrate to Palestine and displace our Muslim brothers.

Ismail became testy, and before his grandchild finished, he interrupted:

> You do not know anything about the world, son! Tell me how many Jews you
> know and how many Jews you met. There is nothing wrong with Jews. I spent
> more than half of my life around them. They went to Jerusalem before the
> French arrived and came back to Akka. They could have stayed there. They
> did not because they have always believed that they belonged here. The French
> turned them against us after they returned. And later after independence people
> like you pushed them to migrate.

This conversation highlights the conflict between the generations of great-
grandparents and grandparents on the one hand and the young adults on the
other hand regarding how and why the Jews left after World War II. Members of the great-grandparent and grandparent generations believed that
local Jews were not affected by the Holocaust and that no Jew from Akka or
another neighboring village was sent either to the European or Vichy camps
established in the Sahara between 1939 and 1945.[39] The late French arrival
in Akka and the important role of Jewish peddlers in the local economy de-
terred the Vichy authorities from imposing its anti-Semitic laws. Any applica-
tion of these laws would have negatively affected the local economy, which
survived on the intermediary role of the Jewish peddler and artisan. Lahcen,
a farmer in his mid-eighties, highlighted the centrality of the Jews in the following way:

> When Jews began to leave the south, you could go for a week without a black-
> smith who could sharpen your sickle or repair your farming equipment. When
> they left, you could find villages without a single artisan—they had to wait for
> outsiders for weeks if not months to repair their stuff. It took Muslims many
> years to fill the gap that Jews left after they joined their brothers in Palestine.

Encountering European Jews

The historical connection with the sacred land would be highlighted as European Jews became interested in the political and social conditions of the Jews
of North Africa in the nineteenth century.[40] In 1790, Jews in France gained their
civil rights and became French citizens.[41] Over the course of the century, Jews

in Europe were no longer part of a separate and dispersed nation—at least until the Dreyfus Affair erupted—as they became members of civic societies and identified with secular nations, especially France, England, Holland, and Germany. Their political emancipation resulted in the beginning of the erosion of traditional Jewish society as a result of secular education.[42] As Jews came to be accepted in modern secular European society, they saw themselves in terms of an Enlightenment discourse. Schroeter believes that this era meant the beginning of the end of the Sephardic world order, in which Sephardic Jews no longer saw themselves "as part of the same trans-national identity in which being Jewish transcended any type of national affiliation."[43] At the same time, a patronizing discourse emerged among European Jews toward non-European Jews,[44] laying the foundation for a rising, European-centered Zionism that produced negative stereotypes of North African Jews and drew attention to a perceived evolutionary gap between "enlightened" European Jews and "primitive" Asian and African Jews.

This discourse began in the late Enlightenment with the development of patronizing views about the Jews of North Africa and the Ottoman Empire. Romanelli, an Italian Jew who traveled throughout North Africa around 1786, drew a disparaging picture of his North African co-religionists.[45] His visit to North Africa coincided with the French Revolution and the beginning of the emancipation of European Jews. With an arrogant sense of superiority, he commented on the conditions of North African Jews, noting:

> The lack of books and news mires their hearts in the mud of ignorance and superstition. They tend to view all new and mysterious things previously unknown to them as miracles. The sciences are too lofty for them. Their ignorance is bliss, for they say that many victims have been thrown into the pits of heresy and atheism by science. The light of knowledge does not shine upon them, nor has it even reached them until now to eradicate their moral failings and their immature vanities. A veil of obscurantist faith corrupts their hearts and blinds their eyes.[46]

Romanelli's adventures in North Africa from 1787 to 1790 set a tone that was reflected in most Jewish literature written by western Europeans who visited the region during the nineteenth and twentieth centuries. Asian and North African

Jews were seen as backward and primitive, and colonial discourse about savage societies influenced the form of writing that characterized de Foucauld's narrative of southern Moroccan Jewry.

The Enlightenment project for these primitive Jews was to be achieved through education and political liberation. Jews were encouraged to join the AIU, an extensive network of schools that concentrated on "civilizing" them through secular education.[47] Although the AIU did not reach the majority of southern hamlets till the late 1940s, once it did, it played a major role in empowering many local Jews by providing a secular modern education, which helped them secure jobs in the colonial administration. It should be mentioned that well before there were schools in the south, the AIU played a political role, speaking out on behalf of the Jews in some of the southern communities, often in conjunction with the European councils.

Starting in the second half of the nineteenth century, many Jews sought out the political protection of European consuls, especially in coastal cities, and some were naturalized by European states.[48] As I mentioned in Chapter 1, on his return from Palestine through Algeria, Rabbi Mardochée Aby Serour received a French passport from the French consulate before he went back to Akka. The legal status of Jews under the sultan of Morocco was blamed for their social and political inferiority. This "desperate situation" would lead Sir Moses Montefiore, the president of the London Committee of British Jews, to travel to Morocco in 1863 to meet Sultan Sidi Mohammed and intervene on behalf of his co-religionists in Morocco.[49] Montefiore, a Sephardic Jew whose ancestors came from Italy and the most prominent leader of London's Jewish community, asked the sultan to grant Moroccan Jews more rights by lifting the restriction of the *dhimmi* status and granting the Jews the same rights as enjoyed by Muslims. Montefiore was familiar with North African Jews, for a trickle of Jews from the Maghreb settled in London in the late eighteenth and early nineteenth centuries, joining the Sephardic community. In the eighteenth century, some Moroccan Jewish merchants—such as Meir Macnin—went to London to serve as the sultan's Jewish agents in Europe.[50] These Moroccan Jews were largely seen as exotic, "picturesque Orientals," although they assimilated to Western society.[51] A handful of Moroccan Jewish merchants were agents of the sultan, but other Moroccan Jews were not.

Organized Zionist Activity and
Southern Moroccan Jewry

Although Montefiore did not visit the southern rural communities, his trip to Marrakesh and Essaouira reverberated throughout the Jewish community of Morocco. The relationship between European Jews and southern Moroccan Jewry took a new direction after the first Zionist Congress (1897) in Basel, Switzerland. Zionist activity started in southern Morocco before the French Protectorate after a Zionist society was established in Essaouira (Mogador) in 1900. The presence of European consulates and many members of elite Jewish society might have been behind the choice of Essaouira. However, despite the connections between Essaouira and other Jewish communities throughout the south, Zionist activity in remote areas of southern Morocco would not start until 1919, after the Balfour Declaration (1917) called for the establishment of a national home for Jews in Ottoman Palestine. The British Mandate over Palestine in 1922 signaled a new era for many Jews of southern Morocco. Some rabbis played a major role in the dissemination of Zionist information and propaganda, stressing the urgency of establishing a Jewish nation in Eretz-Israel. With the rabbis' local assistance, the French Zionist Federation (FZF) began circulating documents and enlisting members.[52] The material was translated into the Judeo-Arabic dialect and distributed to the communities south of Marrakesh and Essaouira.[53]

During the early stages of French military rule in Morocco, the colonial government restricted the activities of the FZF. General Lyautey had a strict approach to Zionism in Morocco.[54] Under his administration, the French authorities were hostile toward the development of any Jewish nationalism and limited Jewish migration to Palestine.[55] However, Théodore Steeg, who replaced Lyautey as the new general resident (1925–1929), had a more lenient approach and allowed Zionist organizations to be relatively active throughout the colony.[56] In fact, under his rule Zionist activity was promoted through newspapers. L'Avenir Illustré appeared in Casablanca in 1926. Its founding director was Jonathan Thursz, a Polish Jew with a British passport. During the late 1920s and early 1930s, Thursz abstained from discussing Zionism as a political solution for Moroccan Jewry. In 1928, he argued that Moroccan Jews should become good Jews in order to be good Frenchmen, providing evidence for the expectation that the Jews would seek French citizenship.[57] In response to Moroccan Muslim and Jewish nationalists and assimilationists, he noted that his paper did not need to disseminate Zionist propaganda to send Moroccan Jews to Palestine. He went as far as arguing that "Zion is Morocco."[58] Thursz refrained from openly expressing his views because the French authorities were careful not to incite Muslim hostilities in North Africa[59] and discouraged Jewish migration to Palestine.

In Essaouira, the coastal gateway to the southern Jewish communities, Zionists focused on the collection of donations to philanthropic projects in Palestine. In 1897, the Zionist Organization established the "*shekel*" membership fee, symbolically using the term of Hebrew currency. Thursz arrived in Morocco as a representative of the British company Kittel and Cie in the mid-1920s. Some rabbis from Marrakesh and Tarudant played an important role in this period, given the strong relationship between the local populations and religious figures who arrived from Jerusalem. A central figure in the Zionist activity in the early 1920s was Rabbi Pinhas Khalifa Ha-Cohen Azogh, a descendant of a famous religious family from Sus.[60] The resettlement of Rabbi Pinhas Cohen from Tarudant, where his family was established, to Marrakesh was strategic. Marrakesh was the Jewish capital of southern Morocco; it served as the economic gateway to Essaouira, the rest of the Sus region, and the pre-Saharan hamlets. Equally important, it played a major role in the religious life of the Jews who aspired to further their rabbinical schooling.[61] For example, Aby Serour received some of his rabbinical training in Marrakesh before he left for Jerusalem. Slouschz noted during his visit to Marrakesh: "The Talmud is taught in a Yeshibah under the renowned Rabbi Azar, but there are very few true scholars in Morocco, although there are gathered here the Jewish youths from all parts of the Atlas for instruction in the Law."[62] In April 1919, Rabbi Cohen established a Zionist office in Marrakesh and began distributing leaflets and collecting money. After a short period, his fund-raising activities shifted from Marrakesh to the communities of Sus. Nevertheless, despite his success in collecting donations among the oasis Jewry, the depressed economic situation in southern Morocco at the time led to the decrease in the number of *shekel* buyers, "causing a deep disappointment among the emissaries who occasionally visited the area and whose financial expectations were not always met by the realities of North Africa."[63] Many claim that the economic hardships that affected the Jews of southern Morocco after World War II played a central role in their migration to Israel. Still, I would argue that the Zionist ideology and its play on the messianic discourse of return remains the basic cause of the massive Moroccan Jewish migration to Israel, compared to the histories of migration from Algeria and Tunisia.[64]

National Mistrust: Political Parties and Jewish Loyalty

While many attempts were made to bridge the political gaps between Jews and Muslims, the international political situation increasingly encouraged a culture of mistrust and intolerance. During World War II, nationalist leaders formed new political movements and established new newspapers. A vigorous debate ensued around Moroccan independence, Islam, and the relationship between Morocco and other Middle Eastern countries, especially in light of the creation of the Arab League in Cairo on March 22, 1945.

The establishment of the Moroccan press owed much to the national political leaders, who were influenced by the ideas of Chakib Arsalane[65] and managed to mobilize the general population about the armed struggle against French colonialism. Starting in the 1930s, the circulation of Arabic and French newspapers was primarily done through four main political parties: the Parti National pour la Réalisation des Réformes (PNRR), led by 'Allal al-Fassi; the Mouvement National (MN) of Hassan al-Wazzani; the Parti de l'Unité Marocaine (PUM) of Muhammad al-Makki al-Naciri; and the Parti des Réformes Nationales (PRN), chaired by Abdelkhaleq Torres. These parties were the offshoots of the first political organization established by the nationalist leaders, Le Comité d'Action Marocaine (CAM). The CAM emerged in 1934, setting the stage for the development of a political consciousness through the media.

Al-Istiqlal, formerly PNRR, emerged in 1943 as the leading nationalist party, headed by Ahmad Balafraj. Its leadership would gain a strong legitimacy among Moroccans after its role in drafting the Independence Manifesto in 1944. The party founded the daily Arabic newspaper, al-'Alam, in September 1946 and a French paper, L'Opinion du Peuple, in March 1947. These publications were banned before resurfacing, in some cases, under different names. In opposition to al-Istiqlal, Muhammad Hassan al-Wazzani established Hizb al-Shura wa al-Istiqlal (the Parti Démocratique de l'Indépendance/PDI) in 1946. Unlike the religious conservatives of al-Istiqlal, the PDI was largely composed of intellectuals, including doctors, lawyers, and administrators. Some were secularists and strongly influenced by Western and liberal ideas. However, like the PDI, they called for the end of the protectorate and the establishment of a constitutional monarchy. The PDI's Arabic newspaper, *al-Ra'y al-'Am*, voiced its support for the king of Morocco, even though it was concerned about a system of government controlled by the monarchy and a single political party. Under the leadership of al-Wazzani, the PDI maintained good relations with al-Istiqlal despite their competition over national membership, political leadership, and the control of national resources.

The third party that played a major role in the debate over Jewish-Muslim relations was the Parti Communiste Marocain (PCM). The PCM was created in July 1943 and led by Léon Soltane (1905–1945), a French Algerian lawyer. Based in Casablanca, it included many European immigrants, who were joined by Moroccan Jews such as Simon Lévy, Albert Ayache, Germain Ayache, and Edmond Amran El Maleh. Al-Istiqlal used the religious makeup of the party to instigate anti-Semitic feelings in the general population. Although the PCM tried to break away from the French central communist party,[66] it was not able to compete with al-Istiqlal in enlisting large numbers of sympathizers from the traditional groups of Moroccan society. Like the PDI, the PCM's members had been educated in French schools and were generally considered pro-French by the conservatives. This was also affected by the position that the party took in its early years against the January 1944 Independence Manifesto, when it described the call for independence from France as a political initiative that would lead to a new American hegemony. The close ideological relationship between the PCM and the French Communist Party also hindered the new Moroccan communists from bridging their cultural and social gaps with the masses, even though they were heavily involved in the Union Générale des Syndicats Confédérés du Maroc (UGSCM), where they stressed workers' rights.

Al-Istiqlal's leadership used the same political strategy through which it had marginalized the PDI in order to make the PCM appear less legitimate. It stressed its own ideological focus on the independence of Morocco under the 'Alawi Dynasty, the territorial unity of the country, its Islamic heritage and pan-Arab links, as well as its loyalty to the monarchy. Therefore, by focusing on the traditional Islamic attributes of the population, al-Istiqlal invalidated the modernity of the PDI and its Western beliefs. As for the PCM, al-Istiqlal was able to criticize and effectively debunk the program of its leadership because of the early lukewarm position of the party toward independence, its French leadership, and its Jewish membership, as well as its connection and ties to the French colonial communist ideologies.[67]

The second phase of political debate between Muslims and Jews in the public press emerged after the end of World War II and the creation of Israel in 1948. The debate over the position of Jews in Moroccan society took place in the columns of al-Istiqlal, PDI, and PCM newspapers. *Al-Ra'y al-'Am*, the weekly newspaper of the PDI, showed moderation in its views compared to al-Istiqlal's, although its editorials tended in many instances to confuse Zionism with Moroccan Judaism. Therefore, its main criticism focused on Jewish migration and its Zionist supporters, especially the Cadima (Forward), an immigration agency in Casablanca funded by the Jewish Agency. One example of these editorials, published on February 22, 1956, argued:

> The world press wanted to present the national struggle for the independence of Morocco as a religious war. So it brainwashed the Jews here into believing they were exposed to a greater danger. In America, too, people think that the Moroccan regime endangered the life of the Jews in this state. However, in spite of the opinion of the world press, the truth is that the Arab nation does not want to discriminate on the basis of race and creed. Eloquent proof of this is the fact that a Jew has been appointed as a Minister in the first Moroccan government. Therefore the Moroccan Jews should not flee to other countries in fear. This fear stems from a misconception on the part of the Moroccan Jew, who thinks that his future in this country will not be safe.[68]

The PCM's ideological clash with al-Istiqlal was largely related to the issue of the Jewish question in Morocco. Al-Istiqlal used the Palestinian issue and the 1948 war to mobilize the masses as well as to strengthen its stature as a supporter of Arabism. In 1948, *L'Opinion du Peuple* contended that the Zionist movement declared war on the Palestinian people and the rest of the Arab world. Its editorials also stressed its pan-Arab links and the necessity of fighting Zionism. Ali Yata, the secretary-general of the PCM, responded by criticizing members of al-Istiqlal as backward and asked Moroccans not to view Moroccan Jews as enemies of Muslims. While the PCM tried to limit the emotional side of the Palestinian war, the media of the nationalist parties used the occasion to mobilize their adherents.

King Mohammed V sought to limit the rising attitude against Jews in many groups in the Muslim community. On May 29, 1948, *L'Opinion du People* published a message from the king in which he stressed that Muslims in Morocco should support their Arab brothers in Palestine and asked Moroccan Jews not to help the "Zionist aggression." At the same time, he called on Moroccan Muslims not to forget that the Jews were also Moroccans and that they should engage them through dialogue and denounce violence.[69] The PCM continued to caution against al-Istiqlal's political discourse, accusing other nationalist leaders of encouraging hatred and social animosities between "Moroccan Muslims and Moroccan Jews."[70] Many Moroccan Jews continued to voice their allegiance to the country and the king. Others, worried about the political situation, heeded the warnings of the Zionist representatives and left.

We can conclude from this early phase that the discourse in the media about Moroccan Jews between 1930 and 1950 was largely characterized by a debate about the status of Jews as *dhimmi* versus Jews as potential citizens. While the king maintained his role as the protector of the Jews, the traditional religious status of Jews as *dhimmi* was of a symbolically moral rather than practical significance, since many Jews began to reject its legality either by applying for foreign citizenship or by emigrating to Israel. Given the French colonial laws, which called for legal transformations in the status of Jews, the *dhimmi* status lost its significance in the national discourse. Yet, although the king and the political parties never debated the *dhimmi* status per se, many Zionists spoke out against it. Moroccan political leaders, however, continued to frame the debate in terms of a common national agenda in which Jews and Muslims were partners with similar rights. After independence, King Mohammed V and his successor, Hassan II, recognized Jews as citizens and put an end to the discourse about *dhimmi*. The idea of a common national destiny for Jews and Muslims was jeopardized in Morocco in the late 1950s after the emergence of Gamal Abdel Nasser in Egypt as a pan-Arab leader. The ensuing debate once again revolved around the issue of Zionism and whether Jews could be Moroccans and Zionists at the same time. In 1959, Moroccan Jews began to withdraw from the national public sphere and chose a closed internal system that enforced conflicting religious categories rather than nationalist partnerships. At the same time, many left the country.

After World War II, and in light of the establishment of Israel in 1948 and the independence of Morocco in 1956, leaders in both Morocco and Israel competed for the allegiance of the Jewish communities of Morocco. The story of the North African Jewish communities became largely a narrative of integration and emigration. During the late 1950s, southern Moroccan Jewry had to decide whether to move to Eretz-Israel or to continue living in "little Jerusalems" throughout southern Morocco. As political animosities in the Middle East intensified, these Jewish communities felt insecure as the distinction between Zionism and Jewishness became blurred. Unlike Moroccan nationalists, Zionist leaders made Moroccan Jewish symbols into instruments of a larger spiritual Jewish consciousness. The success of political Zionism among southern Moroccan Jews rested on the politicization of religious symbols for the construction of a national Israeli feeling. Moroccan nationalists, on the other hand, tried to support the settlements of Jews in Morocco while downplaying their spiritual relationship with Israel.

I have argued that the combination of Zionist symbols that resonated in the rural Jewish communities and the social, economic, and political stresses propelled the emigration of the southern Jews when the opportunity arose. On the other hand, we should not minimize the agency of these Jewish communities in their historical decision to leave their southern oases. Had the Jews stayed in their hamlets, it probably would not have been because the Moroccan nationalists had been more successful in including Jews in the post-colonial world or the Zionists less effective in manipulating messianic religious symbols. Greater prosperity, stability, opportunities, and less fear about the future would have been crucial to providing conditions amenable to these rural Jews.

Shadow Citizens

JEWS IN INDEPENDENT MOROCCO

"A Blind Eye to Jews!"

Ibrahim Nouhi, a grandfather who lived during the struggle for independence, challenged the public perception of Jews in Akka in particular and Moroccan society in general. Throughout my stay in southeastern Morocco, I had many conversations with Ibrahim, the curator of Chaykh Omar Museum (COM) in Akka. Named after his grandfather, COM was established by Ibrahim in the early 1990s as an individual effort to represent the history of Saharan Jews and encourage the national acceptance of their contributions. Although the COM showed different aspects of the region's history and culture, a section on the Jews of Akka and the Sahara dominated his permanent exhibit. Ibrahim said that this was a deliberate choice. His goal, he said, was to highlight the multi-ethnic character of the oases in southern Morocco and the importance of the Jews in these Saharan societies as well as the whole nation.

During one of my trips to Akka in 2004, I enlisted Abdelhaq, a Muslim elder in his early eighties, as my guide. Abdelhaq showed me around different Jewish neighborhoods with their collapsing synagogues, abandoned houses, and closed commercial and artisan shops. As we walked through these empty places with cracked walls and crumbling ceilings, he pointed to the COM building in the far distance in a valley thick with palm trees. Motivated by the perceived injustices of contemporary Arab-Israeli politics against Muslims, Abdelhaq was quick to express his displeasure at the inclusion and focus on Jews in this museum. In a deep voice tinged with anger, he noted:

> It is a shame that the same Jewish individuals we are celebrating in these museums have stolen the property of our Palestinian brothers. Why do we need to commemorate them? Why does our state need to remember its so-called Jews? They are not citizens of this country anymore, so they do not deserve to have a place inside any museum or public place in this land.

This experience illustrates a dominant reaction among the largest proportion of the parents and youth cohorts. Although the Jewish settlement in the Sahara predates Islam, the Jews of Akka, according to Abdelhaq, are outside the Arab-Islamic national narrative of Morocco.

Ibrahim defended his inclusion of Jewish history in his museum. He noted that Moroccans are socialized to express their grievances through *'ayn mika* (the plastic eye).[1] In today's Darija (Moroccan colloquial Arabic), *'ayn mika* (or *tmyak*) stands for things that might be important but should be ignored because of the trouble the observer can experience if he notices them. During one of my first encounters with Ibrahim, he noted:

> *'Ayn mika* is a dangerous practice. *Tmyak* betrays the consciousness of the citizen to speak his mind in society. We cannot claim responsibility if we do not identify what is wrong with us and accept who we are. That is how we improve. Museums are institutions that I think should teach us our history and identity just like schools do. Our textbooks sometimes fail to do so; our museums do the same. That is why I built my museum. To tell the children of my village that Akka was once a vibrant place with many groups, including Jews and slaves. I refuse to *dir 'ayn mika 'al-udayn ou l-'bid* [not represent Jews and slaves in my museum]. The Jews of Akka live in Israel today. I do not agree with how Israel is treating Palestinians on a daily basis. But I will never refuse the Jews of Akka their place in this museum, because once upon a time their home was here. I do not like *tmyak*.

This chapter will analyze Jewish representation after the independence of Morocco through the concept of *'ayn mika*. The COM museum of Akka is a site through which Ibrahim observed what he called the *'ayn mika* of the young generation, the collective intentional act of ignoring Moroccan Jews and their history when it conflicted with state policy about the Palestinian question and simultaneously acknowledging the same heritage when politically expedient. *'Ayn mika* legitimizes issues like corruption and other social ills by ignoring instead of confronting them. For instance, the phrase *kay miyyak 'l-mawdu'* (he gives the issue the plastic treatment) is used to talk about interpersonal issues and relations, where recognition is avoided in public for all sorts of complicated reasons. Ibrahim emphatically noted that *tmyak* was at the heart of the way most national institutions—such as schools and museums—handle (and choose not to represent) Morocco's cultural and social taboos.

After independence in 1956, as noted earlier, the majority of Moroccan Jews emigrated to Israel, France, and Canada. The relative absence of Jews from Moroccan society since independence has left a large social and cultural vacuum. Today, without intensive daily interactions between Muslims and Jews, most of the Muslim debates about Moroccan Jews have taken place in national and international media, including newspapers. Thus, here I use newspapers as another source to situate mainly the parents generation's perceptions about Jews in a modern context. Newspapers are valuable documents for rewriting the histories of North African Jewry.[2]

Jews and the National Public Sphere After Independence

The Habermasian idea of a bourgeois public sphere is about the formation of political debate and rational consensus among bourgeois individuals in opposition to absolutist states. Although a full utopian public sphere can never be realized, the ideal public sphere was thought to emerge from rational and uncoerced discussion among individuals to hold the state accountable.[3] However, the inclusive egalitarian and democratic nature of these open forums was replaced by managed discussions and staged displays. In eighteenth-century Europe, newspapers, replacing salons and coffeehouses, emerged as the new public sphere, providing a medium through which individuals could express their views. Initially, the content of these early newsletters and broadsheets was strictly censored by the state. In response to mounting pressure, however, censorship was relaxed, and the newsletters became relatively open spaces of debate.

The Habermasian notion of the public sphere is useful in understanding national debates about Jews in the context of an independent Morocco. Like generational narratives, newspapers are one of the few media through which we can trace Jewish representation longitudinally by observing the development of the secular and religious perceptions of Jews through the colonial and postcolonial decades. Although mass media and communication played a crucial role during the Moroccan liberation movement, newspapers have not received serious attention as historical sources from scholars of modern Moroccan history and politics. However, newspapers have recently become valuable for rewriting the histories of North African Jewry.[4]

Jews, Political Parties, and the National Elite

In order to analyze the centrality of the media in the social construction and transmission of meanings of Jewishness in Morocco, we must first examine the charismatic political figures behind the parties that sponsored this press, both during and after the protectorate (1930s–1980s). During the colonial era, in both the French- and Spanish-controlled zones, a number of political leaders emerged as major national figures whose influence would be central even after independence. They included 'Allal al-Fassi, Muhammad Hassan al-Wazzani, Abdelkhaleq Torres, Muhammad al-Makki al-Naciri, Ahmad Balafraj, and Ali Yata, among others. I believe that these nationalists played a significant role in the production and dissemination of the ideas of their parties, not only on general political issues, but also about the Moroccan Jews and their relationship to Morocco, Zionist organizations, and Israel. Using the press to publicize their nationalist ideologies, they formed a community of disciples who helped disseminate their views about Jews in Morocco and how the Jews should act if they were allowed to remain within the Arab-Islamic boundaries. Accordingly, descriptions of Jews and Judaism in the context of Moroccan independence and the emergence of Israel have been partly established by these leaders and propagated by their disciples. To understand how the nationalists rationalized their discourse about Jews, it is important to view this discourse within the context of the historical emergence of the national political parties and their press since the 1930s.

The emergence of the Moroccan press in a primarily colonial environment turned out to have a lasting effect on the nature of the press after independence. On April 27, 1914, the French colonial authorities introduced the first *dahir* (decree) that regulated the media, granting permits for the establishment of newspapers. Although the protectorate introduced other laws to control the nationalist press and restrict its influence, the press and the radio empowered the urban nationalist leaders to create a new public sphere informed by local, regional, and international events.

In a study of the leftist Moroccan press during the protectorate (1912–1956), Ihrai-Aouchar postulated that the press remained tightly linked to the political parties even after independence.[5] Despite the potential of the press and other forms of modern media as an industry to have their own agenda in Morocco, the press was later largely co-opted by the central government and political parties to disseminate their political, economic, and cultural programs.[6] The conscious engineering of public opinion through editorial control was central to the Moroccan nationalists' mission. The Palestinian question, Jewish emigration, and the Arab wars with Israel have long served as basic issues for the monarchy and the leadership of the political parties to stress a set of attitudes toward Moroccan Jewry. The recent shift of influence from leftist communist and socialist parties in the 1960s and 1970s to Islamic movements and voices is an example of the inability of the socialist and the traditional conservative parties to adapt to new political and social realities. A few leaders and families maintained their political dominance in traditional historical political parties. Whereas in pre-colonial times the king and tribal leaders protected Jews in their status as *dhimmi*,[7] the monarchy maintained its control over the official religious discourse and power in the era after independence as protector of the Jews, not as *dhimmi* but as citizens. Thus the national political leadership's influence, which was stable for three decades (late 1950s to early 1980s), is losing its influence to a new Islamic charismatic leadership, which has different views about Jews and Judaism in Morocco. In this new environment, which is partly Islamist in tone and attitude, the few remaining Moroccan Jews are caught between their historical *dhimmi* status, attitudes of peaceful coexistence, and community isolation in a nation that aspires to appear multicultural.

After 1956, the debate on the place of Moroccan Jews in the post-independence national plan continued to be affected by internal and external historical events. After a period of anti-Jewish discourse both before and after the creation of Israel on May 15, 1948, the two main parties—the Independent Democratic Party (PDI)[8] and al-Istiqlal—expressed a temporary leniency toward Moroccan Jews. This period of political rapprochement, initiated at the level of al-Istiqlal leadership, coincided with the al-Istiqlal political struggles with the PDI over national leadership.[9] In 1956, in order to demonstrate its good intentions toward Moroccan Jews, al-Istiqlal encouraged Jews to join its political ranks. The Jews, Laskier notes, "were addressed as Moroccan brothers and called upon to build the new Morocco together with the Muslims. In several cities, Jewish leaders were invited by either al-Istiqlal or the PDI to join their ranks."[10]

This rhetoric was followed by some concrete, positive actions at the level of the political and social representation of Moroccan Jews in society. Dr. Léon Benzaquen, a Moroccan Jewish physician, became the minister of posts and telegraphs. Others were assigned high government positions in the ministries of Education, Finance, Commerce, Industry, Public Works, and Agriculture.

The pro-entente movement between Moroccan Jews and Muslims in the al-Istiqlal party was called al-Wifaq (Agreement). Armand Asoulin, David Azoulay, Marc Sabbagh, Joe O'Hana, and Albert Aflalo were the main Jewish figures in this movement. They called for an integration of Jewish communities in the new nation. Nevertheless, the official membership of Morocco in the Arab League in October 1958 and an internal schism within al-Istiqlal would rekindle the discourse against the Jews in its media. Divisions within the party led to the creation of the Union Nationale des Forces Populaires (UNFP) by a leftist and progressive group headed by Mehdi Ben Barka in December 1959.[11] This leadership took a strong stand against Zionist activity in Morocco and espoused a position against Jewish migration. Morocco was asked by the Arab League, under Gamal Abdel Nasser's leadership, to end Jewish migration to Israel. In 1958, Mohammed V appointed Ahmed Balafraj as the second prime minister after independence, replacing the Bekkai government (December 7, 1955–April 15, 1958). A critical political campaign was directed at Jewish migration in 1959. Still, al-Istiqlal's press tried to distinguish between Judaism and Zionism. For instance, in January 1958, an article called "Tolerance in Morocco" appeared in al-'Alam. It claimed:

> Our Arab brothers in the East constantly urge us to support them in their fight against the Jews, and demand that Morocco align itself with the pan-Arab world. While there is no room in Morocco for racial fanaticism, intolerance, and anti-Semitism, we shall continue to support these Arab heroes who wage a bitter struggle against the Jewish State. *Al-Istiqlal* is still able to distinguish between Judaism and Zionism and therefore is fighting Zionism in Morocco on the same terms and with the same weapon as our brothers in the East. At the same time, we are also fighting against antidemocratic tendencies, under which we include anti-Semitism.[12]

By 1959, although al-Wifaq became ineffective, al-Istiqlal managed to enlist the services of Albert Aflalo as a Moroccan Jewish voice critical of the *aliya*.

Pointing to the recent riots of Moroccan Jews in the Wadi Salib slum in Haifa, Aflalo wrote a piece in *L'Avant-Garde*, the newspaper of the Moroccan labor union, Union Marocaine du Travail (UMT), in which he claimed that Israel's policies toward North African Jewish immigrants were discriminatory. These riots, he declared, "have demonstrated beyond any shadow of doubt that Israeli political leadership, stimulated by racial policies, condemned Moroccan Jews to a life of poverty bordering on hunger and starvation."[13]

This new political climate was not helpful for Moroccan Jews in their struggle for national acceptance and integration. King Mohammed V, al-Istiqlal, and the UNFP entered into a new power struggle. The conservative and leftist parties tried to please outside Arab forces for their own political gain, so they minimized their Jewish support and continued to adopt the same political standpoint toward anti-Zionism and Jewish migration. The three political forces were forced to bow in different degrees to the pressure of the Arab League. At the same time, national political forces tried to maintain a positive attitude toward Moroccan Jews and Judaism while they criticized Israel. In response to a correspondent of the *Jerusalem Post* regarding Moroccan Jewish migration to Israel, Ben Barka asserted:

> We need all our human potential. We want all Moroccan patriots, whether they are Muslims or Jews, to dedicate themselves to the common task of national renovation. We expect the Jews to turn their eyes to Israel as we turn ours to Mecca, but if they want to change their nationality, that is bad. The departure of our citizens would mean a loss of Moroccan blood. We have a true brotherhood between Muslims and Jews here. We have equality, not just verbal but actual equality. When some Jews go off, the atmosphere is spoiled for those who remain. It creates a malaise.[14]

In February 1961, the Jewish publication *La Voix des Communautés*, which had disappeared in January 1956, reappeared with an Arabic supplement; it became the only Moroccan Jewish newspaper to reemerge in the new political reality dominated by a largely Moroccan Muslim press. *La Voix des Communautés* argued:

> The only reason for the resumption of our paper was our constant pursuit using our own means to restore the happy dialogue initiated at the dawn of indepen-

dence. We owe our promotion of citizenship to the solicitude of our beloved sovereign, and it is our responsibility to partner with our Muslim brothers in the task of regenerating our country and its reconstruction. . . . It belongs to us using the press to establish a climate of mutual trust and symbiosis that should exist between citizens committed with equal fervor and loyalty to His Majesty Mohammed V and their homeland, Morocco.[15]

The public debate about the Moroccan identity of Jews reappeared in a climate where pan-Arabism was gaining ground. In January 1961, before the reestablishment of *La Voix des Communautés*, two major political events drew Arab and international attention and put pressure on the Moroccan government to block Jews from migrating to Israel. First, on January 3, 1961, Mohammed V hosted the Casablanca Conference, which discussed issues relating to Israel and the struggle of Third World countries against colonialism as well as the Algerian struggle against French colonialism. Gamal Abdel Nasser participated in the African-Arab meeting, triggering considerable anxiety among the Moroccan Jews.[16] Second, on January 9–10, 1961, the sinking of *Pisces*, a ship smuggling forty-three Moroccan Jews from the Gulf of Al-Huceima to Gibraltar as part of a Zionist mission, sharpened national and international focus on the Moroccan Jews. On February 18, 1961, international pressure and scrutiny about the social and political conditions of the Moroccan Jews led Mohammed V to meet with a delegation of the Conseil des Communautés Israélites du Maroc (CCIM). The Jewish leaders submitted a memorandum requesting:

1. unconditional and unrestricted freedom of movement [the memorandum included a description of some of the difficulties that had been met in this regard];

2. action to stop forcible abduction and conversion of Jewish girls to Islam; and

3. a new, fully legal status for the Jewish communities and the CCIM, suitable to independent Morocco.[17]

In response, Mohammed V ordered the Bekkai government to ease the restrictions on Jews and to respect the Jewish movement both in and outside Morocco, proclaiming that the movement of Moroccan Jews was guaranteed by law and that the only factor that could lead to revoking their citizenship would be traveling to Israel. Despite the king's guarantee, the political climate, characterized by the influence of Nasserism and the pan-Arab laws of the Arab League about Jewish migration, encouraged many feelings against the Jews in Morocco, pushing many of them to leave the country.

At the same time, many political parties failed to oppose this anti-Jewish movement, making it easy for Zionist organizations in Morocco to convince the Jews that their safety lay in Israel. A few Jews reacted by republishing *La Voix des Communautés* as a political forum that could dispute the ideology of al-Istiqlal and the media of other political parties.[18] The newspaper tried to focus on the attachment of the Jews to Morocco, putting their citizenship before their religious identity. In fact, a number of young Jews, especially in the Moroccan Communist Party (PCM), had stressed their Moroccan allegiance before independence in the nationalist newspapers such as *Maroc-Presse* and *L'Espoir*. For example, Edmond Amran El Maleh, a member of the political bureau of the PCM, described Jews as simply "Moroccans." Abraham Serfaty, an officer of the Ministry of Industry and a leading member of the workers' union, noted that he was "more Arab than Jewish." He also commented in *Maroc-Presse*: "I am an Arab-Jew and I am Jewish because I am an Arab Jew." *La Voix des Communautés*, Berdugo argued, became "a real forum of expression while during the Protectorate it had tried to maintain a neutral stand towards the national political debate."[19]

A critical debate that emerged from the first years of independence was whether Jews could be viewed through the prism of religion or secular nationalism. Many Jews who decided to stay resisted all attempts to be separated from the national scene. By claiming their Moroccan identity stronger than their Jewish spiritual life, some Jews called for a new definition of Moroccan society that would set aside religious identity as secondary to Moroccan nationalism.[20] At the same time, they resisted any attempt by political players and parties to define them simply as Jews whose identity is tied to Zionism and its core belief in the idea of return. However, for the large number of Jews who decided to leave Morocco, the possibility of Moroccan Judaism (as described by El Maleh and Serfaty)[21] in the context of a resurgent nationalism was not an option because they felt that Muslims were trying to force their view of a Moroccan nation that stressed Islamic and pan-Arab views and limited the full integration of Jews in a democratic Moroccan nation. In a recent interview,

Simon Levy, one of the early members of the PCM, argued that communist Moroccan Jews were forced by al-Istiqlal to swear on the Qur'an as a condition of joining the party.[22]

During the 1960s, political parties took advantage of the freedom of the press guaranteed by the 1961 constitution to make Jews one of their main targets. The focus of *al-'Alam, al-Tahrir, Akhbar al-Dunya*, and *al-Fajr* on Moroccan Jews was intensified because of the Arab defeat in the 1967 war. After the war, *al-'Alam* targeted Moroccan Jews such as Marc Sabbagh, David Azoulay, and David Amar. These Jewish leaders, who had benefited from a momentary acceptance in al-Istiqlal as members of the al-Wifaq movement, became an easy target of the national media, especially after the UNFP broke away from the conservative wing of the party.

The closing of *La Voix des Communautés* in 1963 removed the last Jewish newspaper that spoke out against anti-Semitism. In its absence, the newspapers of other political parties called for boycotting Jewish merchants and businesses after the 1967 war. King Hassan II, who came to power in 1961, and some members of the government became concerned about the growth of xenophobia toward the Jewish community in the Muslim population. Following the steps of his father, Mohammed V, King Hassan II and his government decided to take a clear legal position against racist discourse, announcing: "The Jew has fulfilled all his obligations towards Arabism and Islam but the sentiments of the population have unfortunately been exploited by some elements whose only concern is to sow confusion and disorder and to brand Jews with treacherous slogans."[23]

Although King Hassan II reiterated his father's objection to Zionism, he defined himself as a protector of the Jews in the late 1960s using the legitimate authority that the constitution gave him as the Commander of the Faithful and, therefore, the protector of the Jews—not as *dhimmi*s but as Moroccan citizens with the same rights as Muslims. The trope of *dhimmi* as a religious concept was used symbolically in the same way Mohammed V used it during the early years of independence. By implicitly invoking the status of *dhimmi*, Hassan II legitimized his relationship with Moroccan Jews in and outside Morocco. The monarchy maintained both secret and overt lines of communication, and Israelis of Moroccan heritage benefited from the unofficial diplomatic relations to visit and practice their cultural lifestyles in Morocco without fear of attack. In the independent Moroccan state, the concept of *dhimmi* lost its legal use. Yet it continued to be invoked because it established a historical legal and religious connection between the king and his Jewish subjects. This connection was challenged by some religious figures, who felt that Jews should not be granted protection because they lived in Israel, which was purportedly at war with the Arab world.

In the early 1960s, a growing leftist movement empowered by pan-Arab Nasserite support threatened the rule of King Hassan II. In order to protect himself, Hassan II sought a strategic alliance with the United States and Israel to limit the political reach of leftist dissidents trained in the Middle East, especially in Syria and Algeria in the early 1960s. In return for allowing Moroccan Jews to migrate to Israel, he was promised military and economic support by the United States. As a result, the issue of Moroccan Jews and their migration was rarely discussed, and the monarchy exercised its control over the Jewish question. Even Moroccan historians stayed away from the recent history of the Moroccan Jews, focusing on the period before Israel was established.[24] Accordingly, Moroccan Judaism moved out of the public sphere of the press after the monarchy continued to exercise its hegemony over the political system, especially after two failed coups d'état. The government's control of the press also led to a period of silence about the Zionist ties of the Moroccan Jews between the 1970s and the late 1980s. In fact, if we look at the national media, the debate over the connection between Hassan II and Israel did not emerge again until the late 1990s, after the government limited its control of the media. The king continued to maintain the Moroccan citizenship of Jews, both those who stayed and those who left. In 1989, during a visit to Spain, he met with the leaders of the country's Jewish and Muslim communities from Morocco and announced his special relationship with Moroccan Jews all over the world:

> I do not consider you Jews of Moroccan descent because Moroccan nationality is never lost. We consider you and all your brothers who live from Israel to Canada, in Venezuela, France, England, America, Latin America and elsewhere, as Moroccan subjects who enjoy all the rights that the Moroccan constitution grants you. . . . Your rights are guaranteed by the Constitution because there are two events in the reign of my father Mohammed V and mine. . . . Mohammed V made you Citizens. In my Constitution, I made you full Moroccans.[25]

This relationship between the monarchy and its Jewish subjects would guarantee for the remaining Jewish community many rights, including freedom of movement, even during the first Palestinian Uprising (Intifada) and the First Gulf War. Although the Second Gulf War saw a resurgence of anti-Jewish discourse in the media, it has continued to be framed as a criticism of Israel and its policies in the Palestinian territories. After 1991, political Islam began to emerge as a political force in Morocco and started to exercise its influence over the student body. The continuous flow of images from al-Jazeera and other satellite channels, such as al-Manar, gained ground over the traditional controlled media of the state. In this context of *tmyak* toward Jews, the project of Ibrahim Nouhi emerges as a critique of the national blind eye toward Moroccan Jews and a celebration of their historical achievement. Throughout the period of the 1960s–1980s, Jews remained largely absent from the Moroccan public sphere.

A Jewish Museum in Akka

Early on the morning of February 12, 2004, I arrived in Akka for the first time in my ethnographic study. Some rain had fallen in the night. The wind was blowing east, though mildly, and the heat was already oppressive. As I got off the only bus between Akka and Ouarzazate that day, I headed toward the local government office, where I dropped off photocopies of my research clearance. After I explained the nature and objectives of my research to the state representative, he recommended that I visit the local museum and interview its owner. I was surprised to hear that Akka had a museum that contained material about the Jews in this part of the country. The museum was located between the village of Tagadirt—which housed the main *mellah* until the middle of the twentieth century—and the administrative center of Akka. Although it was accessible by car, I decided to walk through the oasis. As I strolled through the shady palm grove, swarms of locusts flew over my head, abandoning the small farming plots they had left without grass. When I emerged from the dry riverbed of Oued Akka, I saw the only building on the right side, a mud and cement brick compound surrounded by plots of maize, mint, and vegetables. Outside the building, a round yellow sign announced in Arabic and French: Chaykh Omar Museum: National Memory and Communication. At the compound, a young boy was turning on a water pump while scaring away small swarms of locusts with the other hand.

Ibrahim Nouhi, the owner of the museum, emerged out of the new cement side of the compound and greeted me warmly before he ushered me into the sole exhibition hall. As he asked me about my background, roaring and dusty winds started picking up and blowing through the cracks of the windows. All the plastic-coated documents on the cracked tables and unfinished walls were covered with layers of dust. After I briefed him about my research, he boasted how his museum included a whole section just on the Jews of the region.

As Ibrahim left to fetch tea from the adjacent compound where he lived with his family, I took a brief look at his displays. The museum was a wide room with two broken windows that let in the wind. It had a distinctive, homemade feel: its displays were a mixture of newspaper reports about different stages of Moroccan colonial and post-colonial history. Carefully stacked, there were hundreds of manuscripts and old books in wood and metal boxes. Between the boxes and piles at various intervals were assortments of stones from the prehistoric period, arms and weapons from the national liberation movement, and hundreds of pictures of national and local figures, both Jewish and Muslim. In the far right corner of the room, a whole section was reserved for documents and artifacts relevant to the Jewish community of the village and the surrounding oases.

Ibrahim said that few museums around Morocco celebrated the Jewish component of the nation. He felt that this neglect was shameful, since museums played an important role in nation-state building. When I told him about the Jewish Museum of Casablanca (JMC), he said he knew it quite well, but even though it was the only other museum that shared his view on the importance of exhibiting the contributions of the Jewish community to Moroccan history, he nevertheless expressed reservations about its national significance. Ibrahim commented:

> The Jewish Museum of Casablanca was a very courageous step. I think it was inaugurated at the end of the 1990s. My museum was built before that because I knew that our students and teenagers needed to be introduced to Moroccan history and its complexity. People are getting only one story these days. They need to know that the world is more complex than what the media feeds them. But my only problem with the Jewish Museum of Casablanca is that it is not at the center of Casablanca where everybody can see it and then can react to it instead of being built in a hidden villa in the Oasis neighborhood.

Unlike the JMC, Ibrahim said that the COM is centrally located in Akka and that every primary and secondary school child was aware of its location and mission.

Ibrahim was clearly an unusual man. He had no background in museology, and despite his clear views on the representational problem the Casablanca museum was facing, he was not trained as a modern curator. Born in Akka in 1932, Ibrahim served as a member of the southern liberation movement in the 1950s. Later he joined the Union Socialiste des Forces Populaires (USFP) newspaper *al-Tahrir* as an assistant. He became a political dissident and collaborated with many socialist leaders and rebels, such as Fqih Basri and Mehdi Ben Barka, against the monarchy and the leadership of the Istiqlal party in the first decade of independence. Although he never played a major role in the political strategy of the socialist opposition against the monarchy and its allies, his skills as a mechanic put him at the center of the underground movement against the post-independence political establishment. Later, he collaborated with Chaykh al-Arab, a Berber political dissident against the new state. After the dismantling of the movement in the mid-1960s, he left Casablanca and moved back to the south, where he remained until he became interested in salvaging the historical memory of his home region. Ibrahim, it would seem, was an example of what Kreps terms "the traditional model of the indigenous collector and curator."[26]

In 1982, Ibrahim visited Marrakesh with a delegation of former freedom fighters and was received by King Hassan II. These representatives of the southern Moroccan liberation movement called for the improvement of the conditions of retired soldiers. While in Marrakesh, Ibrahim accidentally found in one of the secondhand bookshops a volume *Khilal Jazula*, by al-Mukhtar al-Susi, a scholar and a member of the national independence movement. While leafing through the dilapidated book, he found a section on al-Susi's visit to Akka in the 1940s. Ibrahim said:

> In Marrakesh, we rented a big house waiting for the king to meet us. There were many key figures in the delegation including the father of Abdelaziz, the head of the Polisario, the separatist movement that calls for the independence of Western Sahara. During the days before the king met us, I started reading *Khilal Jazula*. I was amazed to see the name of my grandfather and ancestors from the ayt-Wirran tribe described in the book with biographies and sections about their relationship with the other tribes, their role in the trans-Saharan trade, and their relations with

local and urban Jews. That particular event affected me, and I decided to set up a museum in my house in Akka once I got my first check from the government.

In 1986, Ibrahim received from the government about US$6,000 as compensation for his military service during the period of the national liberation. He bought a camera, a tape recorder, and a jeep and started traveling around the Anti-Atlas, collecting manuscripts and recording its history by interviewing members of the older generations. He visited all the villages described by al-Mukhtar al-Susi, stressing his scientific connection with al-Susi by describing his project as part of "a regional-history and heritage salvage operation" (al-tarikh al-jihawi wa inqad al-turath).

Ibrahim's interest in the representation of Jewish history in museums is a logical extension of his clan's history of political and economic alliances with the Jewish community of Akka. During one of our meetings, Ibrahim explained why he decided to include a section for the Jews of Akka in his museum:

> They were from Akka, therefore they deserve a space in this place. They were our neighbors, our friends, and our companions in the national liberation movement. Why should I not include them here? Akka would never have been as famous as it is now without both its Jews and Muslims. When I was in the national liberation movement they funded us with their trucks, money, and even supported us with food. I was there and I saw how many sandals they bought, how many heads and beards they shaved. They even drove their trucks to the battles. So why should I deny them the place they helped not only protect but also build?

The museum provides a unique perspective when the Jewish text is part of a historical narrative with different subtexts.

Despite the non-Western nature of the COM, my conversations with Ibrahim revealed thematic concerns that are central to Western models of museums and curation, especially the politics of representation and amnesia in the museum.[27] While Ibrahim had never had any formal museum training, he saw museums as a "national" space that educated citizens about the complexities of their identities and diverse historical narratives. He objected to a dominant national narrative that emphasized solely a glorious past. This narrative in the nation's museums, he explained, "has to recover and reconstruct Moroccan history by representing the Berber, Arab, African, Jewish pasts and cultures." COM of Akka challenges the concept of *'ayn mika*. As "counternarratives" to state museums, COM, and to some extent the JMC, are "the means by which groups contest that dominant reality and the framework of assumptions that support it."[28]

A Secret Jewish Museum

I visited the Jewish Museum of Casablanca in the spring of 2004, after I had seen Ibrahim's museum. Located in a prosperous, quiet residential area under government surveillance, nothing outside the building communicates its existence apart from a golden sign outside the door: Museum. As I approached, two security agents (a policeman and a *makhzani* [municipal guard]) stopped me. When I produced my official papers, they informed the curator and I was let into the building. In an article in the independent revue *TelQuel*, Maria Daïf, one of the most outspoken Moroccan journalists about the position of Jews in the Moroccan nation-state, described the situation:

> The museum of Judaism is under high surveillance since the terrorist attacks of May 16. With the exception of a small sign where the word "museum" is written, nothing indicates that Moroccan Jewish cultural treasures are exhibited here. This constitutes a discretion that Simon Lévy, director of the museum, explains first by a witticism: "When we created the museum, it was the only one in the city, there was no need then to specify that this is a museum of Judaism. Why then all these measures of security? Fear of eventual anti-Semitic aggressions? Of the 'bearded of the neighboring school'? To shock the majority? Certainly a little of all that, which explains why the museum of Judaism is not well placed."

Zhor Rehihil, the Muslim curator, greeted me. She had been the curator since the establishment of the museum in the 1990s.[29] Unlike Ibrahim, Zhor had received undergraduate training in archaeology at the Institut National des Sciences de l'Archéologie et du Patrimoine. For her thesis, she wrote an anthropological and ethnological study on the Jewish minority of Morocco. She argued that she "wanted to understand the other, to know it, and to discover if there is a difference between the Moroccan Jew and the one who lives in Israel."[30] Her sympathetic attitude toward what she described as the justice of the Palestinian cause has never been an obstacle to her belief in the right of having a Jewish voice in the national narrative.

The JMC is not only celebrated as the only Jewish museum in the Islamic world, but its site has historical importance for the Jews of Casablanca. The building was first constructed in 1948 as an orphanage for Jewish children, established by Celia Bengio in memory of her husband, Murdock Bengio. At the end of the 1970s, the orphanage was transformed into a *yeshiva* (orthodox Jewish school) for a decade. By the end of the 1980s, Casablanca's Jewish community decided to turn the building into a museum of Moroccan Judaism.

The museum, which occupies an area of seven hundred square meters, consists of a large room used mainly for exhibitions, three rooms where aspects of religious and family life are displayed, two rooms where two replicas of a Moroccan synagogue are exhibited, and a library. The focus of the permanent exhibition is chiefly historical and ethnographic. The exhibits are an amalgam of religious, historical, traditional, and ethnographic relics. Some of these articles include oil lamps, Chanukah lamps, Torahs, Torah covers, traditional clothing, paintings, sculptures, and photographs.

Unlike Akka's museum, the JMC represents Moroccan Jews in complete political and cultural isolation; it does not engage in any historical explanation of Jewish-Muslim relations. The Jews of Casablanca established the museum in 1997 with the support of the Foundation of Jewish Moroccan Cultural Heritage (FJMCH), an organization created in 1995 to safeguard the disappearing Moroccan Jewish culture and promote the distinctive characteristics of Moroccan Judaism. Approved by the government of Abderrahman El Youssefi on February 9, 2001, the decree recognized the FJMCH as an association with public benefits and therefore gave it the necessary legal footing to achieve its goals. It also limited its capital to US$50,000. The income for the museum's annual budget comes either from interest on this capital or from private donations from members of the Jewish community in Morocco and abroad.

Despite the official recognition of the FJMCH as having public benefits, the JMC has not received the same recognition as other private museums. For instance the Belgahzi Museum, Morocco's first privately run museum, was officially recognized in 1996; Princess Lalla Meriem attended its opening. The limited extent to which the JMC is officially recognized in Morocco is in sharp contrast to its appreciation internationally.

Jews in the National Public Sphere

The culture of visiting museums in Morocco in particular and in the Arab world in general is not highly developed.[31] Accordingly, national museums are designed to contribute to the economic development of Morocco by attracting international tourists and promoting an image of Morocco as tolerant and peaceful.[32] The JMC is no different in this regard. Its goal is clearly to attract foreign tourists, especially Israeli tourists of Moroccan origin, by displaying their cultural heritage. However, the state is careful not to broadcast this to a wide audience, and it is difficult to find reliable statistics of Moroccan-born Israeli tourists. Many arrive in Morocco with a second passport, either American or European. However, according to Moroccan officials, about 40,000 Israelis visited Morocco during the first few years after the Oslo Agreement. Once the al-Aqsa Intifada started in 2000, formal relations were cut. In 2003, the suicide bombing in Casablanca occurred, and the number of Israeli tourists dropped at least by half. Both the official website and leaflets from the Ministry of Tourism and the National Office of Tourism fail to list the JMC as one of the country's national museums, even though it, like other private and public museums, presents aspects of the national cultural heritage. In fact, according to the museum's brochure, its mission is to present "religious, ethnographic and artistic objects that demonstrate the history, religion, traditions and daily life of Jews in the context of Moroccan civilization." The JMC's absence from the list of national museums is a way that official Morocco turns "its plastic eye" ('ayn mika) toward the JMC while condoning and funding it. On the national level, the museum is perceived as *Jewish* not Moroccan. The identity of its visitors makes it clear that it primarily serves constituencies of local and foreign Jews or international tourists. At the same time, the museum is advertised only to outsiders. For example, Royal Air Maroc, the official national airline, featured an article about the "Jewish" museum in its magazine as a testimony of national tolerance and Jewish-Muslim coexistence in Morocco.[33] What explains this ambivalence toward the JMC at the official level?

In the shadow of the Palestinian-Israeli conflict, it has become difficult to celebrate the cultural accomplishments of Moroccan Jewry without also commenting on Israeli policies toward Palestinians. Morocco's Jewish community is well aware that its image is linked to that of Israel and its policies toward the Palestinians. For Simon Lévy, it is hard to be Jewish in Morocco because "every time something happens in Palestine we get asked about it here and sometimes blamed for it." In order to understand the difference between the JMC and Ibrahim's COM, it is essential to look at them in their historical contexts.

The JMC opened at a particular historical juncture, when a Palestinian-Israeli entente was about to take root after the Oslo Agreement. Noting the promises for peace after the Madrid meeting and the Oslo Agreement, King Hassan II took a hitherto unusual step when he nominated Serge Berdugo as the tourism minister in 1993.[34] In 1998, Berdugo became the secretary-general of the council of Moroccan Jews. He also heads the World Assembly of Moroccan Jewry and serves as the president of the Jewish Community of Casablanca. In March 2006, King Mohammed VI appointed him ambassador-at-large. Berdugo's tourism appointment (1993–1995) was part of the general development plan to fortify the economic and cultural ties between Israel and Morocco. The opening of the liaison office with Tel Aviv in Rabat was made final in November 1994. By listing a Moroccan Jew for a national cabinet post, Hassan II aspired to attract international support for economic development. Equally important, he issued orders to open a Moroccan liaison office in Gaza. Although there were many economic, agricultural, and cultural exchanges between Israel and Morocco, tourism emerged as the most important. With the support of Berdugo, the liaison office of Tel Aviv issued thousands of tourist visas to Morocco to Israelis who wished to visit their ancestral land. Tourism agencies were even successful in attracting Ashkenazi Jews. According to a recent article in an Israeli paper, an Israeli tour company spokesman says that the market is currently 5,000–7,000 a year.

Despite the clearly political causes behind its existence, the JMC—like all other officially recognized national museums in Morocco—was silent about the politics of its birth and generally apolitical about its content. The curators of the museum consciously ignored topics that were publicly controversial. There were no references to the post-independence period of legal and illegal Jewish migration to Israel. For instance, the post-1948 period and the waves of emigration that followed were not part of the exhibition. Instead, the museum showed Jewish life in Morocco during the colonial and pre-colonial period. It avoided sensitive subjects and controversial Jewish narratives in the history of Morocco. The focus on artifacts instead of stories depersonalized the Jewish experience in Morocco, and Jewish-Muslim relations were idealized. In the words of Alonso, "The past is cleaned up, rendered palatable and made the embodiment of nationalist values. Death and suffering are purged of terror and pain: fratricide is transformed into fraternity."[35] The decisions to exclude these stories were driven by the politics of the Arab-Israeli conflict. Since the first Intifada, there has been an emerging feeling against Israel in some sectors of the general Moroccan public. This attitude conflates Israel with Jews, and consequently Moroccan Jews are occasionally targeted as supporters of Israel and its policies toward Palestine. As the Jewish community of Casablanca tries to safeguard its religious and cultural landmarks, it continues to keep a low profile in the national public sphere.

As we have seen, Ibrahim's museum took a different strategy based on what he called *tarbiya b-lmuwajaha* (educating by confronting). By establishing a museum where he exhibits all the different narratives of Morocco as they relate to the history of Akka, his intent is to build a regional "museum of coexistence." Museums of coexistence focus on ways to avoid confrontation. For instance, after the Oslo Agreement, Palestinians and Israelis attempted to build museums where both groups could express their opinions. The Beit Tourjeman Museum in Jerusalem represented one of the first attempts to create such a museum. Ben-Ze'ev and Ben-Ari defined the project as

> an establishment where narratives of two or more groups marked by confrontations are set side by side. Given that the Israeli directors wanted to set up a museum depicting a *"contemporary* history of Jerusalem," the central story of the museum could not avoid the ongoing reality of the city. Because the focus of the museum was to deal with the meeting point between the city's Palestinian and Jewish parts, this narrative could not escape these relations' confrontational character.[36]

The awareness of a pluralistic society that museums might try to represent was at the center of Ibrahim's life work. Ibrahim did not charge an entrance fee to his museum; he relied on visitors' donations. He was also aware of the shortcomings of his project, noting that the geographic remoteness of the COM restricts its message. Yet he claimed that "this project is local and regional," and that if children became aware that "Jews and Muslims lived once in Akka as neighbors and shared mint tea and exchanged bread," he had succeeded in delivering his educational message. When I met Ibrahim, he expressed his concern over the loss of the memory of past Jewish-Muslim relations in Morocco. In his words:

> The museum gives perspective. When a Muslim visitor enters this space and sees a picture of a Moroccan Jew from Akka dressed like him, he can see himself in that picture. It is the same culture. The Jew in the picture is as Moroccan as the Muslim who observes him. . . . Once this is established, the Muslim, who has never seen a Jew, becomes tolerant, and he can criticize Israeli policies towards Palestinians in the spirit of debate without being anti-Jewish.

While the state takes a marginal role in its involvement with the narratives of some Moroccan museums, it publicly associates itself with Jewish museums outside Morocco. One of the leading figures of this "outside remembering" of Moroccan Jews is Paul Dahan, who was born and raised in Fez before he moved to Belgium. King Mohammed VI nominated him in 2009 as the only Jewish member of the Council of Moroccan Community Abroad. Like the work of the museum of Ibrahim and the JMC, Dahan founded the Centre de la Culture Judéo-Marocaine (CCJM) to represent Moroccan Judaism, in this case from outside national boundaries. Moroccan Jewish heritage is emphasized to enhance the image of Morocco as a place of tolerance and therefore a positive destination for tourists. It is also widely celebrated by the state, especially as "Jewish subjects" in Europe, like Dahan, are behind the celebration of their acceptance by the Moroccan state.

The conflicting narratives in the vignettes of the curator Ibrahim and the elder Abdelhaq earlier in this chapter highlight tensions in the national debate about the status of Jews in Morocco. They expose the challenges that Moroccan society faces in its attempts to represent the national past in museums and other state institutions. They also demonstrate the discrepancies between official discourse and public sentiments about minorities. Since the 1950s, when a majority of the Moroccan Jews left for Israel, an ambivalence has developed in the state's official attitude toward its Jewish population, an ambivalence that is shaped by the state's idea of popular Muslim sensibilities and a changing political context of Muslim-Jewish relations. Internationally, the government promotes Morocco as a nation of Jewish-Muslim historical symbiosis and contemporary tolerance. Nationally, the state has maintained a relative silence about its Jewish history and culture. This ambivalence is made all the more difficult by new economical and political conditions: while more than 99 percent of Morocco is Muslim and popular opinion is slanted in favor of Palestinians, the Jews of Moroccan descent constitute one of the largest groups in Israel and make up a sizable part of Morocco's burgeoning tourism industry. This ambivalence at the government level is reflected in the lack of any official Moroccan-Israeli diplomatic relations, although Morocco is one of Israel's largest trading partners in the Arab world.[37]

I have suggested that the Moroccan state effectively turns "a plastic eye" ('ayn mika/ tmyak) as a strategy to deal with this ambivalence toward the historical importance of Moroccan Jews to the nation-building process. Publicly, neither past Jewish migration nor current conflicts are addressed. The risks are too high, given a highly negative public attitude toward Jews who happen to be in the middle of a clash over land ownership and rights in the Middle East. Tacitly allowing the representation of Moroccan Jews to be "outsourced" to self-made curators and a Jewish association has been the pragmatic way of turning one's plastic eye while appearing tolerant and inclusive. The private Muslim museum of Akka and the Jewish Museum of Casablanca have allowed the state to portray itself to the international community as celebrating its Jewish past and its culture of tolerance. The Moroccan state has also effectively allowed private curators and Moroccan Jews abroad to take the lead in the portrayal of the Moroccan Jewish heritage. As the state engages in engineering positive perceptions and an acceptance of Jews in modern Moroccan society, youth narratives reflect a different worldview, characterized by the conflation of Moroccan Jews and Israelis, and their mistrust of Jews as Moroccan citizens.

6

Between Hearsay, Jokes, and the Internet

YOUTH DEBATE JEWISH MOROCCO

Young Rebels and Generational Authority

Throughout my fieldwork, members of the generations of great-grandparents, grandparents, and even parents complained about how Moroccan youth show little respect for their elders, rejecting their knowledge as backward and outdated. This generational gap was clear at the level of historical memory in general and in knowledge about Jewish communities in particular. Ahmed, a member of the grandparents' generation, provided the following perspective:

> In the old days, Akka used to be a booming commercial center where hundreds of trade caravans exchanged salt and other sub-Saharan products for dates and other articles on their way to the northern coastal port of Essaouira. Families still own historical documents describing a strong relationship with other regional economic centers such as Ifrane and Tazarwalt. Today, Akka has nothing to offer to its local population! The majority of households live below the poverty line. The center of political and commercial power has shifted to interior urban places where a largely Western-educated urban elite run our daily lives. In the past, Akka produced its own local scholars who not only played a significant role in managing the region's daily legal and political activities, but also provided an example for the younger generation to follow. Family education, largely supported by traditional Muslim scholars and schools, was built on respect of elders and our traditional Islamic heritage. Today our youth ignore their parents and see their knowledge as backward and useless. They want to live in the West and relinquish their ancestors' way of life. They have their own version of Islam. They have their own version of education. Unlike other regions, our local youth have not benefited from the state educational system. Therefore, they have not been able to access key administrative positions. We live in an economic and social crisis!

This cameo highlights among other issues a generational gap and a crisis of transmission and interpretation of knowledge that transformed social relations between different generations in the communities of southeastern Morocco. Youth socialization, traditionally influenced by older people, was being replaced by emerging forms of Western knowledge, the state, and modern political parties. In the eyes of the great-grandparents and grandparents, the generational "conflict is represented (by the elders) as a disrupted process of evolution, or the discontinuation of a 'natural' process of reproduction."[1] For the youth, however, there is a general belief that the traditional model of authority, whereby children should consider their parents' knowledge sacred, not only breeds subjugation but also empowers the corrupt. Hamid, a second-year graduate student of geography in Agadir, said:

> After independence the monarchy used our illiterate and religious grandparents and later parents to challenge its enemies in major cities. The religious local elite struck an alliance with the central government, and nobody has ever questioned the government and its economic, educational, and social policies. Today is different. The countryside is struggling; people have to migrate to find jobs in the city; the local elite is broken; the government is running short of solutions and the youth feel betrayed by their corrupt government.

His narrative invokes Leveau's *Le fellah Marocain: défenseur du throne*, which describes how after independence the state sought to control the rural population through the local elite by combining the religious authority of the monarchy and a system of economic and political patronage. Benali argues that Moroccan society, and especially rural communities, have undergone drastic social transformations and that the old system of patronage has seen major fractures, leading to drastic changes in the belief systems and values of the younger generation.[2] The individual revolt is not limited to family structures but extends to question state power and the privileges of political leaders.

Like many student movements worldwide, Moroccan high school and university students have expressed widespread criticism of their government over economic and political issues since the 1960s.[3] Violent riots and movements of civil dissent appeared with increasing frequency in Moroccan cities after the dramatic failure of the state's planned economic development programs of the 1960s and 1970s. Faced with higher external debt, budget constraints, and major deficits, the government took the unpopular decision to cut public spending in education and health.[4] These structural adjustments also threatened entitlement programs and the provision of basic goods. One of the immediate results was an increase in food prices, leading to intermittent outbursts of violence in 1981, 1984, and 1990.[5] At the center of these violent moments was Casablanca's youth.[6]

By the 1980s, with the rapidly growing population of university graduates, the Moroccan public sector was not able to absorb them all, and riots against the central and local governments erupted.[7] Frustration and anger began to dominate the country, especially as both corruption and economic disparities grew. When the government failed to provide jobs, its *hiba* (authority) was questioned. Hammoudi contends that the traditional system of social and cultural behavior was built around a master-disciple relationship in which "signs of femininity—in the form of submission and service—are displayed in the relation of domination between father and son or superior and subordinate."[8] Culturally, the small-scale parallel is that as the father fails to provide for the family, his authority is also challenged. The younger generation's access to other forms of knowledge threatened the authority of the generations of great-grandparents, grandparents, and parents.

The father-son disagreement has been exposed at the level of the neighborhood, where young people have produced a different type of knowledge and paradigm of social interaction. The street and its Internet cafés as well as coffee shops have become the place where the authorities of the family and state are challenged, denounced, and sometimes ridiculed. The paterfamilias and the state have both lost their mandate; they have little to offer a growing population of disenfranchised youth. Meijer argues:

> The traditional pillar of stability and accepted opinion, the family is being severely eroded, while the modern, alternative source of education, employment and security, the state, has proved unable to fulfill its tasks and has lost a great deal of its legitimacy. . . . During the past decades, the influence of the street on youth has greatly expanded, whether in the form of the Islamist movement or alternative cultural expressions.[9]

In her study of Moroccan youth, Bennani-Chraïbi used the term "internal *siba*"[10] (dissidence) to express how Moroccan youth were able not only to question the authority of the state and its political and economic discourse but also to free themselves from its paternalistic cultural order. The *hiba* (respectful fear) of state authority and the elders, an essential factor of Hammoudi's master-disciple model, is less present among rebellious youth. In this process of debunking the traditional master-disciple relationship, they created a new discourse by:

> Mixing up the languages they speak under the influence of close and far-away images and music. . . . Moroccan youths no longer believe in the founding myths of power, and when they look for a collective meaning which would give more content to their individual quests, it is more likely to be within the small groups and communities that they create in the secondary school, in the university or in their neighborhood that the discourse rejecting the society in which they are living is elaborated.[11]

Moroccan youth deploy a modern discourse that appropriates Western cultural references through the development of a new cultural model of knowledge. Younger generations are reproducing new Moroccan ideas about Jews by importing external religious and political thought and adapting it to the social, cultural, and historical realities of Moroccan society. In his work on the plight of poor Malaysian peasants, Scott makes the point that studies of youth have focused on violent means of protest and ignored everyday forms of resistance.[12] He describes subtle ways of resistance (such as gossip) as common methods used by those with little power to challenge hegemonic systems. In this context, Scott's term "weapons of the weak" can be applied to understanding how Moroccan youth talk about Jews in terms of jokes (*nukat*), gossip, and rumor (*tbarguig*).

If we approach the knowledge about Jews produced by youth as part of a set of rumors, with varying degrees of truth, we can argue that the pattern of transmission of these rumors, though they set the younger and older generations apart, bears similarities to the way the social memories of older cohorts about Jews are disseminated. Allport and Postman write:

> As rumor travels, it tends to go shorter, more concise, more easily grasped and told. In successive versions, more and more of the original details are leveled out, fewer words are used and fewer items are mentioned. . . . As leveling of details proceeds, the remaining details are necessarily sharpened. Sharpening

refers to selective perception, retention and reporting of few details from the originally larger context.[13]

The leveling of selective perception, the reporting, and the retention of stereo-types about Moroccan Jews are sharpened among the youth cohort because they meet two essential conditions of rumor transmission: importance and am-biguity. On the one hand, the Palestinian issue is a critical political issue in their daily discussion. On the other hand, Jews as a group form an ambiguous social category used as the laughingstock of youth. Similar to the vignette described in the Prologue, young people talked about Jews largely in terms of sick humor mixed with racist violence. Like Dundes, I chose to reproduce one example of these jokes "not to popularize and further circulate them [but] to examine the slurs to see what the stereotypes are."[14] One of the widely circulated jokes goes:

> There is a saying by the Prophet asking Muslims to change a wrongdoing, if they can, by their hands, if they cannot then by their mouth, and if they cannot by their heart as the least of the choices. Following this Prophet's tradition, one Muslim went to the Jewish cemetery and started peeing on their tombs while shouting loudly: "This is all that I can do for you Palestine!"

This joke exemplifies what Billig calls sick religious humor, which continues to be perpetuated among Moroccan youth because the political context in the Mid-dle East serves as a breeding ground for its reproduction. Accordingly, the joke has a historical and political significance. It both positions the addressee within the Arab-Israeli conflict and acts as a form of popular resistance to disparage and ridicule Israel and the Jews, against whom the "impotent" Arab govern-ment could not do anything. Billig argues that, although the violence of the joke could never take place and could be a fantasy of unreal violence, "it assumes the psychological reality that the fantasy will be shared by recipients of the joke."[15] The joke is the only "effective" weapon that has replaced traditional violent acts or the daily humiliations when Muslim children used to harass the Jew-ish children every time they stepped outside their neighborhoods, as the great-grandparents reported.

In traditional contexts, Jews were described as weak and cowardly. A popu-lar adage read: "The Jew and the woman are alike; they are cowards and they do not show respect [*hishma*]." The feminization of the Jew is a way to express the traditional nonthreatening nature of a Jew to Muslim women.[16] This is why a Jewish peddler had access to Muslim households without the presence of the Muslim patron, while a Muslim peddler did not. On the contrary, a few informants of the young adults cohort criticized the notion that Jews are cowardly. "Look at what they are doing all over the world," Hassan, a young adult from Akka, explained:

> They are not powerless and not cowardly. They managed to beat us in three wars with a limited number of soldiers. They are not cowards as my ancestors think. They have one of the most sophisticated armies in the world. We are the cowards because we cannot even make a last stand against the Americans in Baghdad. The Americans entered the great land of Harun al-Rashid [Baghdad] with their tanks like entering a brothel. Jews have turned Jerusalem into a brothel.

In the eyes of young adults, Jews are no longer the asexual members of the Muslim communities where they used to live. Hassan's image of a brothel is very significant because it describes the situation in which Moroccans' frame of reference about impotent Jews, both politically and sexually, is not true anymore. Similar to Haidt's study of the construction of masculinities in the Spanish Enlightenment, the construction of Muslim masculinity versus Jewish femininity becomes a "foundational cultural maneuver through which relational political categories are sexed and embodied by individuals in society."[17] Therefore, Muslim masculinity, as my young informants construct it, is stressed through Jewish political and military situations. Jamal, an undergraduate student of Islamic studies, summarized this relationship indignantly: "We have lived to witness the weak dirty peddler of Akka becoming the powerful soldier and master under whose feet America and impotent Arab leaders tremble."

Moroccan Youth and the Palestinian-Israeli Conflict

Less than two months after the March 22, 2004, assassination of Ahmed Yassin, the founder and spiritual leader of Hamas, I visited the Faculty of Letters at Cadi Ayyad University in Marrakesh to interview a group of Amazigh (Berber) activists from Berber communities in southeastern Morocco, about their views of the Palestinian-Israeli conflict. Departing from its practice during the first decades of independence, the Ministry of Education established many public universities as part of the national plan to meet the needs of a growing population of high school graduates.[18] After the opening of the University of Ibn Zohr in Agadir in 1986, southern Moroccan students came to Marrakesh to pursue their education in fields not available in Agadir. During my study, I had many encounters with students in the public universities of Agadir and Marrakesh, not only about their views of Moroccan Jewry but also about their attitudes toward the place of Jews in the modern Moroccan state, the relationships between Moroccans and Palestinians, their views of Moroccan Jews in Israel, and their feelings about the Holocaust. Although I met them in the villages of southern Morocco, we also met on the campuses in Marrakesh and Agadir.

A few police trucks patrolled outside the campus walls of the Cadi Ayyad Faculty of Letters to keep demonstrators from marching—this while hundreds of students streamed onto the campus, paying no heed to the security presence. Inside the Faculty of Letters, fliers in Arabic and Tamazight were displayed on columns and walls. A few banners stressed the Palestinian struggle against Jewish Zionists, emphasizing the Islamic rights over al-Quds, praising Hamas as the legitimate Palestinian representative, and denouncing the bureaucratic collaboration of American imperialism, the Palestine Liberation Organization (PLO) leadership, and Arab dictatorships. Others acclaimed the martyrdom of Ahmed Yassin and called for *jihad* against Israel. A few students sat on the ground and displayed sets of recorded Islamic sermons, taped readings of the Qur'an, and interpretations of the Hadith. As they sold their wares, they played songs that celebrated Palestine and al-Quds by Fairuz and Julia Butrous, and poems that mocked Arab political leadership by Shaykh Imam and Ahmed Matar. In one of the hallways, a student delivered an emotional speech about Muslims' obligation toward Palestine, venting his anger against what he called the Moroccan state policies of normalization with the Zionist state. He captured the attention of a larger audience of men surrounded by a handful of veiled women.

A dozen students wearing T-shirts inscribed with letters in Tamazight script closely followed the speech from afar as they occasionally expressed feelings of disagreement. I leaned against a column facing a large window plastered with images of Ahmed Yassin and Abdel Aziz al-Rantissi (the Hamas political leader who faced the same fate on April 17, 2004). A few fliers depicting al-Aqsa Mosque surrounded by Moroccan and Palestinian flags littered the hallways. In another corner of the campus, two veiled women sold Palestinian *kufiya*s (scarves) to a large crowd of students as a Qur'anic tape was played in the background and two security officers watched from a distance. Some students checked the only bookstand with Hadith books, Qur'anic interpretations, books by Moroccan Islamic intellectuals, mainly Ahmed Raissouni and Abdessalam Yassine, and other material, including an abridged Arabic translation of *The Protocols of the Elders of Zion*, published in Egypt in 2002.

Sponsored by the Union Nationale des Étudiants Marocains (UNEM),[19] the event was largely dominated by the Islamic student faction, especially members of al-'Adl wa al-Ihsan (the Justice and Spirituality Movement). Strolling down a hallway to the dean's office, my informant finally called and suggested meeting in the cafeteria. Born in the oasis of Tissint, Hassan represented a growing trend in the university that subscribed to the ideas of the banned Parti Démocratique Amazigh (PDA) and its secretary-general, Ahmed Daghrani. The PDA was officially launched in 2005, but the government banned it in 2007 on the grounds that it advocated an ethnic identity of the nation. Wearing a T-shirt with Amazigh symbols, Hassan expressed contempt for the event:

> These people are not that different from the leftist and Marxist student factions of the 1960s, 1970s, and 1980s. As Amazigh we fought along their side, and many of our parents and brothers got jailed, assassinated, or disappeared. The leftist movement never stood for our cultural and linguistic rights. For these Islamists, everything is about pan-Arab and pan-Islamic ideals. They claim that they are democratic but they have refused Amazigh and Saharawi peoples a fair representation in the UNEM. They are fighting for Palestinian rights but they denied us our own language and cultural rights. As for Moroccan Jews, they have never treated them as nationals. That's probably why they left. Now they criticize them for fighting for Israel. At the same time, they think that every Moroccan Jew today is a spy and untrustworthy foreigner working for America and the Jewish state.

Unlike the majority of students, who identified as Arab, Hassan expressed positive yet controversial feelings toward Moroccan Jews and Israel. He claimed that the UNEM has failed to accept the diversity of the Moroccan identity and has focused on the Arab and Islamic dimensions of the nation, limiting the rights of Berbers, Jews, women, and other minorities. He also argued for establishing cultural and economic relationships between the Amazigh communities throughout the Anti-Atlas Mountains and Jews from the region who now live in Israel. In other conversations, Amazigh students claimed that Amazigh culture in Morocco and North Africa faces "cultural genocide by their Algerian, Libyan and Moroccan states" as well as forms of Amazighophobia which had historically relegated them to second-class citizenship in relation to Arabs. Accordingly, Ali, a third-year French studies undergraduate, noted:

> Since Hassan Nasrallah drove Israel from southern Lebanon, the Islamists have been emboldened. They attacked us as infidels, supporters of colonialism, and sympathizers with Zionism. How do you want me to be for these Arab racists, when they are as anti-Semitic as Amazighophobic? These Islamists argue every day that Israel is racist, but if you listen to their discourse about Jews and Berbers and any other group, their state vision never accepts these groups as citizens with full rights and obligations.

Ali and Hassan represent a Berber faction within the student movement that gained momentum mainly in the last decade. In the 1980s, the UNEM was still under the control of socialist and communist activists.[20] In 2010, Islamist groups seemed to have the upper hand over the student body council. In many Moroccan public universities, where Islamic and secular socialist ideas have long clashed, a new Berber consciousness has emerged at the edge of the secular and religious frontiers of the UNEM.

Internet Activism and Resistance

Eickelman says that new media such as the Internet have the potential to create a space for public debate, eroding the authority and legitimacy of the state and creating an alternate vision of society. He notes how through "fragmenting authority and discourse, the new technologies of communication, combined with the multiplication of agency facilitated by rising education levels, contribute significantly to reimagining Middle Eastern politics and religion."[21] The recent evolution of communication technologies indirectly empowered youth and student movements in Morocco. Their ability to move their message on Palestine outside the walls of the universities weakened state control and authority over the issue. Students no longer limit their transcripts on Palestine to campus conversations. The availability of alternative media, such as Facebook, Twitter, and YouTube, has irrevocably challenged the state discourse about the Palestinian-Israeli conflict. Between the 1960s and late 1980s, public conversations about the Palestinian issue were largely displayed in newspapers and media controlled by the state and political parties. Since the 1960s, the state has been able to control the UNEM and its factions and limit the students' influence on national politics. In the last decade, students have played an instrumental role in developing Moroccan media that challenge the state siege, checkpoints, and curfew imposed on universities nationwide.[22] The geographic isolation has been broken by a student cybercommunication movement, which created a virtual Moroccan student community. By expressing their views through a new counterpublic—in this case, virtual spheres—the student body freed itself from the state-controlled walls of campuses and allowed students nationwide and worldwide to share information, create global and regional connections with other student bodies, and express their views with limited state restrictions. Hamid wrote:

> In the past, we could not express what we think about what our brothers in Palestine are going through. The state radio and TV broadcast every night their version of what was going on in Palestine without questioning what Morocco has done to protect *al-Quds*. The Internet is a blessing. It has allowed us to tell our weak and corrupt leaders that we do not agree with their type of lies and double talk. You cannot be for Palestine and Moroccan Jews in Israel at the same time. You have to choose.

Hamid and other students with an Islamic and secular ideological leaning claimed that Arab governments had used the Palestinian issue as a political tool for the interest of the corrupt leadership. Berber students, mostly from southeastern Morocco, including Akka, argue that these policies have legitimized the economic marginalization of the poor regions of southern Morocco. By calling for political detachment toward the Palestinian-Israeli conflict, Amazigh students revolt against the pan-Arab and Islamic foundation of the Moroccan nation-state. According to Daghrani, Berbers

> do not harbor any hatred against Jews or Israel, and everybody knows that the relation between Jews and Amazighs was always brotherly and strong, and

characterized by cooperation. What is new is that Middle Eastern Arab media, regimes, and political parties disseminated enmity. . . . We do not want to sever our contacts with Jews who migrated to Israel and elsewhere from Tamazgha. We want Palestinians to live in peace. We do not hate Jews and Arabs and any other nation. . . . We do not use the concept of *tatbi'* [naturalization], as it is known among Arabs of the Middle East, instead, we use the term peace.[23]

The views of Daghrani and his Amazigh followers could be interpreted as signs of indigenous political grievance. They are open public transcripts of resistance to the dominance of certain national narratives.[24] They are part of the everyday resistance of the subaltern and new "strangers" to the national hegemonic cultural, political, and economic borders in the post-independence government dominated by the Istiqlal party. The region of Tata and Akka in particular is one of the poorest in Morocco, for it has suffered years of political and economic marginalization since independence. These Amazigh voices of (re)constructed identities could be seen as ways to challenge the Moroccan government's economic and political marginalization of minority groups. Accordingly, the reinvention of identity becomes a form of resistance to national hegemonic models.

For Moroccan youth, cyberspace has emerged as a useful tool, where political and social grievances over the Arab-Israeli conflict are circulated without censorship. Facebook and YouTube have, at least partially, helped both rural and urban Moroccan youth go beyond the limited media traditionally regulated by the state and political parties to express themselves freely about Israeli policies toward Palestinians and Morocco's unofficial diplomatic relationship with Israel. In the last decade, Moroccan youth have targeted a number of official Israeli and American websites as a response to the Arab-Israeli conflict, becoming some of the most active hackers of virtual communities. In their support of the Palestinians, Moroccan hackers deploy "hacktivism" to generate publicity for their cause. Hacktivism includes automated e-mail bombs, virtual sit-ins, site blockades, and web hacks.[25] By using cyberspace, Moroccan youth, I believe, have managed to escape the political and cultural Panopticon[26] that traditionally limited students' activism to the confines of public universities. Accordingly, I contend that youth not only react to their exclusion from the public sphere but also protest the globalized discourse of the conflict. Finally, I claim that these networks of cyberresistance have allowed young people to create through blogs new landscapes of contention over the ownership of memory, the politics of remembering and forgetting, and the interpretation of the histories of the Arab-Israeli conflict, especially as many Moroccan Jews have built their online communities to express Moroccan identity.

From Walled Campuses and Virtual Spaces

Well before the late 1970s, large numbers of students were strongly attracted to radical ideologies, with as many as half supporting parties with leftist agendas.[27] During the UNEM's twelfth conference and following the Arab defeat of 1967, the government prevented the union from holding its meeting on the ground that it was planning to discuss national political issues. The conference was postponed until July 1968 after the global student uprisings and the emergence of the Moroccan Marxist-Leninist faction on many university campuses. The nascent leftist nucleus supported worldwide national movements of liberation and freedom, including that for Palestinian liberation. A few voices in the movement went as far as supporting the right of Sahrawi for an independent state in the Western Sahara. By 1968, the liberation of Palestine became not only a core principle of the UNEM but its national issue as well, and it continued to hold festivals in support of Palestine. For instance, in 1987, the UNEM called for a year of student resistance for Palestine, challenging a speech of King Hassan II's that denied any form of solidarity with the Palestinian people in response to the PLO's invitation to the Polisario during its annual meeting in Algiers. Large demonstrations took place on many university campuses. In Fez, students protested in poor neighborhoods and the government used security forces to suppress the riots.

In the late 1990s, the growth of satellite media, and later the online social networks, blogs, and social media, challenged the state's hegemonic powers and control over the arenas of contention, as the amateur video clip replaced the official national television. For Moroccan youth, YouTube and other tools of cyberspace helped to support a participatory culture of resistance, including the posting of anti-Israeli news and Palestinian flags as profile pictures. According to Jenkins, "participatory culture is one in which fans and other consumers are invited to actively participate in the creation and circulation of new content."[28] Struggles over the meaning and value of politics are symptoms of deep transformation in modern Moroccan society. In the case of student movements, these shifts are linked to changing class politics, cultural production, access to education, and disenfranchised unemployed youth. The students' opposition to the government was shown in its critique of the monarchy's role in the Camp David Accords, as well as King Hassan II's reception of the Israeli prime minister, Shimon Peres, in his palace in Ifrane on July 22–23, 1986. At the same time, Moroccan Jews became part of this debate, as young people perceived Moroccan Jews as potential Israeli lobbyists and spies; accordingly, to them a Jewish allegiance to the Moroccan nation was impossible. In the last decade, Moroccan youth—many of whom are undergraduates in public universities—have reacted to the Palestinian-Israeli conflict by targeting official Israeli and American websites, becoming some of the most active hackers worldwide.

In 2006, a group of Moroccans attacked many Israeli and American websites as a way to express their anger about the Israeli invasion of Gaza. These attacks were referred to as *net-intifada* and *e-jihad*. The Israeli government cautioned against Moroccan hacking activities to the extent that American and Israeli authorities went to Morocco to discuss the issue with the authorities. This culture of online war began to dominate the electronic world, where Moroccan youth are now engaged in an electronic activism, interpreted as *electronic jihad*, against Israel and the United States. On June 28, 2006, and after more than 850 sites were attacked by young Moroccan hackers called Team Evil, a message was posted: "As long as you kill Palestinians, we will kill your servers."[29]

In his work on Palestinian cyberresistance, Khoury-Machool notes that the increase in the use of computers at home and the rise of personal computers allowed Palestinians to "stay together" as virtual friends and communicate their feelings and messages against Israel despite the siege.[30] In Morocco, the surge in the number of Internet cafés has attracted younger adults, since many families cannot afford personal computers and Internet connections. The younger generation has shifted to an active electronic political protest of Israel. It does not express its views about Americans and Jews solely through electronic blogs in major Arabic newspapers and satellite channels; instead, youth see themselves as part of the militant activism in cyberspace whose objective is to fight the United States and Israel. Unemployed urban youth are now active participants instead of idle and impotent gossipers (*bargaga*) on Moroccan streets.[31] They contrast their political protest with the impotence of Arab and Islamic failures and their inability to challenge Israel and the United States at the political, economic, and scientific levels. In this area, according to an Israeli participant in online blogs, Arab youths are as "intelligent as Israelis."

In response to the Moroccans' hacking of the Israeli and American websites, Israeli teenagers called on their government to take these hackers seriously. This challenge is celebrated by Moroccan youth as ridiculing the "Israeli Goliath" by a "band of kids." In this context, their e-mails were virtual bombs, distributed with the aid of automated tools to jam Israeli websites and limit their communication. According to Denning, "an email bomb is . . . a form of virtual blockade. Although email bombs are often used as a means of revenge or harassment, they have also been used to protest government policies."[32] This emerging discourse about Jews among the younger generation shows a drastic shift, not only at the level of generational knowledge, but also of social and political authority. As much as there is a crisis of the transmission of discourse about Jews, there is also a breakdown of traditional authority.

"Moroccan Jews are spies and agents of Israel"

As in the early decades of independence, Moroccan Jews are debated among youth today largely in newspapers and today cyberspace, although there has been a growing movement to represent Moroccan Jewish history in schools and the cinema.[33] A close look at a large number of Moroccan newspapers in the last decade reveals a reemergence of the pre-independence debate about the place of Jews in Moroccan society; it is largely expressed through issues related to a few prominent Moroccan Jews with distinct life histories and different ideologies. For instance, *Attajdid*, which has an Islamist-leaning editorial policy, has established a strong link between a Moroccan Jew, namely, André Azoulay, the economic adviser to Hassan II (and later Mohammed VI, who succeeded Hassan II in 1999) and Israel. In its editorials, Azoulay has been viewed as a chief player in Israeli-Moroccan politics and a critical ally of Israel. Therefore, *Attajdid*'s editorials have repeatedly depicted André Azoulay as an "agent" of foreign forces in Morocco.[34] The most common accusation has repeatedly been Azoulay's perceived involvement as an "agent of Zionism and Israel."[35] Instead of looking at the larger Moroccan policies about the Palestinian issue, Azoulay becomes a representative of all Moroccan Jews, and since, according to these voices, he is a foreign agent, all Moroccan Jews could be foreign agents.[36]

Although Azoulay has maintained his support for a Palestinian state and openly criticized the Israeli governments of Begin and Sharon, he continues to be a target of political slogans during protests against Israel. At the start of the al-Aqsa Intifada, a protest was held in Rabat in 2000 where more than a million people marched. Anti-Jewish slogans were shouted: "Death to Jews," "Jews leave Morocco," "This is a shame! This is a shame! A Zionist is an adviser."[37] All this debate about the position of a Jew in the government raises the issue of whether it is possible for Jews in the dominant Muslim Moroccan nation to serve the "Muslim population." Azoulay argues that as a Moroccan with traditional roots, his citizenship cannot be questioned:

> I feel more than 2000 years old. As a Jew here I belong to a community that arrived long before Islam. I have complete legitimacy in this country. . . . Until the Palestinian is afforded identity and dignity, my Jewishness is weakened. . . . I am an adviser to the Commander of Faithful who is a direct descendant of the Prophet Mohammed. . . . There is no other Arab or Moslem country where you have a Jewish person in such a responsibility. It's not by accident and has nothing to do with [me as a] person, just a continuation of a long tradition.[38]

These words are significant because they emphasize Azoulay's position as a servant of the king, just like any Muslim. The use of "Commander of Faithful" places Azoulay and any Jew in Morocco within its boundaries. Azoulay accepts the Islamic identity of Morocco, but he frames it as inclusive. He interprets Muslim discourses about the protection of Jews so that he can use Islam as an inclusionary rather than exclusionary element of Moroccan nationalism. Accordingly, his viewpoint is similar to the historical position taken by Mohammed V and Hassan II.

Independent and private newspapers critical of *Attajdid* have made the same point. They responded to the criticism about Azoulay and other Moroccan Jews by labeling it "a wave of anti-Jewish racism" and called on the Moroccan public to denounce it. *Al-Bayne*, one of the few political newspapers that continue to show support for Moroccan Jews (which reflects its history as the continuation of the former PCM), has sided with many independent voices and published a petition against anti-Jewish articles.[39] *Attajdid* continues to criticize Azoulay for his central role in the recent contacts with the Israeli government and the last visits of its former minister of foreign affairs, as well as the Moroccan native Amir Peretz, then the head of the Workers' Party. In 2004, the World Congress of Imams and Rabbis for Peace planned its meeting at al-Akhawayn University to discuss ways to bring Jews and Muslims together. *Attajdid* launched a campaign against the congress, even though it was to be held under the patronage of King Mohammed VI. The assassination of the spiritual leader of Hamas, Ahmed Yassin, in March 22, 2004, by Israel and the war in Iraq forced the government to move the meeting to Brussels in January 2005.

Although Azoulay continues to be optimistic about establishing communication between the Palestinians and the Israelis, *Attajdid* continues to be critical of his Israeli relations and any other Moroccan who professes a difference between Moroccan Jews and Israel. *Attajdid* has featured articles about what it calls the Zionist discourse (*al-khitab al-mutasahyin*) in Morocco. In one article, "al-sahyunifuniyya" (Moroccan voices of Zionism), the newspaper argued that a pro-Zionist movement that justified itself as a reaction against anti-Semitism was led by French-educated intellectuals. In 2002, Idris El Kanburi commented:

> The Palestinian who fights for his honor, land, and religion in Palestine does not know that he is fighting Zionists, and he does not know that Zionists are his killers. Instead he knows one thing: Jews. And I have never heard any Palestinian who says differently. As for the term Zionist and Zionism, this is part of the role of those who theorize and deal with books, not those who are burnt and killed.[40]

A similar article, written by Ahmed El Ouajdi on April 18, 2002, asked if "discourse about anti-Semitism" is the new characteristic of the "pro-Zionist discourse in Morocco." It used a discursive strategy similar to that used by al-Istiqlal in its traditional competition with the PCM in the 1940s. It stressed that Morocco's Jews have chosen to establish relations with enemies of the Palestinians, after they were protected for centuries in Morocco.

Apart from the general debate about the relationship between Moroccan Jews and the state of Israel, the other main discussion has revolved around the contacts between the Berbers and Moroccan Jews in Israel. In June 2006, a group of Berber (Amazigh) activists founded an association for economic, political, and cultural cooperation in Sus between Berbers and Jews of Berber origin who live in Israel. Daghrani, the secretary-general of the unofficial Parti Démocratique Amazigh (PDA), has been the most visible and outspoken member of the movement since July 31, 2005. Daghrani claimed that Berbers in Morocco and North Africa face "cultural genocide by an Arab state" as well as forms of Amazighophobia, similar to Judaeophobia, which had historically relegated the Berbers to second-class citizenship in relation to Arabs. He argues that "North African agents" of pan-Arabism, pan-Islamism, Ba'thism, and Nasserism have forced a policy of cultural assimilation on Berbers. This critique of the pan-Arab-Islamic attitude of the "de-valorization" of the Berber is the central argument of Daghrani's political grievance.

In order to counter this Arab-Islamic hegemony, Daghrani has publicly expressed the group's political disengagement from the Palestinian issue, which is seen as "an Arab cause" that does not reflect the economic, cultural, and political aspirations of the Berbers. Daghrani and his followers have shifted the debate about Moroccan Jews from Islam and pan-Arabism to secularism. Unlike the traditional parties that framed their discourse in terms of Islam, Arabism, and nationalism, this movement took a secular approach and called for integrating Jews and Berbers in the modern Moroccan nation. *Attajdid* has been one of the leading critics of this association. A debate about the group's objective erupted in newspapers of different political parties, al-Jazeera, and in online blogs. In an article titled "Amazighi Movement as a Means Towards Normalization with Israel," *Attajdid* denounces the movement because it undermines the Palestinian struggle and accepts the Israeli policies toward the Palestinians.[41]

However, for Boubaker Oudaadid, one of the founders of the Berber-Jewish Friendship Association in Sus, its goal is to fight against "the culture of anti-Semitism" in Morocco and to develop Amazigh culture among Amazigh Jews in Israel. This association signals an effort to make a major shift in the public discourse toward a "critical 'humanist' or 'universal' approach." However, because of its progressive nature, its members "find themselves set apart from the accepted intellectual, cultural and emotional levels within the history of 'their' society."[42] They are ostracized. Therefore, this emerging voice in the Moroccan public sphere is trying to navigate between the national collective memory of the Israeli occupation of Palestinian lands and the humanist as well as universal discourse about Jews. These opposite voices are part of a new discourse that is central, not only to the acceptance of the "Jews" as full citizens in Morocco, but also to other social and cultural issues at the heart of the public debate in the post–Hassan II era.

This broader discourse is concerned with the issue of Jewish representation in the Moroccan public sphere and the acceptance of difference in Moroccan society. Oudaadid claimed: "In Sus, where I grew up, there was no difference between Muslims and Jews. We had close relations with our Jewish brothers. When I settled in Casablanca, I was astonished by the anti-Semitic attitude of people who use phrases such as (Jews, God forbid!). It is one of the reasons that led us to create this association."[43] This comment is reminiscent of a short personal witness account, *Les juifs vont en enfer* [The Jews go to Hell], published in 1965 by Said Ghallab, about the attitude of Moroccan Muslims toward their fellow Jewish citizens. Ghallab emerged as one of the first Moroccans among Arab Muslims after independence to raise the issue of racism and negative attitudes held by Muslims toward Jews in Morocco. He discussed not only his childhood memories but also "what [he] saw, knew, learnt when [he] was a young man about the Jews."[44] His account received little attention from either national or Western scholars, although it raised the issue of how generations of Moroccan Muslims have been socialized to uphold certain beliefs about Jews. Ghallab was writing from the perspective of someone who saw how ethnocentric and racist attitudes contributed to wholesale massive extermination and genocide, such as the Holocaust. His account brought to the public sphere a discussion about how Moroccans get socialized through neighborhood, family, school, and society in general to nurture certain negative attitudes and racist tendencies toward Jews. Ghallab argues that as he grew up, he abandoned the practice of insulting Jews as they walked through Muslim neighborhoods. Still, he confessed:

> The worst insult that a Moroccan could possibly offer was to treat someone as a Jew. . . . My childhood friends have remained anti-Jewish. They hide their virulent anti-Semitism by contending that the state of Israel was the creation of European imperialism. . . . A whole Hitlerite myth is being cultivated among the populace. The massacres of the Jews by Hitler are exalted ecstatically. It is even credited that Hitler is not dead, but alive and well, and his arrival is awaited to deliver the Arabs from Israel.[45]

Oudaadid contends that many Muslims still regard Jews as Ghallab described in the 1960s. Despite continuous criticism, the Amazigh association continues to organize trips for Berbers and Israeli Jews of Berber descent to promote Berber culture in both countries. Many members have even participated in conferences about the teaching of the Holocaust in Yad Vashem, the official memorial of the Holocaust in Jerusalem.[46]

The Holocaust in Youth Narratives

I sat outside the doorway of a large mud-brick compound in the village of Allougoum when a big red rooster crowed as it scratched the rocky ground looking for food. Three little girls combed their handmade dolls as they conversed in Berber. A group of boys were busy fixing the tires of their cars, made from sardine boxes. While I waited for Hassan, who insisted on fetching a bottle of Coke and cookies, groups of men headed home after the midafternoon prayer. Hassan had just finished his bachelor's degree in Islamic studies; I had not seen him since 2004, when I interviewed him for the first time. (I visited Hassan and many villagers at my ethnographic sites whenever I went back to Morocco.) He emerged with a tray and poured a strong, sweet mint tea into a chipped cup. Two young adults joined us. On this trip I tried to gather more data about French policies in the region during World War II. I got little information about how successful French soldiers were in implementing the discriminatory policies toward Jews during the Vichy period. Nonetheless, I was surprised by the circulation of an abridged translation of *The Protocols of the Elders of Zion* among some students and their strong belief in its message.

I sipped my tea while Hassan introduced me to the two young adults. Realizing that I study the Jews of Morocco, Said, also a recent graduate of Islamic studies and a member of the widely popular Justice and Charity Group, wasted no time in expressing his opinions about Jews in general. The twenty-four-year-old stated with confidence that six Jewish rabbis are running the world through a network of Freemasons. I made an effort to maintain my neutral position while engaging his views:

> Aomar: Do you really believe six Jews would be able to run as complex a world as we know it today?

Said: Yes I do. Jews are by nature untrustworthy and shrewd. Their history in the Arabian Peninsula shows that, and the Qur'an, Allah's word, is clear about it. Of course they are a few, but their power is not in their numbers, it is in their treacherous minds. Look at how they rule America today! Look at how they turned the Holocaust into a commodity. They are profiting from their suffering just like they profit from prostitution and other vices. You should read Ahmed Rami's website.

Aomar: If you mean Radio Islam, I did. It is full of fallacies and rumors even about our monarchy.

Said: I am sorry, but you just refuse to acknowledge that Jews are untrustworthy because they fund what you do.

Aomar: It's not as simple as you think. Doing research is not about telling people what they want to hear. Instead, it is about showing the world what people, like you, think about certain issues. I do not hide my funding agencies, and I told you that since 2004, and I do not shy from mentioning it.

Said: Then I hope you tell them what I just told you now.

Aomar: But do you agree that the Holocaust took place and that Jews suffered and lost millions of people?

Said: Hitler did kill some. I remember my father telling me in the 1960s about Germans burning Jews and making soap out of their corpses. But there is no way that six million Jews were lost during World War II. Even my teachers questioned the number.

Aomar: I do not claim to be a historian of the Holocaust, but I can tell you that after spending four months in the United States Holocaust Memorial Museum, I saw enough historical records that show that Hitler did kill more than some Jews.

Said: I am glad you came out of your shadow and expressed where you stand. Just like these petty Berbers who have been visiting Israel's Holocaust memorial [Yad Vashem] and who want to teach Holocaust subjects in Moroccan schools, you are not working on behalf of Palestinians like Ahmed Rami and other respectable Moroccan scholars are doing. You are nothing but a pawn for the global Zionist and Freemasonry project.

By the end of World War II, the Holocaust had become a prominent issue in Arab political and intellectual discourse. Although this issue largely played out in Egypt, Syria, and Lebanon, it had also been an integral part of the North African debates in general and the Moroccan Zionist discussions in particular by the early years of independence. In recent years, a few Muslim intellectual and political leaders, notably President Mahmoud Ahmadinejad of Iran, have alternately minimized, contested, or challenged the historicity of the Holocaust, setting off worldwide reactions of condemnation (and occasionally of support from some parts of the Muslim world). In response to the 2005 Danish cartoons of the Prophet Mohammed, this Holocaust denial movement culminated in the Iranian government's sponsoring a conference on the Holocaust and a cartoon contest. Abdellah Darkaoui, a Moroccan cartoonist for *al-Maghribia*, won the contest. Although his winning cartoon did not deny the Holocaust, it compared it to Israeli policies toward the Palestinians. Since independence, Moroccan views about the Holocaust have been shaped by the Palestinian-Israeli conflict, creating a culture of Holocaust denial and acceptance that is both inter- and hypertextual: Moroccan youth appropriate indigenous and foreign signs. Through a patchwork of different ideologies and cultural texts—ranging between Christian anti-Semitic views and Islamic discourses about Jews—younger Arab Moroccans, like Said, are today using Internet hypertextuality to blur the religious, ideological, cultural, and historical boundaries of indigenous and foreign texts that have become

> a multi-dimensional space in which a variety of writings, none of them original, blend and clash. The text is a tissue of quotations. . . . The writer can only imitate a gesture that is always anterior, never original. His only power is to mix writings, to counter the ones with the others, in such a way as never to rest on any one of them.[47]

Ahmed Rami, one of the most controversial North African Muslim immigrants in Europe, epitomizes the trend of Holocaust denial. Born in southeastern Morocco like Yassine and the majority of my informants, he grew up in a socialist and Marxist era in Morocco before he became a supporter of political Islam. He participated in two failed coups d'état against the monarchy. Today, through Radio al-Islam's website, he describes himself as a critic of Israel, Zionism, and the Jewish community of Europe. By claiming that Rami espouses an ideological syncretism, I contend that he reconciles contradictory systems of belief by blending unrelated histories, disparate local geographies, and different cultural philosophies. I also argue that he represents a normative modern "Islamic" view about Jews, which changes according to the ideological period in which each Muslim generation came of age. This juxtaposition of contradictory philosophies becomes a form of revolutionary romanticism and puritanical idealism, which fuels extremist political views and discourages attempts by European Muslims to nurture a moderate Islamic view in Christian Europe.

Jewish "guilt" and Muslim "innocence" are the basic elements of the Islamists' ideological message about Israel and its "naturally satanic and evil Jewish supporters all over the world." This ideology finds its roots, according to Yassine, in the extremely strained relations between the Prophet Mohammed and the Jews of al-Medina. The underlying message is that Jews betrayed Muslims in the formative period of the Islamic Empire after they struck a pact with Muslims, and they ended up being driven out from the Prophet's city. Today, according to him, they have struck another alliance with the enemies of Islam (for example, the United States), and they will be driven out once again. Yassine bases his prophecy on a Qur'anic verse from "The Children of Israel," outlining Jewish arrogance and the retribution that will follow.[48] According to Yassine, Jewish arrogance is also manifested not only in a historically negative attitude toward the Prophet, but also in the recent harm inflicted on Muslims in general and Palestinians in particular. It is manifested, Yassine notes, in the

> knavery and scheming of a rich and cunning minority, Jewish alliances with the Muslims' enemies, betrayal of the pact of solidarity that the Prophet had concluded with the Jewish tribes upon arriving in Medina. After years of evasion and offences, above all after the Jewish betrayal of their Muslim allies at the "battle of the trench" (*al-khandaq*), the Jews were definitively driven from Medina. Elsewhere, they did not forget this trench in the history of their people, and today, Zionist pretensions do not stop at the biblical territories of Palestine, Syria, Iraq, and Egypt; they stretch toward Medina, which they consider to be part of their patrimony. Talk about the covetousness and rapacity of the tiny Israeli state![49]

The "wound of Palestine," Yassine espouses, is caused by a Jewish conspiracy supported by Western colonial forces. Had it not been for this bleeding injury in the Arab-Islamic entity, Jews and Muslims would continue "to live side by side," as they did in Muslim Spain and other Islamic territories. Like Yassine, Kader thinks that Jews that were once protected and respected in his village are now killing his own brothers. He spoke at length:

> When they lived among us, they never raised their voice. They never raised their arms on women and children. Now the snakes are biting the hands that served them. They are killing unprotected children and old men, even crippled defenseless men like Sheikh Yassin and the shahid Muhammed Durra and his son. They are monsters. You cannot give them power; even the Qur'an said it. Power breeds their arrogance and they became like Hitler and the Pharaoh.

Kader believes that by nature Jews are hostile once they achieve power. His attribution of animalistic behavior (snake, monsters) to Jews is a linguistic strategy used to divert the blame from the in-group. Therefore, he argues, it is in the nature of Jews to kill innocent and defenseless people. If they are not "tamed," they can lead the world to ultimate destruction.

Yassine believes that "Europe needed a reservoir where it could dispose of its overflow of Jewry: [because] the Jew is too shrewd, too active, too able a businessman—and so, too annoying."[50] Europe, according to Yassine, was afraid that the emergence of the Jew after World War II and the rising of sympathy toward his plight after the Nazi defeat provided an opportunity for Europe to get rid of him and to free its "European soul" from his demonic nature, and also provide the "historic opportunism, in the pragmatic interests of British and imperialist politics, [to accommodate] Zionist ambitions with a home in Palestine."[51] Yassine comments that Jewish persecution is not a Muslim problem; it is a Christian and European issue. Muslims did not kill Jews in the war. Therefore, they should not be responsible for Europe's anti-Semitic political history. He comments:

> Not only would Arab lands be occupied and split up to receive Jews called to the land of their ancestors, but the same myth that lies at the base of the Jewish claim is preserved at any cost. The Gayssot-Fabius law, enacted in France

and promulgated in 1990, severely sanctions all criticism of the Zionist political creed; casting doubt on the existence or extent of the "Holocaust" is a crime, and the doubter is persecuted at law.[52]

Like Ahmadinejad, Yassine questions the Holocaust as a historical event. Although he uses some discursive strategies to denounce the killing of a single Jew because Islam forbids the killing of innocent people, Jew or Muslim, he continues to shift the blame to Jews because of their Hollywood connections and their purported skillfulness at falsifying historical facts.[53] Yassine writes that "inflating the number of victims adds nothing to the horror of Hitler's carnage; a single victim, Jew or not, is already one too many according to our deeply-held Islamic convictions."[54] However, his argument covertly suggests that the Holocaust "might" be a Jewish fabrication and that the West denounces anybody who tries to examine its scientific evidence. Iran's attempt at sponsoring a future Holocaust conference is part of Ahmadinejad's and other Islamic leaders' discursive strategies to repackage the laws and terms of memory. For Yassine, America and its Western allies, with strong support from Hollywood, have managed to advocate, fund, manufacture, and sell powerful and captivating movies and documentaries:

> Making the Jewish cause . . . omnipresent in the world conscience while other causes are erased forever. . . . Neither side erects plaques to mourn the sixty million Native Americans exterminated by the white Protestant American pioneer. No stele commemorates the hundred million dead black Africans packed in the compartment of the slave ships. . . . Who thinks anymore of them? Only the Jewish state lays claim to attention and memory![55]

Unlike this extremist Islamic ideology, Hassan II was faithful to the positive approach toward Jews as Moroccan citizens espoused by his father, Mohammed V, and he upheld the promotion of a Jewish-Muslim peace process.[56] Arab media criticized him for his viewpoint. In the wake of Sadat's visit to Jerusalem, he was described as "a pillar in the Egyptian-American-Moroccan strategy to legitimize Israel's continued occupation of Arab territories."[57] Today, King Mohammed VI faces similar criticism for his approach toward recognizing the Holocaust and sympathizing with the Jewish plight. It is in this context that the king has recently supported politically and financially a national initiative to restore and maintain historical Jewish sites, and cemeteries in particular, throughout Morocco. This initiative has included the creation of Internet sites that highlight Moroccan Jewish cultures.

This secular movement, whose membership is mainly Berber, has positioned itself as anti-Arab and anti-Islamic. By identifying with Zionism, its Berber activists broke from the Arab-Islamic foundation of the Moroccan nation. They also challenged the historical discourse of many political parties that made establishing any connection with Zionism and Israel not only a national taboo but also a crime. This shift moves Jews back into the national scene, not as Zionists or pro-Israel agents and spies, but as Moroccan citizens. As Silverstein argues, this Berber philo-Semitism reflects "a racial project to redefine the Moroccan nation as inclusive" of Berbers, Arabs, Jews, and Muslims.[58] In this new context, young Berber activists have set themselves apart from what they see as a historically intolerant nation, which makes Muslim faith and Arab identity a priority.

In 2010, I ran into a Berber student at the University of Cadi Ayyad in Marrakesh. When he realized that I studied Moroccan Jewry, he proceeded to express his personal opinion about the issue:

> Moroccan Jews are like a valuable mortgage that cannot be afforded. Moroccans talk a lot about their Jewish subculture to outsiders and boast about their history of tolerance; yet, they refuse to accept that Jews can be Moroccan citizens with full rights and obligations. Our full support and sympathy toward the Palestinian cause have blinded us, hindering our acceptance of Moroccan Jews. If we believe that Moroccan Jewish history can be an economic asset worth mortgaging, then we should accept their full rights. Otherwise, we have to put it up for sale and stop using it for our economic advantage.

For this informant and many Amazigh students from different parts of Sus, Moroccan society must rethink its attitude toward its Jewish population and accept Jews as part of its wider multicultural, ethnic, and religious fabric without looking at them through the lens of the Palestinian issue. This comment stresses the relationship between the economics of Moroccan Judaism and its politics, putting the government as well as ordinary citizens into a self-contradictory situation. My Amazigh informant claimed that as a society, Moroccans engage in "political hypocrisy," arguing that Moroccan Jewry, despite their love for Morocco, are being unjustly labeled as unpatriotic. Accordingly, as Moroccan Jews continue to leave their communities, their cultural heritage and mainly their cemeteries have been both vandalized for being a "Jewish" property and marketed for being a "national treasure" worth visiting.

Conclusion

In the physical absence of Jews from the majority of Moroccan cities and hinterlands, Moroccans are left with the memories of a Jewish life that once existed. The great-grandparent and grandparent generations continue to discuss nostalgically the richness of Jewish-Muslim life in the past; the younger generation demonstrates narrow and misinformed perspectives of Jews. I have described and analyzed how four generations of Muslims, equally comprising Arab and Berber, *shurfa* and *haratine*, perceive and construct their understandings of Jews. I have presented transcriptions gathered during my fieldwork and discussed them in historical contexts by bringing to bear different primary sources, from the earliest French travel narratives to media and legal manuscripts. I have analyzed each generation's worldview in the context of the period in which it came of age. I have also theorized my position as a native ethnographer by providing examples of my daily interactions with informants who approved of my project as well as others who disagreed with my work.

Circulated representations of Jews are usually organized, stored, and transmitted through the daily acts of narration around television, in cafés, and in public spaces. These disseminated representations vary from one generational group to another both in content and in their channels of mediation. Generational groups have demonstrated a significant difference in their representation of Jews. On the one hand, the older ones mainly invoke a repertoire of images, discursive tropes, and a lexicon from the traditional worldview when Muslims and Jews were neighbors. On the other hand, the disenfranchised Arab youth rely on a different knowledge, which is largely influenced by a set of imagined ideas of "Jewishness." I have demonstrated that although members of young and old generations have lived in the same households for a long period of time, their narratives about Jews are at variance. Members of the older cohorts tend to express feelings of friendship and amicable relations toward Jews. By contrast, younger cohorts mostly describe them as evil and threatening to Muslim values and traditions.

Sampled members of the youth cohort have never lived with Jews, nor have any of them even met any Jews. This might seem to be the reason for the high frequency of their negative attitudes towards Jews. However, negative exemplar representations of Jews among the youth are rampant because of the fracturing of memory and knowledge transmission. In fact, although members of the grandparents' generation have not socialized on a daily basis with Jews, their representations are still influenced by the intimate knowledge transmitted through the great-grandparents. The great-grandparents and grandparents are less negative in their representations because their knowledge of Jews is not responding solely to the media and the Palestinian-Israeli conflict. They have other perceptions based on real experiences that challenge media reports and stereotyping.

These dichotomous views of Jews are part of a shift in identity referents in contemporary Moroccan society. Culturally, Moroccan youth are rebelling against the limiting social and cultural values of the family, which restrict their social and political movement. They are constructing a new self that is still anchored in Islamic values while adapting to and appropriating foreign ideas. The traditional hierarchical transmission of knowledge and authority is broken, giving way to more individual freedom and the appropriation of other cultural forms. Foucault contends:

> The episteme may be suspected of being something like a world-view, a slice of history common to all branches of knowledge, which imposes on each one the same norms and postulates, a general stage of reason, a certain structure of thought that the men of a particular period cannot escape—a great body of legislation written once and for all by some anonymous hand.[1]

The restricting power of the episteme, or worldview, which justifies the sacredness of the religious text in the case of the politicized view of the younger generation, does not put pressure on the individual and the state to challenge common ideas about Jews. Therefore, contact with Jews is seen as an act of breaching the normative Islamic social rules and cultural regulations. In this context, a debate in Moroccan society about the status of Jews as citizens is still a national taboo. For example, when one studies Jews, he or she could be seen not only as a Jewish supporter but also an Israeli sympathizer. Edward Said deconstructs this perspective, arguing that it is "fatuous" to reject everything "Israeli." After all, he contends, there are "one million Palestinians who are Israeli citizens: are they also to be boycotted, as they were during 1950? What about Israelis who support our struggle? Are they to be boycotted because they are Israeli?"[2]

Nevertheless, the Islamic nature of knowledge about Jews, influenced by Moroccan leaders such as Yassine and Rami, does not restrain certain Moroccans from rebelling against the system and questioning the cultural bias against Jews. Although the social critique of perceptions toward Jews and other minorities has been usually left to important members of the political establishment, journalists, artists, and ordinary citizens have joined the movement of national auto-critique. There is a growing movement generally mediated through an independent press that highlights the possibility of being critical of Israeli policies without being anti-Jewish.

This debate can be primarily noted, as I have discussed in Chapter 5, in an emerging liberal media. Since the May 2003 bombing in Casablanca, a set of liberal and independent Moroccan newspapers have lifted the collective silence over the question of Moroccan Jewish identity and published, intermittently, articles that looked at the Moroccan Jewish community from social, political, religious, or cultural angles. This discourse and debate have the potential to reintroduce the Jewish voice in the predominant Muslim debate and to encourage heteroglossia in the national public sphere.[3] Although many journalists and media outlets resist this movement, the monarchy's continuing support and protection of Moroccan Jews suggests this debate will continue despite the opposing forces of the Palestinian-Israeli conflict.

Epilogue

PERFORMING INTERFAITH DIALOGUE

Few Moroccans publically recognize the existence of racist attitudes and stereo-types toward Jews and Christians. State agencies such as the Ministry of Education have done little to change these attitudes and educate young adults to accept cultural and ethnic differences. The task of responding to stereotypes about Jews is left to a few individuals while the state takes a back seat. As the Palestinian-Israeli conflict continues to enlarge the gap of misunderstanding and limit dialogue among Jewish, Christian, and Muslim communities through-out the world, a few Jewish, Christian, and Muslim "artisans of peace" continue to hold partnerships and dialogues of reconciliation between Israelis and Palestinians.[1] In this context, Jewish-Christian-Muslim *convivencia* during Islamic Spain has emerged as their historical reference.[2] For instance, the Foundation for the Three Cultures and the Three Religions, based in Seville, Spain, has become an annual pilgrimage for these traders of peace. This interfaith dialogue has largely been a performance, despite its message of tolerance and understanding. It can end abruptly when it does not have an audience and when its actors exit the national stage. Accordingly, these annual festivals and meetings of tolerance remain simply moments of reification of imagined communities of tolerance.[3] These meetings of tolerance are Turnerian moments of *communitas*, when Muslims, Jews, and Christians gather in an imagined space of toleration, free from violence, and invoke this past of coexistence through Andalusian music.[4]

In 1948, Américo Castro coined the word *convivencia*, referring to the symbiotic relationship among Jews, Christians, and Muslims in medieval Spain.[5] A number of scholars have argued that the focus on medieval Spain's religious tolerance has emerged in the context of "rising concern about religiously framed acts of violence."[6] The focus on the romantic representation of the period of coexistence was partly a reaction to Europe's hatred toward Jews in general and the focus on multicultural and liberal ideas. Therefore, the so-called Andalusian period of coexistence became a leitmotif and a trope of tolerance for Muslim, Jewish, and Christian apologists who have critiqued the treatment of minorities in their societies. It is in this context that elites from the Arab world have tried to argue for liberal ideas in the Arab and Islamic world. Accordingly, medieval Islamic Spain emerges as the memory of a sacred Islamic space in which groups are tolerated. As a *lieu de mémoire*, Seville is the incarnation of the spirit of *convivencia*.

In 2006, as an organization that seeks to initiate rapprochement between Judaism and Islam, the World Congress of Imams and Rabbis for Peace held its meeting in Seville through the support of the Swiss foundation Hommes de Parole (Men of Their Word). It tried to hold its first meeting in Ifrane, Morocco, in 2004, but it was canceled due to pressures from some Islamic groups after Israel's assassination of the Hamas leader Ahmed Yassin. In addition to these meetings, other organizations have made Seville their destination and a platform of *convivencia*. The Andalusian city of Seville has become a Turnerian liminal space that other different groups are invited to enter: the king of Saudi Arabia, the king of Morocco, the Palestinian president, as well as rabbis and imams met in Seville because of its reputation of tolerance and multiculturalism. As a place of *communitas*, Seville represents the revival of religious togetherness and respect of the rights of others. The presence of rabbis and imams in Seville represents a rite of passage that allows these "enemies" to experience a transient humility and therefore reach a position of mutual respect.

For many Arab leaders, the historical reference of medieval Spain acquires an ideological significance as its historical tokens are used selectively to promote peace and dialogue. On July 17, 2008, Saudi king Abdullah, the Custodian of the Holy Mosques of Mecca and Medina, along with Juan Carlos, the king of Spain, sponsored and inaugurated the World Interfaith Dialogue in Madrid. Although the meeting did not take place in Seville, the romantic view of al-Andalus and its space was selectively cited as a utopia of religious tolerance and peace. The myth of al-Andalus and Seville in particular is not limited to the geographic space of Spain, for it can be relocated and reimagined in different geographic settings. In Morocco, the memory of al-Andalus and Seville in particular is at the core of national festivals of sacred music in Fez, Essaouira, and other cities.

Since 2003, the Festival of the Atlantic Andalusias, held annually at the end of October in the coastal city of Essaouira, has been one of the most celebrated events that evoke the memory of medieval Spain and Jewish-Muslim coexistence. The festival has been linked to André Azoulay. For Azoulay, Essaouira represents the extension of the Andalusian culture of tolerance. In 2010, he invited Jewish and Muslim singers to share Andalusian Arabic and Hebrew songs on the stages of Essaouira. He claimed that the occasion was meant "to say to the world that we in Morocco have an ancient heritage in the field of tolerance and coexistence. We also want to preserve that heritage and to protect it against oblivion and marginalisation, and against the negative impacts and pollution resulting from the circumstantial political turmoil."[7]

Andalusian music has been the subject of other festivals—in Rabat, Casablanca, Fez, and Tangiers. The relationship between Jews and Muslims has been highlighted as the central focus of these meetings. Each year Jewish and Muslim icons of Andalusian music (such as Rabbi Samy El Maghribi and Abdessadeq Cheqara) are honored through performances that include living symbols of this tradition, such as Mohammed Briouel of Fez and Rabbi Haim Louk of Los Angeles. These performances highlight the linguistic and musical traditions of North Africa and medieval Spain by mixing Spanish, Moroccan and classical Arabic, and Hebrew while singing ancient Andalusian melodies. Azoulay sees this annual event as "an invitation to recall the joint memory which we seem to have lost; an invitation to recover that golden age of co-existence and the building of joint civilization and culture; an invitation to dance together and to give a different picture other than the catastrophic image conveyed daily by the media about Jewish-Arab relations."[8] For Moroccan elites, there is a strong connection between Morocco and medieval Islamic Spain that is reflected in the symbiotic relations that characterized relations between Jews and Muslims in medieval Spain. However, one of the main obstacles that these performers of *convivencia* face is how attentive they are to others' voices. I claim that, as performers of peace, Moroccan and Arab elites enter for a short moment what Turner calls a "liminal" time, a threshold period. For instance, these meetings have rarely improved the relationship between Jews and Muslims except for rare interactions. In 2006, during the World Congress of Imams and Rabbis for Peace in Seville, Renwick McLean noted, "the meeting . . . led to some uninhibited displays of camaraderie, like rabbis and imams singing and dancing together during an impromptu musical performance in the hotel lobby near midnight."[9]

As "enemies" fighting over claims to Jerusalem and sacred lands, imams and rabbis, among other elites, enter a "time outside of time," where alternative modalities of social relatedness appear. These modalities center on the common ground of music (Gharnati and Andalusian), which Jews and Muslims shared and sometimes sang together. The performance renders Seville a liminal space and therefore a place of *communitas*. As opposed to *societas*, or structure, *communitas* is characterized by equality: Jewish and Muslim musicians sit on the same stage and share the rituals of *convivencia*. A leveling process takes place and brings about the dissolution of structure, the absence of social distinctions, a homogenization of roles, the disappearance of political allegiance, the breakdown of regular borders and barriers. For example, during the 2006 meeting in Seville, Ashour Kullab, a Muslim leader from Gaza who had never spoken with a rabbi before, said he spoke with two rabbis on the first morning of the conference. "There were no problems with them," he said. "They listened and I listened. They are my friends now."[10]

Through these festivals, André Azoulay tries to build a ritualized and institutionalized system of toleration.[11] Anna Bigelow looks at the community of Malerkolta as an Indian sacred site, where different religious groups manage to avoid violence and maintain a level of peace between the residents. She argues that the collective commemoration of the Sufi saint Haider Shaykh is what defines the community's enduring ethos of toleration and peace. Azoulay attempts to create a similar model through the commemoration of the alleged ethos of al-Andalus. In many festivals, he highlights the memory of al-Andalus as central to his project and other national festivals. This is what Edward Casey refers to as "carrying the past forward" through memorialization. The past here is the al-Andalus model of *convivencia*. Casey writes:

> [I]n acts of commemoration remembering is intensified by taking place *through* the interposed agency of text (the eulogy, the liturgy proper) and *in* the setting of a social ritual (delivering the eulogy, participating in the service). The remembering is intensified still further by the fact that both ritual and text become efficacious only in the presence of others, *with* whom we commemorate together in a public ceremony.[12]

In our case, Andalusian music and space trigger the possible actualization of toleration. The collective identity of Essaouira—a historical extension of al-Andalus—revolves around the harmonious coexistence of Jews and Muslims. The idea is to create, through these symbolic interactions in the context of the festival, a future culture of toleration. Bigelow asserts that "the common sense approach to living with religious diversity is the norm in Malerkolta, but the approach is made normal through practice and repetition."[13] This, however, is not the case in Essaouira, where meetings are seasonal. The absence of Jews from the context of Essaouira and other Moroccan cities and villages makes the whole projection of practicing toleration also difficult because, as Bigelow observed in her Indian case, social meetings around food and weddings are a critical index to the level of understanding.

If Morocco replaced medieval Islamic Spain as the sacred space of Jewish-Muslim symbiosis, why do intellectuals and politicians invoke Muslim Spain in their celebrations of the sacred instead of focusing solely on sacred spaces in Morocco, such as Fez? The politics of representation of this symbiosis show that a different kind of sacred space is in operation here: these festivals of the sacred have been imagined through a reified space, which finds its historical continuity in Morocco. That is to say, although Jews and Muslims coexisted in medieval Islamic Spain, both found their final home in Morocco, especially when Jewish persecution leading to the Inquisition forced Jews to migrate partly to Morocco. Therefore, Zafrani argues, "The antisemitism of . . . medieval and modern Europe is foreign to the history of Muslim thought in the Maghrib, and especially Morocco."[14] These festivals are meant to challenge the fundamentalist Arab-Islamic narrative that makes them, at least on a superficial level, festivals of the normalization of relations with Israel. Their organization allows the state and its elite to maintain its official Arab-Islamic discourse without looking pro-Israel. At the same time, this strategy enables the state to project an international image of democratization and respect for minorities.

Al-Andalus, as a sacred space of Jewish-Muslim dialogue, enables these organizers to imagine the possibilities of dialogue. This is what Deborah Kapchan refers to as the "promise of sonic translation." In her article on the festive sacred in Morocco, she asks the following questions: "How do international music festivals like this one [Fez] perform sacred imaginaries for multi-faith audiences? What is their part in creating transnational communities of affect?"[15] She maintains that by drawing on the religious sentiments of sacred music, sacred festivals "create [a] transnational (thus mobile) notion of 'the sacred' that is in many ways a counterpoint to the specificity and ideology of more orthodox forms of religious practice."[16]

The elite personal belief in the possibilities of cultural and social dialogue between Jews and Muslims is one of the driving forces behind invoking medieval Islamic Spain at the local and international levels. Muslim and Jewish elites, such as al-Hassan Ibn Talal, André Azoulay, and King Abdullah of Saudi Arabia, are trying through festivals and conferences to reverse the social order of things in which a natural Jewish-Muslim enmity is assumed. Such cultural celebration might, as Turner underlines with reference to ceremonies in general, "bring about a temporary reconciliation between conflicting members of single community. Conflict is held in abeyance during the period of ritualized action."[17] In the eyes of many critics, this effort amounts to a call for the normalization of relations with Israel. These rituals of toleration remain an idea and are still far from being a practice of toleration. There is no indication that this elitist discourse of tolerance manifests itself during these festivals in the form of real dialogue between Jews and Muslims at the youth level. In many interviews, Azoulay goes as far as to think that Essaouira not only provides an instance of coexistence between different faiths and cultures but becomes an example for Israelis and Palestinians to follow as they negotiate a future peace agreement.

Some argue that when people meet during these festivals they might become lifelong friends. However, the experience of this friendship is transient and short because it has not changed the beliefs of other members of Middle Eastern societies, which remain to be convinced of the importance of the memory of medieval Spain as a haven of toleration. In 2010, as Azoulay expressed his dreams of the importance of the festivals of Andalusia as exercises that reunite Jews and Muslims and help them understand each other, Rashid Benmokhtar Benabdellah, a former minister of education and the president of the National Observatory for Human Development, stressed Moroccans' negative ideas about Jews and pointed to "the orchestrated ignorance in education" about Jewish history in Morocco. In the absence of daily interactions between Jews and Muslims in Morocco and other Arab societies today, schools must fill the gap of humanizing the "other" if these projects of promoting toleration are to succeed. Otherwise, they will remain seasonal dances with a limited audience, which will only eulogize the myth of al-Andalus in the cities of Morocco. These eulogies are bound to go unnoticed at the popular level of neighborhood cafés, where young people will continue to tease one another, calling in derogatory jest: "Sharon! Sharon!"

Reference Matter

Methodological Appendix

GENERATIONS, COHORTS, SCHEMAS, AND LONGITUDINAL MEMORIES

Over the past several decades, personal narratives have been widely used by linguists to study language variation and change[1] and cultural meanings.[2] While historical linguists have used language data from different historical periods to explain linguistic transformations, William Labov introduced a theoretical framework that allowed linguists to figure out language variation and change as they happen in apparent time (synchronically across different generations of respondents). Labov was primarily concerned with the reconstruction of the history of vowels on the basis of the correlation of the language patterns and social as well as social-structural variations within the American Eastern seaboard community of Martha's Vineyard. By stressing the relationship between language change and community social transformations, Labov contended that "social pressures are continually operating upon language, not from some remote point in the past, but as an immanent social force acting in the living present."[3]

Using a Labovian longitudinal model, I historicize the social memories of Muslims about former local Jews and discuss how these memories are generated, maintained, and reproduced through social experiences, personal narratives, legal documents, memorial sites, and media (mainly newspapers). In his linguistic work, Labov contends that "language change seems to resolve itself into three separate problems: the origin of language variation; the spread and propagation of linguistic changes; and the regularity of linguistic change. The model which underlines this three-way division requires as a starting point a variation in one or several words in the speech of one or two individuals."[4] The sociolinguistic *actuation, embedding,* and *diffusion* model[5] is applicable to an analytic discussion of different generations of Muslim interviewees' attitudes toward Jews. The historical and anthropological nature of this approach sheds light on the historical contexts in which opinions about Jews develop and are later shared among different members of the community. By situating these attitudes in historical contexts, I argue that Muslim ideas about Jews have changed across generations as Moroccan society continues to be affected by significant national and international historical and social events from the colonial to the post-independence period. Situating historical memories allows us to look at the memories of each cohort in terms of what psychologists call exemplar models, where "the memories of [cohorts] are organized . . . so that memories of highly similar instances are close to each other and memories of dissimilar instances are far apart. The remembered tokens display the range of variation that is exhibited in the physical manifestations of the category."[6] Exemplar theory has the potential to highlight the strong correlation between the historical and ideological period and the attitudes of Muslim cohorts about Jews.

Labov's linguistic methodology has shown that cohort studies can provide the methodological means to make explicit the social and cultural context that frames the experiences, behavior, and decisions of cohort respondents. Through the stories of members of stratified generations, I look at how a cohort's educational experience, socialization, political background, and media preference in the context of profound ideological changes can explain attitudes toward Jews. Therefore, the contextualization of memories of the great-grandparents' cohort, having been shaped in the historical period of pre-colonial and early colonial French presence in Morocco, helps us understand not only these views but also their pattern across the generation.

The Labovian apparent-time technique applied to language variation across age cohorts resonates with another approach that tried to understand "individuals' lives and experiences as arising out of the intersection between individual agency and historical and cultural context [and which] has become articulated as the life course paradigm."[7] The life-course approach attempts to understand individuals' attitudes, experiences, and perceptions through time by correlating their life stages with specific historical contexts and the social ideologies existing at the time. This approach veers away from the generation or the life cycle concepts, which stand for a multi-variate model with many variables in a group regardless of the historical period. The apparent-time and the life-course approaches use a longitudinal design facilitating the understanding of the impact of earlier historical events on the interviewees' attitudes.

In the case of my respondents, the historical-ideological variable proved to correlate with individual perception of Jews within each group. Although the variables affect each individual's experience within the cohort differently, respondents who came of age during specific historical events tended to show common perceptual trends. For instance, while great-grandparents saw Jews as local *dhimmi* and native to the region, younger adults described them as outsiders and conflated Jews with Israelis and Americans. According to Elder and Pellerin, the fact that an individual is a member of a generation "may be less influential on beliefs or behavior than are shared historical location and related experience."[8]

Using the concept of cohort to understand perceptions of Jews among Muslims helps us understand the factors at play in societal transformations in modern Morocco. The data generated through the narratives show how "successive cohorts are differentiated by the changing content of formal education, by peer-group socialization, and by idiosyncratic historical experience."[9] Although longitudinal study looks at the "aggregate of individuals (within some population definition) who experienced the same event within the same time interval,"[10] its main focus revolves around the individual as opposed to the whole group. Each individual narrative generates a corpus of data that leads to a comprehensive summary about the whole cohort. Individual experiences within the cohort might take different social trajectories. However, they tend to exhibit similar social and cultural traits.

In her work on cultural models, Quinn argued against semantic theory because of its failure to capture the larger meanings behind words and the social conventions that govern their life-course.[11] Quinn, a cognitive anthropologist, proposed schema theory to deconstruct cultural frameworks and understand their meanings. A schema, Quinn notes, "is a generic version of (some part of) the world built up from experience and stored in memory."[12] The schema provides a prototypical cultural model for "the cumulative outcome of just those features of successive experiences that are alike. . . . To the degree that people share experiences, they will end up sharing the same schemas."[13] Yet, schemas change as cultural experiences go through internal transformation. Combining the apparent-time technique with the schema and life-course approaches, I explore the transmission and breakdown of inter-generational memory and knowledge about Jews in Morocco from one Muslim generation to another.

Using the concepts of cohort, schema, and life-course to understand attitudes among Muslims towards Jews helps us understand some of the factors at play in societal transformations in modern Morocco, especially with regard to the politics of attitudes towards other minorities. The cohort group is not solely a summation of individual narratives about personal histories. Each cohort, Ryder postulates, reflects "a distinctive composition and character reflecting the circumstances of its unique origination and history."[14] By using this approach, I answer the following question: Can narratives yield a set of longitudinal data and information which would tell us about factors that influence the way the different Muslim cohorts construct their worldviews about Jews in the context of national and global political and social realities?

For interviews in Moroccan Arabic and texts in Classical Arabic, I use a simplified transliteration system based on the *International Journal of Middle East Studies* (IJMES). I do not use any diacritical symbols except for the *'ayn* (') and *hamza* (').

Prologue

1. Rosenberger, "Tamdult, cité minière," 103–141.
2. All translations are mine unless otherwise noted.

Introduction

1. For a good historical overview of the historical Jewish settlements in Morocco, see Hirschberg, *A History of the Jews*; Jacques-Meunié, *Le Maroc saharien*, vol. 1, 60; Zafrani, *Deux mille ans de vie juive au Maroc*, 11–12; Schroeter, "Jewish Communities of Morocco," 27.

2. Laskier, *The Alliance Israélite Universelle*, 321. For a discussion of the Jewish communities in the Atlas mountain villages, see Shokeid, "Jewish Existence"; Goldberg, "The Mellahs of Southern Morocco."

3. Hunwick, "Al-Maghili and the Jews of Tuwat"; Stillman, *The Jews of the Arab Lands*; Schroeter and Chetrit, "Emancipation and Its Discontents."

4. Shokeid, "Jewish Existence"; Meyers, "Patronage and Protection."

5. Bilu and Levy, "Nostalgia and Ambivalence"; Schroeter, "In Search of Jewish Farmers."

6. Geertz, "Suq: The Bazaar Economy in Sefrou."

7. Boum, "Schooling in the *Bled*."

8. Boum, "From 'Little Jerusalems' to the Promised Land."

9. Laskier, *North African Jewry*; idem, *Israel and the Maghreb*.

10. El Mansour, "Moroccan Historiography," 109–120.

11. Shatzmiller, *Nationalism and Minority Identities*.

12. Boum, "Southern Moroccan Jewry."

13. Al-Susi, *Khilal jazula*, vol. 3, 75.

14. There is a large literature on the subject of Haratine-*shurfa* relationships and social hierarchy in southern Morocco. For a detailed analysis, see Ensel, *Saints and Servants*, 110; El Hamel, "'Race,' Slavery and Islam"; idem, "Blacks and Slavery in Morocco"; Jacques-Meunié, "Hiérarchie sociale"; Ennaji, *Serving the Master*.

15. Boum, "The Political Coherence."

16. Ibid.

17. For a study on the concept of Saharan Jewry, see Boum, "Saharan Jewry."

18. Kenbib, *Juifs et musulmans au Maroc*; Baida, "La presse juive."

19. Trevisan Semi and Sekkat Hatimi recently looked at Muslims' views about Jews in Meknès. See *Mémoire et representations*.

20. A large number of European explorers traveled through southern Morocco. Examples include Jackson, *An Account of the Empire*; idem, *An Account of Timbuctoo*; De Foucauld, *Reconnaissance au Maroc*; Caillié, *Travels Through Central Africa*; Davidson, *Notes Taken During Travels*.

21. Boum, "Southern Moroccan Jewry."

22. Ayache, "La recherche au Maroc."

23. Bahloul, *The Architecture of Memory*.

24. Abrahams, "A Performance-Centered Approach"; idem, "Black Talking"; Coates, "Gossip Revisited"; Ghosh, "Symbolic Speech," 251; Gluckman, "Gossip and Scandal"; Handelman, "Gossip in Encounters"; Hannerz, "Gossip, Networks"; Merry, "Rethinking Gossip."

25. Labov, "Rules for Ritual Insults"; idem, *Language in the Inner City*; Kochman, "The Boundary Between Play and Non-Play"; Murray, "Ritual and Personal Insults."

26. Apte, *Humor and Laughter*; Dundes, *Cracking Jokes*; Besnier, "Gossip and the Everyday."

27. For a general discussion on humor as a method to belittle others, see Burma, "Humor as a Technique."

28. Boum, "Southern Moroccan Jewry."

29. Bailey, "Real and Apparent Time"; Labov, *Language in the Inner City*.

30. Miles and Huberman, *Qualitative Data Analysis*, 28.

31. Al-Susi, *Khilal Jazula*.

32. Elliott, *Using Narratives*, 72; Rosenthal, "Reconsideration of Life Stories."

33. Halbwachs, *On Collective Memory*.

34. Campt, *Other Germans*, 86.

35. Trevisan Semi and Sekkat Hatimi, *Mémoire et representations*.

36. *TelQuel* (September 20–26, 2003), 24.

Chapter 1

1. Van Paassen, *Days of Our Years*, 459–469.

2. *Syracuse Herald* (April 6, 1933), 1.

3. Van Paassen, *Palestine Land of Israel*; idem, *Jerusalem Calling!*; idem, *The Forgotten Ally*.

4. Van Paassen, *The Forgotten Ally*, 6.

5. Van Paassen, "Aviator Tells of Peaceful Community Thriving Among Savages . . . Finds Thousands of Jews Living in the Heart of Africa," *New York Evening World* (November 15, 1928), 23.

6. Sémach, "Un Rabbin Voyageur Marocain," 396. Also see Hirschberg, "The Problem of the Judaized Berbers."

7. Van Paassen, "Aviator Tells of Peaceful Community," 23.

8. Williams, *Hebrewisms of West Africa*, 235.

9. Van Paassen, "Aviator Tells of Peaceful Community," 23.

10. Boum, "Saharan Jewry."

11. Boum, "Southern Moroccan Jewry."

12. Flamand, *Diaspora en terre d'Islam*; Goldberg, "The Mellahs of Southern Morocco"; Larhmaid, "Jama'At yahud Sus"; Boum, "Muslims Remember Jews."

13. Davidson, *Notes Taken During Travels*; De Foucauld, *Reconnaissance au Maroc*.

14. Schroeter, *Merchants of Essaouira*; Gottreich, *The Mellah of Marrakesh*.

15. Flamand, *Diaspora en terre d'Islam*; Afa, "Al-yahud fi mantaqat Sus"; Boum, "Muslims Remember Jews."

16. Chouraqui, *Between East and West*; Jacques-Meunié, *Le Maroc saharien*; Hirschberg, "The Problem of the Judaized Berbers."

17. Boum, "Schooling in the *Bled*."

18. Bidwell, *Morocco Under Colonial Rule*, 98–127. Also see Justinard, *Le Caid Goundafi*.

19. Slouschz, *Travels in North Africa*, 464.

20. Schroeter, *Merchants of Essaouira*; Boum, "Muslims Remember Jews."

21. Afa, "Al-Yahud fi mantaqat Sus"; Goldberg, "The Mellahs of Southern Morocco," 61; idem, *Cave Dwellers and Citrus Growers*.

22. Schroeter, "The Jews of Essaouira."

23. For trans-Saharan routes and entrepôts, see Schroeter, *Merchants of Essaouira*; Lydon, *On Trans-Saharan Trails*; Stein, *Plumes*.

24. Al-Susi, *Khilal jazula*, vol. 3.

25. Rosenberger, "Tamdult, cité minière."

26. De Foucauld, *Reconnaissance au Maroc*.

27. Schroeter, "The Jews of Essaouira."

28. De La Porte des Vaux, "Note sur le peuplement du Sous," 448.

29. Miège, *Le Maroc et l'Europe*.

30. De La Porte des Vaux, "Note sur le peuplement du Sous," 450; Schroeter, *Merchants of Essaouira*; Lydon, *On Trans-Saharan Trails*.

31. Jacques-Meunié, *Le Maroc saharien*.

32. Monteil, "Choses et gens du Bani," 393–394.

33. Boum, "From 'Little Jerusalems' to the Promised Land"; idem, "Saharan Jewry"; idem, "Schooling in the *Bled*"; Oliel, *De Jérusalem à Tombouctou*.

34. Aby Serour, *Les Daggatoun*, 9–10. Also see, Morais, *The Daggatouns*, 12–13.

35. Hunwick, *Jews of a Saharan Oasis*; idem, "Al-Maghili and the Jews of Tuwat"; idem, *Shari'a in Songhay*; idem, *Timbuktu and the Songhay Empire*.

36. Bovill, "Mohammed El Maghili."

37. For a discussion of Saharan Jewry, see Boum, "Saharan Jewry."

38. Boum, "Saharan Jewry"; Mauny, "Le Judaïsme, les Juifs," 374; Lydon, *On Trans-Saharan Trails*, 88.

39. Hunwick, *Shari'a in Songhay*.

40. Aby Serour, "Premier établissement des Israélites," 356; Bovill, "Mohammed El Maghili," 30.

41. Hunwick, *Timbuktu and the Songhay Empire*, 281.

42. Oliel, *Mardochée Aby Serour*.

43. Aby Serour, "Premier établissement des Israélites."

44. Schroeter, *Merchants of Essaouira*.

45. Aby Serour, "Premier établissement des Israélites," 356.

46. Davidson, *Notes Taken During Travels*.

47. Caillié, *Travels Through Central Africa to Timbuctoo*.

48. Barth, *Travels and Discoveries in North and Central Africa*.

49. For more information on the ethics of disguised exploration and research, see Denzin, "On the Ethics of Disguised Observation"; Erikson, "A Comment on Disguised Observation"; and Sagarin, "The Research Setting."

50. Boum, "Saharan Jewry."

51. Aby Serour, "Premier établissement des Israélites," 357–359.

52. Bazin, *Charles de Foucauld*, 32–33.

53. Goitein, *Letters of Medieval Jewish Traders*.

54. Levtzion, "The Jews of Sijilmasa."

55. Slouschz, *Travels in North Africa*, 466.

56. McKay, "Colonialism in the French."

57. The same article was translated in German: "Reisen des Rabbi Mardokhaï Abi-Serur nach Timbuktu," *Pettermanns Mitteinlungen* 16 (1870): 335–337.

58. For instance, in *L'Explorateur* 1 (1875): 31, Hertz wrote: "This Jew, born in one of the southern provinces of Morocco, expressed his interest in serving French interests; he was able to establish a Jewish colony in Timbuktu, the capital of the Sudan, which survived for a period of over ten years. We hope that the Commission of the Commercial Geography will recognize the future work of Rabbi Mardochée in the service of the Geographical Society of Paris. Thanks to this ingenious and humble collaborator, Timbuktu may become the head office of our commercial operations between Senegal, Algeria, Niger, and all of Western Africa. Our national influence will reach one third of the African continent."

59. Duveyrier, "De Mogador au Djebel Tabayoudt," 561–573.

60. Duveyrier, "Sculptures antiques," 129–146.

61. De Foucauld, *Reconnaissance au Maroc*; Boum, "Schooling in the *Bled*." Also see Carrouges, *Foucauld devant l'Afrique*; Sémach, "Charles de Foucauld," 264–284.

62. Lenz, *Timbouctou*.

63. In *Travels Through Central Africa*, vol. 2, 84, Caillié described these steps as follows: "To ensure success, the traveller should, I think, make no sort of display; he should externally adopt the worship of Mahomet, and pass himself off for an Arab. A pretended convert would not enjoy so much liberty, and would be an object of suspicion to such distrustful people. Besides, I am of opinion that a converted Christian would not be tolerated among the negro tribes. The best plan would be, I think to cross the great desert of Sahara in the character of an Arab, provided with adequate but concealed resources. After remaining for some time in the Musulman town selected by the traveller as his starting point, where he might give himself out as a merchant, to avoid suspicion, he might purchase some merchandise in that town, under the pretence of going to trade further on, carefully abstaining from all mention of the city of Timbuctoo. Let us suppose Tangiers or Arbate to be the place chosen as the point of departure; mercantile business at Fez might be alleged as an excuse for setting off. Still adopting the same pretence, the traveller might proceed from Fez to Tafilet and, thence to Timbuctoo. At Tafilet there would be no danger of speaking of Timbuctoo, for there a journey to the Soudan is an affair of frequent occurrence and it excites no attention."

64. McKay, "Colonialism in the French," 218.

65. Preminger, *The Sands of Tamanrasset*, 61.

66. De Foucauld, *Reconnaissance au Maroc*, xiii–xiv.

67. Preminger, *The Sands of Tamanrasset*, 77.

68. Fremantle, *Desert Calling*, 94–95.

69. Carrouges, *Foucauld devant l'Afrique*, 79.

70. Chaffal, "De Foucauld saharien"; Merad, *Christian Hermit*.

71. De Foucauld, *Reconnaissance au Maroc*, xiv.

72. Ibid., xv–xvi.

73. Parsons, *The Origins of the Moroccan Question*.

74. De Foucauld, *Reconnaissance au Maroc*, v.

75. Wilson, *Ideology and Experience*, 213–229; Fitch, "Mass Culture," 55.

76. Preminger, *The Sands of Tamanrasset*, 64–65; Gorrée, *Sur les traces de Père Charles*.

77. Sémach, "Charles de Foucauld," 264–284.

Chapter 2

1. In Ibn Rushd, *The Distinguished Jurist*, 325 (n. 163), Nyazee states that "[t]he term rahn has generally been translated into English as pledge or mortgage, by

modern writers, both Muslim and western. The rahn transaction is somewhat different from pledge and mortgage. The contract of rahn . . . is merely a security for a debt that exists, for whatever reason, before the rahn is transacted; the pledge is made when the payment of the loan becomes due. It does not involve pledging, pawning, or mortgaging where something is submitted as a collateral and some value, money or other, is raised as [a] loan to be returned later. Such a contract would amount to a sale, according to Muslim jurists, which is revocable at the termination of the agreed period, with the buyer having the right to dispose of the property during this period."

2. Mezzine, *Le Tafilalt*.

3. Ibid., 15.

4. Bourdieu, "The Force of Law," 814.

5. Hill, "Syncretism." Hill "recognized a *syncretic* practice at all levels of linguistic production in syntax, in phonology, lexical choice, in text construction and in vernacular etymology and other kinds of metalinguistic talk. Through this work speakers constructed the Mexicano language as a '*syncretic* project' that drew on a range of semiotic materials. The *syncretic* project creates a continuum from 'more Mexicano' to 'more Spanish' utterances. . . . Speakers will assert that all their talk is marred by mixing (in reference to legítimo mexicano) and by error (in reference to castellano). Yet while these speakers represented themselves as *defeated* by *structure*, it was clear that they were *manipulating* it at every turn" (emphases are mine).

6. For a broader discussion of these complex legal relations, see Bowie, "An Aspect of Muslim-Jewish Relations," 3–19; Kenbib, *Juifs et musulmans au Maroc*.

7. Al-Manuni, *Al-masadir al-'arabiyya*; idem, *Tarikh al-wiraqa al-maghribiyya*.

8. Boum, "Southern Moroccan Jewry."

9. El Mansour, "Moroccan Historiography."

10. Some of these scholars include Edmund Burke III, Jacques Berque, Paul Pascon, Lionel Galand, Ernest Gellner, and Claude Cahen, among others.

11. Tawfiq, *Al-Mujtama' al-maghribi*.

12. Bourqia, "La caidalité chez les tribus."

13. El Moudden, "État et société."

14. Kenbib, *Juifs et musulmans au Maroc*.

15. Baida, *La presse marocaine*.

16. Afa, *Tarikh al-maghrib*.

17. Perkins, "Recent Historiography," 121.

18. Boum, "Southern Moroccan Jewry."

19. For detailed studies on dendritic markets, see Benet, "Explosive Markets"; Smith, "How Marketing Systems"; Skinner, "Mobility Strategy"; Bonine, *Yazd and Its Hinterland*.

20. Smith, "How Marketing Systems," 130.

21. Schroeter, "The Jews of Essaouira"; idem, *Merchants of Essaouira*.

22. Montagne, *Les Berbères et le Makhzan*; Lorcin, *Imperial Identities*.

23. Smith, "How Marketing Systems."

24. Schroeter, "Trade as a Mediator"; idem, "Royal Power and the Economy."

25. Hess, *Israel au Maroc*, 21.

26. Davidson, *Notes Taken During Travels*, 188.

27. Westermarck, *Ritual and Belief*, 535.

28. Chouraqui, *La condition juridique*.

29. Messick, *The Calligraphic State*.

30. *sharikat a'mal*

31. *sharikat 'uqud*

32. *sharikat mal*

33. *sharikat milk*

34. *sharikat wujuh*

35. Chouraqui, *The Social and Legal Status*, 25.

36. Lorcin, *Imperial Identities*.

37. *tuqayyid al-mutlaq wa tukhassis al-'am*

38. Al-'Uthmani, *Alwah Jazula*.

39. Ibid.

40. Al-Jidi, *Al-'urf wa al-'amal*, 237.

41. Lorcin, *Imperial Identities*.

42. Gellner, *Plough, Sword, and Book*, 73.

43. *m'arfa* and *wasta*

44. Some of these judges are al-Qadi Sidi al-Hasham al-Fasi, Sidi Muhammad ban 'Abd al-Rahman, Ahmad ban al-Madani al-Wakhshashi, Ahmad ban al-Hasham al-Wakhshashi, al-Husayn ban al-Hasham ban 'Abdallah al-Wakhshashi, Muhammad al-'Alam, Si Muhammad Ousaya, and 'Abd al-Rahman al-Wannas.

45. Al-Susi, *Sus al-'alima*; *Iligh qadiman*; *Al-Ma'sul*.

46. Ali Bey, *Travels of Ali Bey in Morocco*, 33.

47. Boum, "Muslims Remember Jews," 232–244.

48. In colonial Morocco, two *riyals* were circulated. The Spanish *riyal* (also called *al-riyal al-kabir*) equaled five *piastres*. The French *riyal* (also called *al-riyal al-saghir*) was five francs.

49. One *riyal hasani* equals ten *dirhams*. And see n. 32.

50. *Qirta* is one piece of anything of twenty-four. A gold *dinar* weighed twenty-four *qirta*. A *qirta* measured 0.1954 gram.

51. One *sa'* is four *mudd* (a *mudd* is a volumetric measure that equaled 25.25 liters).

52. A *dirham* is a silver piece that weighed 50.4 grains of barley that equaled 2,911 grams. A *dirham* was composed of four *muzuna* (a quarter of a *dirham*).

53. Udovitch, *Partnership and Profit*, 170.

54. Udovitch, "At the Origins of the Western Commenda," 198.

55. Ibn Qayyim al-Jawziyya, *Ahkam ahl al-dhimma*, vol. 1, 552–560; vol. 3, 1330–1333.

56. Udovitch, *Partnership and Profit*, 228.

57. Goitein, *A Mediterranean Society*; idem, *Jews and Arabs*.

58. Personal communication, Agadir Uzru, Akka, 2004.

59. Park, "Essaouira," 114.

60. Park, "Essaouira."

61. Legardère, "Histoire et société," 33.

62. Park and Boum, *Historical Dictionary*, 264.

63. Schroeter, *Merchants of Essaouira*, 164–165; Rosenberger and Triki, "Famines et épidémies au Maroc."

64. Park and Boum, *Historical Dictionary*, 264–265.

65. Schroeter: "Anglo-Jewry and Essaouira," "Morocco, England," "Royal Power and the Economy," "Jewish Communities of Morocco."

66. Schroeter, *Merchants of Essaouira*, 23.

67. Ibid., 165.

68. Schroeter, "Anglo-Jewry and Essaouira."

69. Schroeter, *Merchants of Essaouira*, 43.

70. From *sukhra*, which stands for the monetary salaries paid by the different tribes to the Makhzan's lower workers in exchange for the work they perform in the region. For example, a person who works for a *qadi* can benefit from the *sukhra* and is usually referred to as *lamsakhkhar*. After the sultan Mawlay 'Abd al-'Aziz reinstated the *tartib* tax that was first issued by Mawlay al-Hasan on farmers' animals and trees, the *sukhra* was annulled because the government workers were issued special salaries.

71. Also for the Berber word *arqqas*, the person in charge of taking mail from one region to another. He is known for his trust. He can also be in charge of the Makhzan's mail to the interior regions.

72. Derived from the word "intérêt," *lantris* refers to the benefits that traders had to pay when they did not meet their deadlines with European merchants.

Chapter 3

1. Langellier, "Personal Narratives," 243.

2. Tonkin, *Narrating Our Pasts*.

3. For a discussion on the Jewish commemoration of righteous saints, see Kosansky, "All Dear unto God."

4. Flamand, *Diaspora en terre d'Islam*.

5. Shokeid, "Jewish Existence."

6. Boum and Mjahed, "Silencing the Built Environment," 280.

7. Bahloul, *The Architecture of Memory*, 29.

8. Lagardère, *Histoire et société*. Also see Larhmaid, "Jewish Identity and Land Ownership," 59–62.

9. Beck, *Risk Society*, 21.

10. Flamand, *Diaspora en terre d'Islam*.

11. Giddens, "Risk and Responsibility," 3.

12. Levy, "Hara et mellah"; Schroeter, "The Jewish Quarter"; Miller, "The Mellah of Fez"; idem, "Les quartiers Juifs"; Gottreich, "On the Origins of the Mellah"; idem, "Rethinking the Islamic City"; Miller and Bertagnin, *The Architecture and Memory*.

13. As Goitein put it, the world of the Jewish community of Yemen "center[ed] around the synagogue, where simple people, craftsmen and labourers, are versed in religious lore and are able to follow arguments based on the Scriptures." Also see "The Jews of Yemen," 228.

14. Similar issues were discussed by Udovitch and Valensi in their work on the Jewish community of Jerba; see *The Last Arab Jews*, 40.

15. Boum, "The Political Coherence."

16. Goitein, "Jewish Education."

17. Boum, "The Political Coherence."

18. Aubin, *Morocco of Today*, 290.

19. Gottreich, *The Mellah of Marrakesh*, 10.

20. De Périgny, *Au Maroc*, 151.

21. Slouschz, *Travels in North Africa*, 443.

22. Ibid.

23. Zafrani, *Pédagogie juive en terre d'Islam*, 42–43.

24. Sarah Levin, personal comunication, 2010.

25. Harrus, *L'Alliance en action*.

26. Sarah Levin, personal communication, 2008.

27. Ibid.

28. *AIU Archives*, Maroc, Circonscription de Marrakech, 179. Rapport d'Elias Harrus sur l'ouverture de l'école de Guelmim, January 27, 1952.

29. Lydon, *On Trans-Saharan Trails*.

30. Schroeter, *Merchants of Essaouira*; Lydon, *On Trans-Saharan Trails*.

31. *AIU Archives*, Maroc, Circonscription de Marrakech, 179. Rapport d'Elias Harrus sur l'ouverture de l'école de Guelmim, January 27, 1952.

32. Laskier, "Aspects of Change and Modernization," 342.

33. See the Communication of the Assembly General held in July 10, 1867. Cited in Chouraqui, *Cent*, 178.

34. Abramovitch, "Jewish Education in Morocco," 24.

35. A new term was coined for the AIU to become known as Ittihad-Maroc (*Ittihad* means "Alliance" in Arabic).

36. *AIU Archives*, Maroc, Circonscription de Marrakech, 345, n. 11. Correspondance avec Charles Bitton, le directeur de l'école d'Akka, November 16, 1955.

37. *AIU Archives*, Maroc, Circonscription de Marrakech, 179. Rapport d'Elias Harrus sur l'ouverture de l'école de Guelmim, January 27, 1952.

38. *AIU Archives*, Maroc, Circonscription de Marrakech, 212. Rapport d'Elias Harrus sur l'ouverture des écoles de Taounza et Tinerhir, November 13, 1950.

39. Ibid.

40. *AIU Archives*, Maroc, Circonscription de Marrakech, 179. Rapport d'Elias Harrus sur l'ouverture de l'école de Guelmim, January 27, 1952.

41. Personal communication, Sarraf Bardkhin, Guelmim, 2004.

42. Laskier, "Aspects of Change and Modernization," 334.

43. *AIU Archives*, Maroc, Circonscription de Marrakech, 212. Rapport d'Elias Harrus sur l'ouverture des écoles de Taounza et Tinerhir, November 13, 1950.

44. Sarah Levin's interview with Emile Sebban, Casablanca, 1999.

45. *AIU Archives*, Maroc, Circonscription de Marrakech, 212. Rapport d'Elias Harrus sur l'ouverture des écoles de Taounza et Tinerhir, November 13, 1950.

46. Ibid.

47. *AIU Archives*, Maroc, Circonscription de Marrakech, 179. Rapport d'Elias Harrus sur l'ouverture de l'école de Guelmim, January 27, 1952.

48. *AIU Archives*, Maroc, Circonscription de Marrakech, 345. Rapport Annuel à addresser à l'Inspecteur de l'enseignement Primaire de Marrakech. Correspondance avec Charles Bitton, le directeur de l'école d'Akka, June 18, 1956.

49. Ohayon, "Souvenirs du Bled."

50. *AIU Archives*, Maroc, Circonscription de Marrakech, 345. Rapport Annuel à addresser à l'Inspecteur de l'enseignement Primaire de Marrakech. Correspondance avec Charles Bitton, le directeur de l'école d'Akka, June 18, 1956.

51. Laskier, "Aspects of Change and Modernization," 336.

52. Goldenberg, "A Teacher in the Bled," 32.

53. *AIU Archives*, Maroc, Circonscription de Marrakech. "Enquête dans la region sud de Marrakesh: tournée du Tafilalt," *Les Cahiers de l'Alliance Israélite Universelle* 40–41 (1950), 8.

54. *AIU Archives*, Maroc, Circonscription de Marrakech, 345: Colis. Letter of Reuben Tajouri to Charles Bitton, 799I MZ/mc. Correspondance avec Charles Bitton, le directeur de l'école d'Akka, December 5, 1955.

Chapter 4

1. For a discussion of Moroccan colonial soldiers, see Maghraoui, "Moroccan Colonial Soldiers." Also see Gershovish, *French Military Rule in Morocco*; Bimberg, *The Moroccan Goums*.

2. Gavish makes similar claims in her study of the Jewish community of Zakho; see *Unwitting Zionists*, 337.

3. Hatimi, "Al-jama'at al-yahudiyya al-maghribiyya."

4. M'Barek, "La desertion des soldats."

5. For a recent discussion of Jewish migration from southern Morocco, see Larhmaid, "Jama'at yahud Sus"; Boum, "Muslims Remember Jews." For a detailed study of the Jewish emigration in the national context, see Hatimi, "Al-jama'at al-yahudiyya al-maghribiyya."

6. Cohen, "Lyautey et le sionisme"; Bensimon-Donath, *Immigrants d'Afrique*; Laskier, *The Alliance Israélite Universelle*.

7. Tsur, "The Religious Factor," 317.

8. Gellner, *Nation and Nationalism*, 101–109.

9. Tsur, "The Religious Factor," 313.

10. Ibid., 325. Tsur notes that the "fact that both nationalisms, Moroccan and Zionist, penetrated the Atlas preindustrial hinterland from the outside underlines an important similarity between them. Moroccan nationalism, like all third world national movements, did not necessarily require an industrialized environment to spread, it was enough that part of Moroccan society—namely certain elite groups— were industrialized sufficiently to establish a modern national movement. They could serve as a modernizing and national leadership with the potential to reach out to traditional elements of the society. At the right moment, they could mobilize a national turnabout. Zionism . . . also had the ability to enlist preindustrial segments of the Jewish diaspora to the national enterprise."

11. Gilman, "Introduction," 1; Anderson, *Imagined Communities*.

12. Boyarin and Boyarin, "Diaspora."

13. Boyarin and Boyarin, "Diaspora," 713; idem, *Powers of Diaspora*; Wettstein, *Diasporas and Exiles*.

14. Boyarin and Boyarin, *Powers of Diaspora*, vii.

15. Gilman, "Introduction," 12.

16. Ibid., 1.

17. Levy, "A Community That Is," 69.

18. Yehuda, "The Place of Aliyah."

19. Tsur, "The Religious Factor," 325.

20. Hobsbawm, "Introduction: Inventing Traditions," 13.

21. *L'Action du peuple*, "Les israélites et nous," August 18, 1933.

22. Baida, "La presse juive," 177.

23. *L'Action du peuple*, May 20, 1937.

24. Hatimi, "Al-jama'at al-yahudiyya al-maghribiyya," 549–570.

25. Entelis, *Culture and Counterculture*.

26. Jacques-Meunié, *Le Maroc saharien*, 175–188.

27. Schroeter, "Jewish Communities of Morocco," 27.

28. Hirschberg, *A History of the Jews*; idem, "The Problem of the Judaized Ber-

bers." It is worth mentioning that the idea of "Judaized Berbers" is a disputed theory, and Hirschberg refutes it. Daniel Schroeter had a lengthy discussion of this theory; see Schroeter, "La découverte des juifs berbères."

29. Schroeter, "Jewish Communities of Morocco," 27.

30. Gaudio, *Guerres et paix au Maroc*, 90.

31. Hirschberg, *A History of the Jews*.

32. Laskier, *The Alliance Israélite Universelle*, 194.

33. Boum, "From 'Little Jerusalems' to the Promised Land."

34. Kosansky, "Tourism, Charity, and Profit."

35. Ibid.

36. Bar Asher, "The Jews of North Africa," 297.

37. Ibid.; also see Slouschz, "La colonie des maghrabim."

38. This is quoted in Schroeter, "Royal Power and the Economy," 87.

39. Oliel, *Les camps de Vichy*, 2005.

40. Laskier, "Zionism and the Jewish Communities," 124.

41. Benbassa, *The Jews of France*, 94.

42. Katz, *Out of the Ghetto*.

43. Schroeter, "Orientalism and the Jews," 185.

44. Schroeter, "Orientalism and the Jews"; Abitbol, "The Encounter Between French Jewry"; Kosansky, "Tourism, Charity, and Profit."

45. Romanelli, *Travail in an Arab Land*.

46. Ibid., 28.

47. Laskier, *The Alliance Israélite Universelle*, 33–34.

48. Kenbib, "Changing Aspects of State"; Miège, *Le Maroc et l'Europe*; Parsons, *The Origins of the Morocco Question*.

49. Lipman and Lipman, *The Century of Moses Montefiore*.

50. Schroeter, "Morocco, England, and the End of the Sephardic"; idem, "A Different Road to Modernity."

51. Schroeter, "Royal Power and the Economy"; Roth, "The Amazing Clan of Buzaglo"; Hirschberg, "Jews and Jewish Affairs."

52. Yehuda, "Zionist Activity."

53. Ibid.

54. Cohen, "Lyautey et le sionisme."

55. Abitbol, "Zionism in North Africa," 72–73; Goidan, *Le sionisme au Maroc*; Gallard, "Le sionisme et la question juive."

56. Kenbib, *Juifs et musulmans au Maroc*, 493.

57. *L'Avenir Illustré*, July 27, 1928, 3.

58. *L'Avenir Illustré*, September 30, 1929, 13.

59. Laskier, "The Evolution of Zionist Activity."

60. Yehuda, "Zionist Activity," 364; Ben-Ami, *Saint Veneration*, 260–263.

61. Gottreich, *The Mellah of Marrakesh*, 36; Boum, "Muslims Remember Jews"; Oliel, *De Jérusalem à Tombouctou*.

62. Slouschz, *Travels in North Africa*, 443.

63. Abitbol, "Zionism in North Africa," 72.

64. Laskier, *North African Jewry*.

65. In 1930, after the introduction of the Berber Decree of May 16, 1930, Arsalane led a massive critical campaign against the French colonial authorities through his newspaper *La Nation Arabe*, published in Geneva. He believed that a cultural, political, and social reawakening and revival of the Islamic and Arab nations could not be achieved without a struggle for independence. Born in 1869 to one of the most influential families of the druze of Lebanon, Arsalane turned to orthodox Islam after being influenced by the teaching of Mohammed Abdu. He settled in Geneva in 1921, becoming the leader of Arab nationalist consciousness. In 1930, he created the French revue *La Nation Arabe*, which became a springboard of issues relating to the Arab and Islamic world in the Middle East and North Africa. Around 1938, he turned to Nazi Germany and Fascist Italy for help to manage his newspaper and looked for their support against the French and British colonialism of the Arab world. After the Axis defeat in World War II, Arsalane's influence declined, and he went into a self-imposed exile in Brazil, where he died in 1946.

66. Moroccan Muslims and Jews were the main founders and members of the PCM. However, the party was largely an extension of the French Communist Party and its leadership.

67. Ayache, *Le mouvement syndical*; Oved, *La gauche française*; Rézette, *Les partis politiques marocaines*.

68. Quoted and translated in Laskier, "The Instability of the Moroccan Jewry," 50–51.

69. Kenbib, *Juifs et musulmans au Maroc*.

70. Boum, "Muslims Remember Jews"; Hatimi, "Al-jama'at al-yahudiyya al-maghribiyya."

Chapter 5

1. *'Ayn mika* is a commonly used idiomatic phrase. The verb is *dir 'ayn mika l-* (meaning "give the plastic treatment to"). The behavior of *'ayn mika* can also be referred to as *"tmyak,"* a Moroccan Arabic word that comes from the verb *mayak*. Etymologically speaking, *mika* might have come from "mica," which stands for all that glitters. In colloquial Moroccan Arabic, *mika* means plastic or everything that is made out of it. *'Ayn mika* started probably as a phrase used for things that glitter, but because they are not important, they should be ignored.

2. Baida, "Le Maroc et la propagande"; idem, "La presse juive"; idem, *La presse marocaine*; Boum, "Muslims Remember Jews."

3. Habermas, *The Structural Transformation*, 34.

4. Laskier, "The Instability of the Moroccan Jewry"; Baida, *La presse marocaine*; Boum, "Muslims Remember Jews"; Hatimi, "Al-jama'at al-yahudiyya al-maghribiyya."

5. Ihrai-Aouchar, "La presse marocaine d'opposition."

6. Boum, "Muslims Remember Jews."

7. Schroeter, *The Sultan's Jew*.

8. The PDI was created by Muhammad Hassan al-Wazzani in 1946.

9. Rézette, *Les partis politiques marocaines*.

10. Laskier, "The Instability of the Moroccan Jewry," 40.

11. It should be noted that the UNFP splinter in 1972 became the Union Nationale des Forces Populaires.

12. *Al-'Alam*, October 17, 1958.

13. Laskier, *Israel and the Maghreb*, 81.

14. Ibid., 78.

15. *La Voix des Communautés*, February 1, 1961.

16. Laskier, "The Instability of the Moroccan Jewry."

17. Laskier, *Israel and the Maghreb*, 93.

18. Berdugo, *Juives et Juifs*, 87.

19. Ibid., 89.

20. Levy, *Yahud Magharibah*.

21. See Serfaty and El Baz, *L'insoumis*. Serfaty has written numerous works on Moroccan Judaism, Zionism, and his experience as a political dissident. See *Dans les prisons du roi*; *Écrits de prison*; *Lutte antisioniste*; *Le Maroc*. El Maleh's main novels include *Aïlen ou la nuit du récit*, *Mille ans un jour*, *Parcours Immobile*, and *Le Retour d'Abou El Haki*.

22. *Assabah*, January 25, 2011.

23. Malka, *La mémoire brisée*, 65.

24. Kenbib, *Juifs et musulmans au Maroc*.

25. *Le Matin du Sahara*, September 29, 1989.

26. Kreps, "Non-Western Models of Museums."

27. Dubin, *Displays of Power*.

28. Gates, *Thirteen Ways of Looking*, 57; Gilmore and Smith, "Identity, Resistance and Resilience."

29. Malt, "Women, Museums."

30. See Fadwa Miadi, "Zhor Rehihil: musulmane et militante propalestinienne, elle est depuis quatre and conservatrice du Musée juif de Casablanca," *Jeune Afrique*, September 26, 2004. Available at www.jeuneafrique.com/jeune_afrique/article_jeune_afrique.asp?art_cle=LIN26104z (accessed November 28, 2008).

31. Amahan, "Les grands musées"; Erzini, "Cultural Administration in French North Africa"; Kafas, "De l'origine de 'idée"; Rharib, "Taking Stock of Moroccan

Museums"; Bisharat, "Museums Collections and Collecting"; Malt, "Women, Museums."

32. Amahan, "Les grands musées," 299.

33. See the official magazine of Royal Air Maroc, *Ram Magazine* 142 (March–April 2007): 74–78.

34. Park and Boum, *Historical Dictionary*.

35. Alonso, "The Effects of Truth," 45.

36. Ben-Ze'ev and Ben-Ari, "Imposing Politics," 7.

37. Maddy-Weitzman, "Israel and Morocco."

Chapter 6

1. Van Leeuwen, "The Lost Heritage," 201.

2. "Ihtijajat al-shari': thiql al-kalima wa haqiat al-waqi'," *Al-massae*, February 19, 2012.

3. Tessler, "Alienation and Urban Youth"; Moore and Hochshild, "Students Unions."

4. Boum, "The Culture of Despair."

5. Payne, "Economic Crisis."

6. Tessler, "Alienation and Urban Youth."

7. Ibid.

8. Hammoudi, *Master and Disciple*, 5.

9. Meijer, "Introduction," 7–8.

10. *Siba* or *bled al-siba* is the traditional term used to refer to the areas where the sultan is powerless. See Bennani-Chraïbi, *Soumis et rebelles*.

11. Leveau, "Youth Culture and Islamism," 272.

12. Scott, *Weapons of the Weak*.

13. Allport and Postman, "An Analysis of Rumor," 505.

14. Dundes, *Essays in Folkloristics*, 114.

15. Billig, "Comic Racism and Violence," 39.

16. Goldberg, *Cave Dwellers*; Hammoudi, *The Victim and Its Masks*, 148.

17. Haidt, *Embodying Enlightenment*, 9.

18. Park and Boum, *Historical Dictionary*, 347–350.

19. Known in Arabic as al-Ittihad al-Watani li-Talabat al-Maghrib. See Darif, *Al-haraka al-tulabiyya al-maghribiya*.

20. Ibid.

21. Eickelman, "Communication and Control," 42.

22. Khoury-Machool, "Cyber Resistance," 123.

23. Interview by Abdeslam Razzaq with Ahmed Darghani, "Ahmed Daghrani al-nashit al-huquqi al-amazighi: hammuna al-akbar huwa ta'kid hawiyyat al-insan al-maazighi." Available at www.al-jazeera.net.

24. Scott, *Weapons of the Weak.*

25. Denning, "Activism, Hacktivism, and Cyberterrorism."

26. Foucault, *Discipline and Punish*, 198.

27. Park and Boum, *Historical Dictionary*, 212–216.

28. Jenkins, *Convergence Culture*, 290.

29. Available at www.ynetnews.com/articles/0,7340,L-3268449,00.html.

30. Khoury-Machool, "Cyber Resistance," 119.

31. Boum, "Youth, Political Activism."

32. Denning, "Activism, Hacktivism, and Cyberterrorism," 268–269.

33. Kosansky and Boum, "The Jewish Question."

34. *Attajdid*, January 9, 2009.

35. Ibid., July 23, 2007.

36. *Maroc-Hebdo International*, July 19–25, 1997.

37. Boum, "Muslims Remember Jews."

38. Available at www.associatedcontent.com/content.cfm?content_type=article &content_type_id=11145.

39. *Maroc-Hebdo International*, July 26–August 1, 2002.

40. *Attajdid*, May 17, 2002.

41. Ibid., June 20, 2006.

42. Gur-Ze'ev and Pappé, "Beyond the Destruction of the Other's Collective Memory," 105.

43. Hicham Houdaïfa, "Une association berbero-israélienne à contre-courant," *Le Journal Hebdomadaire*. Available at www.lejournal-hebdo.com/article.php3?id_article=8485.

44. Ghallab, "Les Juifs vont en enfer," 2247.

45. Ibid., 2249.

46. Boum, "Muslims Remember Jews"; Silverstein, "Masquerade Politics"; Maddy-Weitzman, "Morocco's Berbers and Israel."

47. Barthes, *Image-Music-Text*, 146.

48. Al-Qur'an, 17:4–8, trans. Ali 1984: 240.

49. Yassine, *Winning the Modern World*, 56.

50. Ibid., 47.

51. Ibid., 48.

52. Ibid., 50.

53. Ibid.

54. Ibid.

55. Ibid.

56. Assaraf, *Une certaine histoire.*

57. Laskier, *Israel and the Maghreb*, 246.

58. Silverstein, "Masquerade Politics," 81.

Conclusion

1. Foucault, *Archaeology of Knowledge*, 191.
2. Said, "Israel-Palestine: A Third Way," 6.
3. Bakhtin, *The Dialogic Imagination*, 368.

Epilogue

1. Boum, "The Performance of Convivencia."
2. Soifer, "Beyond Convivencia"; Ray, "Beyond Tolerance and Persecution"; Cohen, *Under Crescent and Cross*, 6–8.
3. Boum, "The Performance of Convivencia."
4. Shannon, "Performing al-Andalus." For a discussion of the dynamics of the festival, its features, and its manifestations, see Kapchan, "The Promise of Sonic Translation," and Boum, "'Sacred Week'." For festivals in Morocco, see Boum, "Festivalizing Dissent."
5. Castro, *The Spaniards*.
6. Wolf, "Convivencia in Medieval Spain," 72.
7. Available at www.magharebia.com.
8. Ibid.
9. Available at www.nytimes.com.
10. Ibid.
11. Bigelow, *Sharing the Sacred*.
12. Casy, *Remembering*, 218.
13. Bigelow, *Sharing the Sacred*, 219.
14. Zafrani, *Pédagogie juive en terre d'Islam*, 27; also Aouad Lahrech, "Esther and I," 82–84.
15. Kapchan, "The Promise of Sonic Translation," 467.
16. Ibid., 468.
17. Turner, *Celebration*, 21.

Methodological Appendix

1. Labov, *Language in the Inner City*.
2. Hill, "The Voices of Don Gabriel"; Bamberg, *Narrative Development*; Ochs and Capps, *Living Narratives*.
3. Labov, *Language in the Inner City*, 3.
4. Ibid, 1.
5. This model was first proposed in Weinreich, Labov, and Herzog, "Empirical Foundations."
6. Pierrehumbert, "Exemplar Dynamics," 140.
7. Elliott, *Using Narratives*, 72.
8. Elder and Pellerin, "Linking History," 267.

9. Ryder, "The Cohort as a Concept," 843.

10. Ibid., 845.

11. Quinn, *Finding Culture*.

12. Ibid., 38.

13. Ibid., 38.

14. Ryder, "The Cohort as a Concept," 845.

References

Arabic and French Newspapers

L'Action du peuple
Al-'Alam
Assabah
Attajdid
L'Avant-Garde
L'Avenir Illustré
L'Espoir
Jeune Afrique
Le Journal Hebdomadaire
Magharebia
Maroc-Hebdo International
Maroc-Presse
Al-massae
Le Matin du Sahara
La Nation Arabe
New York Evening World
New York Times
L'Opinion du Peuple
Al-Ra'y al-'Am
Al-Tahrir
TelQuel
L'Union Marocaine
La Voix des Communautés

Family Archives in Akka

Ibrahim Nouhi Family Archives
Hmad Ouhamam Family Archives
Najm Lahrash Family Archives
Hassi Ouqandou Family Archives
Al-Jaafari Family Archives

Bibliography

Abitbol, Michel. "The Encounter Between French Jewry and the Jews of North Africa: Analysis of a Discourse (1830–1914)." In *The Jews in Modern France*, ed. F. Malino and B. Wasserstein, 31–53. Hanover, N.H.: University Press of New England, 1985.

———. "Zionism in North Africa." *Jerusalem Quarterly* 21 (Fall 1981): 61–84.

Abrahams, Roger D. "Black Talking on the Streets." In *Explorations in the Ethnography of Speaking*, ed. R. Bauman and J. Sherzer, 337–73. Cambridge: Cambridge University Press, 1974.

———. "A Performance-Centered Approach to Gossip." *Man* 5 (1970): 290–301.

Abramovitch, Stanley. "Jewish Education in Morocco." *Jewish Education* 43 (1) (1970): 23–28.

Aby Serour, Mardochée. *Les Daggatoun: Tribu d'origine juive demeurant dans le désert du Sahara*, trans. Isidore Loeb. 1880.

———. "Premier établissement des Israélites à Timbouctou," trans. Auguste Beaumier. *Bulletin de la Société de Géographie* 5 (19) (1870): 345–70.

Afa, Aomar. *Tarikh al-maghrib al-mu'asir: dirasat fi al-masadir, wa al-mujtam' wa al-iqtisad*. Al-Ribat: Manshurat Kuliyyat al-'Adab wa al-'Ulum al-Insaniyya, 2002.

———. "Al-yahud fi mantaqat Sus: dawruhum al-iqtisadi wa 'alaqatuhum bi al-suwayra." In *Essaouira mémoire et empreinte du présent*. Series Colloques et Journées d'études, no. 3, October 26–27–28, 1990, 131–49. Agadir: Publications de la Faculté des Lettres et des Sciences Humaines, 1994.

Ali Bey [Badia Y Leyblich]. *Travels of Ali Bey in Morocco, Tripoli, Cyprus, Egypt, Arabia, Syria, and Turkey, between the Years 1803 and 1807*. 2 vols. Farnborough, England: Gregg International Publishers, 1970 [1816].

Al-Jidi, 'Umar bn 'Abd al-Karim. *Al-'urf wa al-'amal fi al-madhhab al-maliki wa mafhumuhuma lada 'ulama' al-maghrib*. Muhammadia: Matba'at Fdala, 1984.

Allport, Gordon W., and Leo Postman. "An Analysis of Rumor." *Public Opinion Quarterly* 10 (4) (1946–1947): 501–17.

Alonso, Ana Maria. "The Effects of Truth: Re-Presentations of the Past and the Imagining of Community." *Journal of Historical Sociology* 1 (1) (1988): 33–57.

Al-Manuni, Muhammad. *Al-masadir al-'arabiyya li tarikh al-maghrib min al-fath al-islami ili al-'asr al-hadith*. Rabat: Publications de la Faculté des Lettres et des Sciences Humaines, 1983.

———. *Tarikh al-wiraqa al-maghribiyya: sina'at al-makhtut al-maghribi min al-'asr al-wasit ila al-fatra al-mu'asira*. Rabat: Publications de la Faculté des Lettres et des Sciences Humaines, 1991.

Al-Susi, al-Mukhtar. *Iligh qadiman wa hadithan*. Rabat: al-Matba'at al-Malakiyya, 1966.

———. *Khilal jazula*. 4 vols. Tetouan, n.d.

————. *Al-Ma'sul.* 20 vols. Casablanca: Matba'at al-Najah, 1973.

————. *Sus al-'alima.* Muhammadia: Matba'at Fdala, 1960.

Al-'Uthmani, Muhammad. *Akwah Jazula wa al-tashri' al-islami: dirasat li-a'raf qaba'il sus fi daw' al-tashri' al-islami.* Al-Ribat: Manshurat Wizart al-Awqaf wa al-Shu'un al-Islamiyya, 2004.

Amahan, Ali. "Les grands musées un public essentiellement touristique." In *L'état du Maghreb,* ed. Camille Lacoste-Dujardin and Yves Lacoste, 299–301. Casablanca: Editions le Fennec, 1991.

Anderson, Benedict. *Imagined Communities: Reflections on the Origin and Spread of Nationalism.* London: Verso, 2006.

Aouad Lahrech, O. "Esther and I: From Shore to Shore." In *Morocco: Jews and Art in a Muslim Land,* ed. Vivian Mann, 65–84. New York: Merrell, 2000.

Apte, Mahadev L. *Humor and Laughter: An Anthropological Approach.* Ithaca, N.Y.: Cornell University Press, 1985.

Assaraf, Robert. *Une certaine histoire des Juifs du Maroc: 1860–1999.* Paris: Gawsewitch, 2005.

Aubin, Eugène. *Morocco of Today.* London: E. B. Dutton, 1906.

Ayache, Albert. *Le mouvement syndical au Maroc.* Paris: L'Harmattan, 1982.

Ayache, Germain. "La recherche au Maroc sur l'histoire du judaisme marocain." In *Juifs du Maroc: Identité et dialogue.* Actes du colloque international sur la communauté juive marocaine: Vie culturelle, histoire, sociale et évolution. Paris, December 18–21, 1978, 31–35. Paris: La Pensée Sauvage, 1980.

Bahloul, Joëlle. *The Architecture of Memory: A Jewish-Muslim Household in Colonial Algeria, 1937–1962.* Cambridge: Cambridge University Press, 1996.

Baida, Jamaa. "Le Maroc et la propagande du IIIème Reich." *Hespéris-Tamuda* 28 (1990): 91–106.

————. "La presse juive au Maroc entre les deux guerres." *Hespéris-Tamuda* 37 (1999): 171–89.

————. *La presse marocaine d'expression française des origines à 1956.* Rabat: Publications de la Faculté des Lettres et des Sciences Humaines, 1996.

Bailey, Guy. "Real and Apparent Time." In *The Handbook of Language Variation and Change,* ed. J. K. Chambers, Peter Trudgill, and Natalie Schilling-Estes, 312–32. Malden, Mass.: Blackwell, 2002.

Bakhtin, Mikhail. *The Dialogic Imagination: Four Essays,* trans. Caryl Emerson and Michael Holquist. Austin: University of Texas Press, 1981.

Bamberg, Michael. *Narrative Development: Six Approaches.* Mahwah, N.J.: Lawrence Erlbaum Associates, 1997.

Bar Asher, S. "The Jews of North Africa and the Land of Israel in the Eighteenth and Nineteenth Centuries: The Reversal in Attitude Toward *Aliyah* (Immigration to the Land) from 1770 to 1860." In *The Land of Israel: Jewish Perspectives*, ed. L. Hoffman, 297–315. Notre Dame, Ind.: University of Notre Dame Press, 1986.

Barth, Heinrich. *Travels and Discoveries in North and Central Africa*. New York: Harper & Brothers, 1859.

Barthes, Rolland. *Image-Music-Text*. London: Fontana, 1977.

Bazin, René. *Charles de Foucauld: Explorateur du Maroc, érmite au Sahara*. Paris: Plon-Nourrit et Cie, 1921.

Beck, Ulrich. *Risk Society: Towards a New Modernity*, trans. Mark Ritter. London: Sage, 1992.

Benali, Driss. "ihtijajat al-shari': thiql al-kalima wa haqiat al-waqi'." *Al-massae*, February 19, 2012.

Ben-Ami, I. *Saint Veneration Among the Jews of Morocco*. Detroit: Wayne State University Press, 1998.

Benbassa, Esther. *The Jews of France: A History from Antiquity to the Present*. Princeton, N.J.: Princeton University Press, 1999.

Benet, Francisco. "Explosive Markets: The Berber Highlands." In *Trade and Market in the Early Empires. Economies in History and Theory*, ed. Karl Polanyi et al., 188–217. Glencoe, Ill.: Free Press, 1957.

Bennani-Chraïbi, Mounia. *Soumis et rebelles, les jeunes au Maroc*. Paris: CNRS Editions, 1994.

Bensimon-Donath, D. *Immigrants d'Afrique du Nord en Israel*. Paris: Editions Anthropos, 1970.

Ben-Ze'ev, Efrat, and Eyal Ben-Ari. "Imposing Politics: Failed Attempts at Creating a Museum of 'Co-existence' in Jerusalem." *Anthropology Today* 12 (6) (1996): 7–13.

Berdugo, Arlette. *Juives et juifs dans le Maroc contemporain: Images d'un devenir*. Paris: Librairie Orientaliste Paul Geuthner S. A., 2002.

Besnier, Niko. *Gossip and the Everyday Production of Politics*. Honolulu: University of Hawai'i Press, 2009.

Bidwell, Robin. *Morocco Under Colonial Rule: The French Administration of Tribal Areas, 1912–1956*. London: Frank Cass, 1973.

Bigelow, Anna. *Sharing the Sacred: Practicing Pluralism in Muslim India*. New York: Oxford University Press, 2010.

Billig, M. "Comic Racism and Violence." In *Beyond a Joke: The Limits of Humor*, ed. Sharon Lockyer and Michael Pickering, 25–44. New York: Palgrave, 2005.

Bilu, Yoram, and André Levy. "Nostalgia and Ambivalence: The Reconstruction of Jewish-Muslim Relations in Oulad Mansour." In *Sephardi and Middle Eastern Jewries: History and Culture in the Modern Era*, ed. Harvey E. Goldberg, 288–311. Bloomington: Indiana University Press, 1991.

Bimberg, Edward. *The Moroccan Goums: Tribal Warriors in a Modern War*. Westport, Conn.: Greenwood Press, 1999.

Bisharat, Souhail. "Museums Collections and Collecting in the Arab World: Some Reflections on Today." *International Journal of Museum Management and Curatorship* 4 (1985): 279–87.

Bonine, Michael E. *Yazd and Its Hinterland: A Central Place Theory of Dominance in the Central Iranian Plateau*. Marburg: Im Selbstverlag des Geographischen Institutes der Universität Marburg, 1980.

Boum, Aomar. "The Culture of Despair: Youth, Unemployment and Educational Failures in North Africa." In *Educators of the Mediterranean . . . Up Close and Personal: Critical Voices from South Europe and the MENA Region*, ed. Ronald Sultana, 237–44. Rotterdam: Sense Publishers, 2011.

———. "Festivalizing Dissent in Morocco." *Middle East Report* 263 (Summer 2012): 22–25.

———. "From 'Little Jerusalems' to the Promised Land: Zionism, Moroccan Nationalism, and Rural Jewish Emigration." *Journal of North African Studies* 15 (1) (2010): 51–69.

———. "Legal Syncretism, Private Archives and the Historiography of Southern Moroccan Jewry." In *Le Local et le global dans l'écriture de l'histoire sociale: Mélanges dédiés à Larbi Mezzine*. Coordination Mohammed Kenbib et Jillali Adnani. Essais et Etudes, no. 55, 159–92. Rabat: Publications de la Faculté des Lettres et Sciences Humaines, Université Mohammed V, 2012.

———. "Muslims Remember Jews in Southern Morocco: Social Memories, Dialogic Narratives and the Collective Imagination of Jewishness." Ph.D. dissertation, University of Arizona (Tucson), 2006.

———. "The Performance of Convivencia: Communities of Tolerance and the Reification of Toleration." *Religion Compass* 6 (3) (2012): 174–84.

———. "The Plastic Eye: The Politics of Jewish Representation in Moroccan Museums." *Ethnos* 75 (1) (2010): 49–77.

———. "The Political Coherence of Educational Incoherence: The Consequences of Educational Specialization in a Southern Moroccan Community." *Anthropology and Education Quarterly* 39 (2) (2008): 205–23.

———. "'Sacred Week'": Re-Experiencing Jewish-Muslim Co-existence in Urban Moroccan Space." In *Sharing the Sacra: The Politics and Pragmatics of Inter-communal Relations Around Holy Places*, ed. Glenn Bowman. New York: Berghahn, 2012.

———. "Saharan Jewry: History, Memory and Imagined Identity." *Journal of North African Studies* 16 (3) (2011): 325–41.

———. "Schooling in the *Bled*: Jewish Education and the Alliance Israélite Universelle in Southern Rural Morocco, 1830–1962." *Journal of Jewish Identities* 3 (1) (2010): 1–24.

———. "Southern Moroccan Jewry Between the Colonial Manufacture of Knowledge and the Postcolonial Historiographical Silence." In *Jewish Culture and So-*

ciety in North Africa, ed. Emily Gottreich and Daniel Schroeter. Bloomington: Indiana University Press, 2011.

———. "Youth, Political Activism, and the Festivalization of Hip-Hop Music in Morocco." In *Contemporary Morocco: State, Politics, and Society Under Mohammed VI*, ed. Bruce Maddy-Weitzman and Daniel Zisenwine. London: Routledge, 2012.

Boum, Aomar, and Mourad Mjahed. "Silencing the Built Environment: Colonialism and Architecture in the Ksur of the Dr'a Valley." *Maghreb Review* 36 (3) (2011): 280–307.

Bourdieu, Pierre. "The Force of Law: Towards a Sociology of the Juridical Field." *Hastings Law Journal* 38 (5) (1987): 814–53.

Bourqia, Rahma. "La caidalité chez les tribus Zemmour aux XIXè siècle." *Bulletin Économique et Sociale du Maroc* (1987): 159–61; 131–40.

Bovill, E. W. "Mohammed El Maghili." *Journal of the Royal African Society* 34 (134) (1935): 27–30.

Bowie, Leland. "An Aspect of Muslim-Jewish Relations in Late Nineteenth-Century Morocco: A European Diplomatic View." *International Journal of Middle East Studies* 7 (1976): 3–19.

Boyarin, Daniel, and Jonathan Boyarin. "Diaspora: Generation and the Ground of Jewish Identity." *Critical Inquiry* 19 (4) (1993): 693–725.

———. *Powers of Diaspora: Two Essays on the Relevance of Jewish Culture*. Minneapolis: University of Minnesota Press, 2002.

Burma, John. "Humor as a Technique in Race Conflict." *American Sociological Review* 11 (6) (1946): 710–15.

Caillié, René. *Travels Through Central Africa to Timbuctoo and Across the Great Desert, to Morocco Performed in the Years 1824–1828*. 2 vols. London: Frank Cass & Co., 1968 [1830].

Campt, Tina. *Other Germans: Black Germans and the Politics of Race, Gender, and Memory in the Third Reich*. Ann Arbor: University of Michigan Press, 2005.

Carrouges, Michel. *Foucauld devant l'Afrique du Nord: Essai critique*. Paris: Cerf, 1961.

Castro, Américo. *The Spaniards: An Introduction to Their History*, trans. W. King and S. Margaretten. Berkeley: University of California Press, 1971.

Casy, E. *Remembering: A Phenomenological Study*. Bloomington: Indiana University Press, 2000.

Chaffal, Jean du. "De Foucauld saharien." *Revue Historique de l'Armée* 15 (4) (1959): 89–94.

Chouraqui, André. *Between East and West: A History of the Jews of North Africa*. Philadelphia: Jewish Publication Society of America, 1968.

———. *Cent ans d'histoire l'alliance israélite universelle et la renaissance juive contemporaine*. Paris: P.U.F., 1965.

————. *La condition juridique de l'israélite marocain*. Paris: Presses du Livre Français, 1950.

————. *The Social and Legal Status of the Jews of French Morocco*. New York: American Jewish Committee, 1952.

Coates, Jennifer. "Gossip Revisited: Language in All-Female Groups." In *Women in Their Speech Communities*, ed. Jennifer Coates and Deborah Cameron, 94–122. London: Longman, 1988.

Cohen, D. "Lyautey et le sionisme, 1915–1925." *Revue Française d'Histoire d'Outre-Mer* 67 (1980): 248–49; 269–300.

Cohen, Mark. *Under Crescent and Cross: The Jews in the Middle Ages*. Princeton, N.J.: Princeton University Press, 1994.

Darif, Mohammed. *Al-haraka al-tulabiyya al-maghribiya: qira'a fi azmat al-ittihad al-watani li-talabat al-maghrib 1956–1996*. Al-Dar al-Bayda': al-Najah al-Jadida, 1996.

Davidson, John. *Notes Taken During Travels in Africa*. London: J. L. Cox and Sons, 1839.

De Foucauld, Charles. *Reconnaissance au Maroc, 1883–1884*. Paris: Challamel, 1888.

De La Porte des Vaux, C. "Note sur le peuplement du Sous." *Bulletin Economique et Social du Maroc* 15 (54) (1952): 448–59; 15 (55) (1952): 625–32 (two parts).

Denning, Dorothy. "Activism, Hacktivism, and Cyberterrorism: The Internet as Tool for Influencing Foreign Policy." In *Networks and Netwars: The Future of Terror, Crime, and Militancy*, ed. John Arquilla and David Ronfeldt, 239–88. Santa Monica, Calif.: Rand Corporation, 2001.

Denzin, Norman. "On the Ethics of Disguised Observation." *Social Problems* 15 (4) (1968): 502–4.

De Périgny, Maurice. *Au Maroc: Marrakech et les ports du sud*. Paris: P. Roger, 1918.

Dubin, Steven C. *Displays of Power: Memory and Amnesia in the American Museum*. New York: New York University Press, 1999.

Dundes, Alan. *Cracking Jokes: Studies of Sick Humor Cycles and Stereotypes*. Berkeley: Ten Speed Press, 1987.

————. *Essays in Folkloristics*. New Delhi: Folklore Institute, 1978.

Duveyrier, Henri. "De Mogador au Djebel Tabayoudt." *Bulletin de la Société de Géographie* 10 (July–December 1875): 561–73.

————. "Sculptures antiques de la province marocaine du Sous, découvertes par le rabbin Mardochée." *Bulletin de la Société de Géographie* 12 (July–December 1876): 129–46.

Eickelman, Dale. "Communication and Control in the Middle East: Publication and Its Discontents." In *New Media in the Muslim World: The Emerging Pubic Sphere*, ed. Dale Eickelman and Jon Anderson, 33–44. Bloomington: Indiana University Press, 2003.

Elder, Glen H., and Lisa A. Pellerin. "Linking History and Human Lives." In *Methods of Life Course Research Qualitative and Quantitative Approaches, ed. Janet Z. Giele and Glen H. Elder, 264–94. Thousand Oaks, Calif.: Sage Publications, 1998.

El Hamel, Chouki. "Blacks and Slavery in Morocco: The Question of the Haratin at the End of the Seventeenth Century." In Diasporic Africa: A Reader, ed. Michael A. Gomez, 177–99. New York: New York University Press, 2006.

———. "'Race,' Slavery and Islam in the Maghrebi Mediterranean Thought: The Question of the Haratin in Morocco." Journal of North African Studies 7 (3) (2002): 29–52.

Elliott, Jane. Using Narratives in Social Research: Qualitative and Quantitative Approaches. London: Sage Publications, 2005.

El Maleh, Edmond Amran. Aïlen ou la nuit du récit. Paris: La Découverte, 1983.

———. Mille ans un jour. Grenoble: La Pensée Sauvage, 1986.

———. Parcours Immobile. Paris: La Découverte, 1980.

———. Le Retour d'Abou El Haki. Grenoble: La Pensée Sauvage, 1990.

El Mansour, Mohamed. "Moroccan Historiography Since Independence." In The Maghrib in Question: Essays in History and Historiography, ed. Michel Le Gall and Kenneth Perkins, 109–20. Austin: University of Texas Press, 1997.

El Moudden, Abderrahmane. "État et société rurale à travers la harka au Maroc du XIXè siècle." Maghreb Review 8 (5–6) (1983): 141–45.

Ennaji, Mohammed. Serving the Master: Slavery and Society in Nineteenth-Century Morocco. New York: St. Martin's, 1999.

Ensel, Remco. Saints and Servants in Southern Morocco. Leiden: Brill, 1999.

Entelis, John. Culture and Counterculture in Moroccan Politics. Boulder, Colo.: Westview Press, 1989.

Erikson, Kai. "A Comment on Disguised Observation in Sociology." Social Problems 14 (4) (1967): 366–73.

Erzini, Nadia. "Cultural Administration in French North Africa and the Growth of Islamic Art History." In Discovering Islamic Art: Scholars, Collectors and Collections, 1850–1950, ed. Stephen Vernoit, 71–84. London: I. B. Tauris, 2000.

Fitch, Nancy. "Mass Culture, Mass Parliamentary Politics, and Modern Anti-Semitism: The Dreyfus Affair in Rural France." American Historical Review 97 (1) (1992): 55–95.

Flamand, Pierre. Diaspora en terre d'Islam: Les communautés Israélites du sud marocain. Casablanca: Imprimeries Reunites, 1959.

Foucault, Michel. The Archaeology of Knowledge. London: Tavistock, 1986.

———. Discipline and Punish: The Birth of the Prison, trans. Sheridan Alan. New York: Vintage Books, 1979.

Fremantle, Anne. Desert Calling: The Life of Charles de Foucauld. New York: Holt, 1949.

Gallard, H. "Le sionisme et la question juive en Afrique du Nord." Renseignements Coloniaux, January–February 1918, 3–7.

Gates, H. L. "Thirteen Ways of Looking at a Black Man." *New Yorker Magazine*, October, 23, 1995.

Gaudio, A. *Guerres et paix au Maroc (Reportages: 1950–1990)*. Paris: Éditions Karthala, 1991.

Gavish, Haya. *Unwitting Zionists: The Jewish Community of Zakho in Iraqi Kurdistan*. Detroit: Wayne State University Press, 2010.

Geertz, Clifford. "Suq: The Bazaar Economy in Sefrou." In *Meaning and Order in Moroccan Society: Three Essays in Cultural Analysis*, ed. Hildred Geertz, Clifford Geertz, and Lawrence Rosen, 123–310. Cambridge: Cambridge University Press, 1979.

Gellner, Ernest. *Nation and Nationalism*. Oxford: Blackwell, 1983.

———. *Plough, Sword, and Book: The Structure of Human History*. London: Collins Harvill, 1988.

Gershovish, Moshe. *French Military Rule in Morocco: Colonialism and Its Consequences*. New York: Frank Cass, 2000.

Ghallab, Said. "Les Juifs vont en enfer." *Les Temps modernes*, April 1965, 2247–51.

Ghosh, Anjan. "Symbolic Speech: Towards an Anthropology of Gossip." *Journal of the Indian Anthropological Society* 31 (1996): 251–56.

Giddens, Anthony. "Risk and Responsibility." *Modern Law Review* 62 (1) (1999): 1–10.

Gilman, S. "Introduction: The Frontier as a Model for Jewish History." In *Jewries at the Frontier: Accommodation, Identity, Conflict*, ed. S. L. Gilman and M. Shain, 1–25. Urbana: University of Illinois Press, 1999.

Gilmore, Perry, and David Smith. "Identity, Resistance and Resilience: Counter Narratives and Subaltern Voices in Alaskan Higher Education in 1991." In *Discourses in Search of Members: In Honor of Ron Scollon*, ed. D.C.S. Li, 103–35. Lanham, Md.: University Press of America, 2002.

Gluckman, Max. "Gossip and Scandal." *Current Anthropology* 4 (1963): 307–15.

Goidan, E. *Le sionisme au Maroc*. Rabat, 1948.

Goitein, S. D. "Jewish Education in Yemen as an Archetype of Traditional Jewish Education." In *Between Past and Future: Essays and Studies on Aspects of Immigrant Absorption in Israel*, ed. Carl Frankenstein, 109–46. Henrietta Szold Foundation for Child and Youth Welfare, 1953.

———. *Jews and Arabs: Their Contacts Through the Ages*. New York: Schocken, 1974.

———. "The Jews of Yemen." *Religion in the Middle East: Three Religions in Concord and Conflict*, ed. A. J. Arberry, 226–38. Cambridge: Cambridge University Press, 1996.

———. *Letters of Medieval Jewish Traders*. Princeton, N.J.: Princeton University Press, 1973.

———. *A Mediterranean Society: The Jewish Communities of the Arab World as Portrayed in the Documents of the Cairo Geniza*. Berkeley: University of California Press, 1967.

Goldberg, H. E. *Cave Dwellers and Citrus Growers: A Jewish Community in Libya and Israel*. Cambridge: Cambridge University Press, 1972.

———. "The Mellahs of Southern Morocco: Report of a Survey." *Maghreb Review* 8 (3–4) (1983): 61–69.

Goldenberg, Alfred. "A Teacher in the Bled." *Alliance Review* 46 (1975): 32.

Gorrée, Georges. *Sur les traces de Père Charles de Foucauld*. Paris: Vieux Colombier, 1953.

Gottreich, Emily. *The Mellah of Marrakesh: Jewish and Muslim Space in Morocco's Red City*. Bloomington: Indiana University Press, 2007.

———. "On the Origins of the Mellah of Marrakesh." *International Journal of Middle Eastern Studies* 35 (2003): 237–305.

———. "Rethinking the Islamic City from the Perspective of the Jewish Space." *Jewish Social Studies* 11 (1) (2004): 118–46.

Gur-Ze'ev, Ilan, and Ilan Pappé. "Beyond the Destruction of the Other's Collective Memory: Blueprints for a Palestinian/Israeli Dialogue." *Theory, Culture and Society* 20 (1) (2003): 93–108.

Habermas, Jürgen. *The Structural Transformation of the Public Sphere: An Inquiry into a Category of Bourgeois Society*, trans. Thomas Berger. Cambridge, Mass.: MIT Press, 1991.

Haidt, Elizabeth. *Embodying Enlightenment: Knowing the Body in Eighteenth-Century Spanish Literature and Culture*. New York: St. Martin's Press, 1998.

Halbwachs, Maurice. *On Collective Memory*. Chicago: University of Chicago Press, 1992 [1925].

Hammoudi, Abdellah. *Master and Disciple: The Cultural Foundations of Moroccan Authoritarianism in Comparative Perspectives*. Chicago: University of Chicago Press, 1997.

———. *The Victim and Its Masks: An Essay on Sacrifice and Masquerade in the Maghreb*, trans. Paula Wissing. Chicago: University of Chicago Press, 1993.

Handelman, Don. "Gossip in Encounters: The Transmission of Information in a Bounded Social Setting." *Man* 8 (1973): 210–27.

Hannerz, Ulf. "Gossip, Networks and Culture in a Black American Ghetto." *Ethnos* 32 (1967): 35–60.

Harrus, Elias. *L'Alliance en action: Les écoles de l'Alliance israélite universelle dans l'Empire du Maroc (1862–1912)*. Paris: Nadir, 2001.

Hatimi, Mohamed. "Al-jama'at al-yahudiyya al-maghribiyya wa al-khiyar al-sa'b bayna nida' al-sahyuniyya wa rihan al-maghrib al-mustaqil 1947–1961." Ph.D. dissertation, University Sidi Muhammad ben Abdallah (Fez, Morocco), 2007.

Hess, Jean. *Israel au Maroc*. Paris: J. Bosc, 1907.

Hill, Jane. "Finding Culture in Narrative." In *Finding Culture in Talk: A Collection of Methods*, ed. Naomi Quinn, 157–202. New York: Palgrave Macmillan, 2005.

———. "Syncretism." *Journal of Linguistic Anthropology* 9 (1–2) (2000): 244–46.

———. "The Voices of Don Gabriel: Responsibility and Self in a Modern Mexicano Narrative." In *The Dialogic Emergence of Culture*, ed. Dennis Tedlock and Bruce Mannheim, 97–147. Urbana: University of Illinois Press, 1995.

Hirschberg, H. Z. *A History of the Jews in North Africa*. Leiden: Brill, 1974.

———. "Jews and Jewish Affairs in the Relations Between Great Britain and Morocco in the 18th Century." In *Essays Presented to Chief Rabbi Israel Brodie on the Occasion of His Seventieth Birthday*, vol. 1, ed. H. J. Zimmels, J. Rabbinowitz, and I. Finestein, 153–81. London: Soncino Press, 1967.

———. "The Problem of the Judaized Berbers." *Journal of African History* 4 (3) (1963): 323–39.

Hobsbawm, E. "Introduction: Inventing Traditions." In *The Invention of Tradition*, ed. E. Hobsbawm and T. O. Ranger, 1–14. Cambridge: Cambridge University Press, 1983.

Hunwick, John. *Jews of a Saharan Oasis*. Princeton, N. J.: Marcus Wiener, 2005.

———. "Al-Maghili and the Jews of Tuwat: The Demise of a Community." *Studia Islamica* 61 (1985): 155–83.

———. "The Rights of Dhimmis to Maintain a Place of Worship: A 15th Century Fatwa from Tlemcen." *Al-Qantara* 12 (1991): 133–55.

———. *Shari'a in Songhay: The Replies of Al-Maghili to the Questions of Askia al-Hajj Muhammad*. Oxford: Oxford University Press, 1985.

———. *Timbuktu and the Songhay Empire. Al-Sa'di's Tarikh al-Sudan Down to 1613 and Other Contemporary Documents*. Leiden: Brill, 1999.

Ibn Qayyim al-Jawziyya, Muhammad ibn Abi Bakr al-Zar'i. *Ahkam ahl al-dhimma*. Beirut: Dar al-Kutub al-'Ilmiyya, 1995.

Ibn Rushd [Averroës]. *The Distinguished Jurist's Primer: A Translation of Bidayat Al-Mujtahid*, trans. Imran Ahsan Khan Nyazee. 2 vols. Reading, UK: Garnet Publishing Limited, 1996.

Ihrai-Aouchar, Amina. "La presse marocaine d'opposition au protectorat (1933–1956)." *Hespéris-Tamuda*, 1982: 333–47.

Jackson, James Grey. *An Account of the Empire of Morocco and the Districts of Sus and Tafilelt*. London: Frank Cass & Co., 1968 [1809].

———. *An Account of Timbuctoo and Housa Territories in the Interior of Africa*. London: Frank Cass & Co., 1967 [1820].

Jacques-Meunié, D. "Hiérarchie sociale au Maroc pre-saharien." *Hésperis* 45 (1958): 239–70.

———. *Le Maroc saharien des origines au XVIème siècle*. 2 vols. Paris: Librairie Klincksieck, 1982.

Jenkins, Henry. *Convergence Culture: Where Old and New Media Collide*. New York: New York University Press, 2006.

Justinard, Léopold Victor. *Le Caid Goundafi: Un grand chef berbère*. Éditions Atlantides, 1951.

Kafas, Samir. "De l'origine de 'idée de musée au Maroc." In *Le Patrimoine culturel marocain*, ed. Caroline Gaultier-Kurhan, 39–55. Paris: Maisonneuve et Larose, 2003.

Kapchan, Deborah. "The Promise of Sonic Translation: Performing the Festive Sacred in Morocco." *American Anthropologist* 110 (2008): 467–83.

Katz, J. *Out of the Ghetto: The Social Background of Jewish Emancipation, 1770–1870*. Cambridge, Mass.: Harvard University Press, 1973.

Kenbib, Mohammed. "Changing Aspects of State and Society in 19th century Morocco." In *The Moroccan State in Historical Perspective 1850–1985*, ed. A. Doumou, 11–27. Dakar: CODESIRA, 1990.

———. *Juifs et musulmans au Maroc 1859–1948: Contribution à l'histoire des relations inter-communautaires en terre d'Islam*. Rabat: Publications de la Faculté des Lettres et des Sciences Humaines, 1994.

Khoury-Machool, Makram. "Cyber Resistance: Palestinian Youth and Emerging Internet Culture." In *Being Young and Muslim: New Cultural Politics in the Global South and North*, ed. Asef Bayat and Linda Herrera, 113–24. Oxford: Oxford University Press, 2010.

Kochman, T. "The Boundary Between Play and Non-Play in Black Duelling." *Language in Society* 12 (1983): 329–37.

Kosansky, Oren. "All Dear unto God: Saints, Pilgrimage and Textual Practice in Jewish Morocco." Ph.D. dissertation, University of Michigan, 2003.

———. "Tourism, Charity, and Profit: The Movement of Money in Moroccan Jewish Pilgrimage." *Cultural Anthropology* 17 (3) (2002): 359–400.

Kosansky, Oren, and Aomar Boum. "The Jewish Question in Postcolonial Moroccan Cinema." *International Journal of Middle Eastern Studies* 44 (2) (2012): 421–42.

Kreps, Christina. "Non-Western Models of Museums and Curation in Cross-Cultural Perspective." In *A Companion to Museum Studies*, ed. Sharon Mcdonald, 457–72. Oxford: Blackwell, 2006.

Labov, W. *Language in the Inner City: Studies in the Black English Vernacular*. Philadelphia: University of Pennsylvania Press, 1972.

———. "Rules for Ritual Insults." In *Rappin' and Stylin' Out: Communication in Urban Black America*, ed. T. Kochman, 265–314. Champaign: University of Illinois Press, 1972.

———. *Sociolinguistic Patterns*. Philadelphia: University of Pennsylvania Press, 1972.

Lacan, Jacques. *The Seminar of Jacques Lacan*, trans. Sylvana Tomaselli. Cambridge: Cambridge University Press, 1988.

Lagardère, Vincent. *Histoire et société en occident musulman au moyen âge: Analyse du mi'yar al-wansharisi*. Madrid: Casa de Velázquez, 1995.

Langellier, Kristin. "Personal Narratives: Perspectives on Theory and Research." *Text and Performance Quarterly* 9 (4) (1989): 243–76.

Larhmaid, Abdellah. "Jama'at yahud Sus: al-majal wa al-tamathulat al-ijtima'iyya wa al-siyyasiyya, 1860–1960." Ph.D. dissertation, University of Mohammed V (Rabat), 2002.

———. "Jewish Identity and Land Ownership in the Sous Region of Morocco." In *Jewish Culture and Society in North Africa*, ed. Emily Benichou Gottreich and Daniel J. Schroeter, 59–72. Bloomington: Indiana University Press, 2011.

Laskier, Michael. *The Alliance Israélite Universelle and the Jewish Communities of Morocco: 1862–1962*. Albany: State University of New York Press, 1983.

———. "Aspects of Change and Modernization: The Jewish Communities of Morocco's Bled." In *Communautés juives des marges Sahariennes du Maghreb*, ed. Michel Abitbol, 329–64. Jerusalem: Institut Ben-Zvi pour la recherche sur les communautés juives d'Orient, 1982.

———. "The Evolution of Zionist Activity in the Jewish Communities of Morocco, Tunisia and Algeria: 1897–1947." *Studies in Zionism* 4 (2) (1983): 205–36.

———. "The Instability of the Moroccan Jewry and the Moroccan Press in the First Decade After Independence." *Jewish History* 1 (1) (1986): 39–54.

———. *Israel and the Maghreb: From Statehood to Oslo*. Gainesville: University of Florida Press, 2004.

———. *North African Jewry in the Twentieth Century: The Jews of Morocco, Tunisia, and Algeria*. New York: New York University Press, 1994.

———. "Zionism and the Jewish Communities of Morocco." *Studies in Zionism* 6 (1) (1985): 119–38.

Lenz, Oskar. *Timbouctou: Voyage au Maroc, au Sahara et au Soudan*, trans. Pierre Lehautcourt. Paris: Hachette, 1886–1887.

Leveau, Rémy. "Youth Culture and Islamism in the Middle East." In *The Islamist Dilemma: The Political Role of Islamist Movements in the Contemporary Arab World*, ed. Laura Guazzone, 265–86. Reading, Berkshire: Ithaca Press, 1995.

Levtzion, Nahum. "The Jews of Sijilmasa and the Saharan Trade." In *Communautes Juives des marges Saharaiennes du Maghreb*, ed. Michel Abitbol, 253–64. Jerusalem: Institut Ben-Zvi pour la recherche sur les communautés juives d'Orient, 1982.

Levy, André. "A Community That Is Both a Center and Diaspora: Jews in Late Twentieth Century Morocco." In *Homelands and Diaspora: Holy Lands and Other Places*, ed. A. Levy and A. Weingrod, 68–96. Stanford, Calif.: Stanford University Press, 2005.

Levy, Simon. "Hara et mellah: Les mots, l'histoire et l'institution." In *Histoire et Linguistique*, ed. Abdelhadi Sebti, 41–50. Rabat: Publications de la Faculté des Lettres et des Sciences Humaines, Université Mohammed V, 1992.

———. *Yahud Magharibah man nahnu?* Al-dar al-bayda: Muassasat al-turath al-thaqafi al-yahudi al-maghribi, 2006.

Lipman, S., and V. D. Lipman. *The Century of Moses Montefiore.* Oxford: Oxford University Press, 1985.

Lorcin, Patricia. *Imperial Identities: Stereotyping, Prejudice and Race in Colonial Algeria.* London: I. B. Tauris Publishers, 1995.

Lydon, Ghislaine. *On Trans-Saharan Trails: Islamic Law, Trade Networks and Cross-Cultural Exchange in Nineteenth-Century Western Africa.* Cambridge: Cambridge University Press, 2009.

Maddy-Weitzman, Bruce. "Israel and Morocco: A Special Relationship." *Maghreb Review* 21 (1–2) (1996): 36–48.

———. "Morocco's Berbers and Israel." *Middle East Quarterly* 18 (1) (2011): 79–85.

Maghraoui, Driss. "Moroccan Colonial Soldiers: Between Selective Memory and Collective Memory." *Arab Studies Quarterly* 20 (1998): 21–42.

Malka, Victor. *La mémoire brisée des Juifs du Maroc.* Paris: Editions Entente, 1978.

Malt, Carol. "Women, Museums, and the Public Sphere." *Journal of Middle East Women's Studies* 2 (2) (2006): 115–36.

Mauny, R. "Le Judaïsme, les Juifs et l'Afrique occidentale." *Bulletin de l'Institut Français d'Afrique Noire* 11 (3–4) (1949): 354–78.

M'Barek, Z. "La desertion des soldats de l'armée française à l'armée de liberation du Maghreb (A.L.M.): Role militaire, impact psycho-politique (1955–1956)." *Revue Maroc-Europe: Histoire, Economies, Sociétés* 7 (1994): 235–71.

McKay, Donald Vernon. "Colonialism in the French Geographical Movement 1871–1881." *Geographical Review* 33 (2) (1943): 214–32.

Meijer, Roel. "Introduction." In *Alienation and Integration of Arab Youth: Between Family, State and Street,* ed. Roel Meijer, 1–14. Richmond, Surrey: Curzon, 2000.

Merad, Ali. *Christian Hermit in an Islamic World: A Muslim's View of Charles de Foucauld,* trans. Zoe Hersov. Mahwah, N.J.: Paulist Press, 1999.

Merry, Sally Engle. "Rethinking Gossip and Scandal." In *Toward a General Theory of Social Control,* ed. Donald Black, vol. 1, 271–302. New York: Academic Press, 1984.

Messick, Brinkley. *The Calligraphic State: Textual Domination and History in a Muslim Society.* Berkeley: University of California Press, 1993.

Meyers, Allan. "Patronage and Protection: The Status of Jew in Pre-colonial Morocco." In *Jewish Society in the Middle East: Community, Culture, and Authority,* ed. Deshen Schlomo and Walter P. Zenner, 85–104. Washington, D.C.: University Press of America, 1982.

Mezzine, Larbi. *Le Tafilalt: Contribution à l'histoire du Maroc aux XVIème et XVIIIème siècle.* Rabat: Publications de la Faculté des Lettres et des Sciences Humaines, 1987.

Miège, Jean Louis. *Le Maroc et l'Europe 1830–1894.* 4 vols. Rabat: Editions La Porte, 1989.

Miles, Matthew B., and A. Michael Huberman. *Qualitative Data Analysis: An Expanded Source Book*. Beverly Hills, Calif.: Sage, 1994.

Miller, Susan. "The Mellah of Fez: Reflections on the Spatial Turn in Moroccan Jewish History." In *Jewish Topographies; Visions of Space, Traditions of Place*, ed. A. Nocke, J. Brauch, and A. Lipphardt, 101–18. London: Ashgate, 2008.

———. "Les quartiers juifs de la Méditerranée et leur héritage architectural." In *Identités Sépharades et Modernité*, ed. J-C. Lasry, J. Lévy, and Y. Cohen, 47–60. Montreal: Presses de l'Université Laval, 2007.

Miller, Susan, and Mauro Bertagnin, eds. *The Architecture and Memory of the Minority Quarter in the Muslim Mediterranean City*. Cambridge, Mass.: Harvard University Press, 2010.

Montagne, Robert. *Les Berbères et le Makhzan dans le sud du Maroc: Essai sur la transformation politique des Berbères sédentaires (groupe Chleuh)*. Paris: L'Harmattan, 1930.

Monteil, V. "Choses et gens du Bani." *Hésperis* 33 (1946): 388–405.

Moore, Clement, and Arlie Hochshild. "Students Unions in North African Politics." *Daedalus* 97 (1) (1968): 21–50.

Morais, Henry Samuel. *The Daggatouns: A Tribe of Jewish Origin in the Desert of Sahara*. Philadelphia: Edward Sten & Co., 1882.

Murray, S. "Ritual and Personal Insults in Stigmatized Subcultures: Gay—Black—Jew." *Maledicta* 7 (1983): 189–211.

Ochs, Elinor, and Lisa Capps. *Living Narratives: Creating Lives in Everyday Narratives*. Cambridge, Mass.: Harvard University Press, 2001.

Ohayon, Jacques. "Souvenirs du Bled." In *Témoignages: Souvenirs et réflexions sur l'oeuvre de l'Alliance Israélite Universelle*, ed. David Bensoussan and Edmond El-Baz, 37–38. Montreal: Les Éditions du Lys, 2002.

Oliel, Jacob. *Les camps de Vichy: Maghreb-Sahara 1939–1945*. Montreal: Les Éditions du Lys, 2005.

———. *De Jérusalem à Tombouctou L'odyssée saharienne du rabbin Mardochée, 1826–1886*. Paris: Editions Olbia, 1998.

———. *Mardochée Aby Serour, 1826–1886: Rabbin, caravanier, guide au Sahara*. Paris: Éditions Élysée, 2010.

Oved, Georges. *La gauche française et le nationalisme marocain 1905–1955*. 2 vols. Paris: L'Harmattan, 1984.

Park, Thomas. "Essaouira: The Formation of a Native Elite 1940–1980." *African Studies Review* 31 (3) (1988): 111–32.

Park, Thomas, and Aomar Boum. *Historical Dictionary of Morocco*. Lanham, Md.: Scarecrow Press, 2006.

Parsons, F. V. *The Origins of the Morocco Question, 1880–1900*. London: Duckworth, 1976.

Payne, Rhys. "Economic Crisis and Policy Reform in the 1980s." In *Polity and Society in Contemporary North Africa*, ed. William Zartman and William Habeeb, 148–55. Boulder, Colo.: Westview Press, 1993.

Perkins, Kenneth. "Recent Historiography of the Colonial Period in North Africa: The 'Copernican Revolution' and Beyond." In *The Maghrib in Question: Essays in History and Historiography*, ed. Michel Le Gall and Kenneth Perkins, 121–35. Austin: University of Texas Press, 1997.

Pierrehumbert, Janet. "Exemplar Dynamics: Word Frequency, Lenition and Contrast." In *Frequency Effects and the Emergence of Lexical Structure*, ed. J. Bybee and P. Hopper, 137–57. Amsterdam: John Benjamins, 2001.

Preminger, Marion Mill. *The Sands of Tamanrasset: The Story of Charles de Foucauld*. New York: Hawthorn Books, 1961.

Quinn, Naomi, ed. *Finding Culture in Talk: A Collection of Methods*. New York: Palgrave Macmillan, 2005.

Ray, J. "Beyond Tolerance and Persecution: Reassessing Our Approach to Medieval *Convivencia*." *Jewish Social Studies* 11 (2006): 1–18.

Rézette, Robert. *Les partis politiques marocaines*. Paris: Librairie Armand Colin, 1955.

Rharib, Sakina. "Taking Stock of Moroccan Museums." *Museum International* 58 (1–2) (2006): 229–30.

Romanelli, S. *Travail in an Arab Land*, trans. Yedida K. Stillman and Norman A. Stillman. Tuscaloosa: University of Alabama Press, 1989 [1792].

Rosenberger, Bernard. "Tamdult, cité minière et caravanière presaharienne, IXè–XIVè siècles." *Hésperis-Tamuda* 11 (1970): 103–41.

Rosenberger, Bernard, and Hamid Triki. "Famines et épidémies au Maroc au XVIè–XVIIIè siècles." *Hésperis-Tamuda* 14 (1973): 109–75.

———. "Famines et épidémies au Maroc au XVIè–XVIIIè siècles." *Hésperis-Tamuda* 15 (1974): 5–92.

Rosenthal, Gabriele. "Reconsideration of Life Stories: Principles of Selection in Generating Stories for Narrative Interviews." In *The Narrative Study of Lives*, vol. 1 (1), ed. Ruthellen Josselson and Amia Lieblich, 59–91. Newbury Park, Calif.: Sage, 1993.

Roth, C. "The Amazing Clan of Buzaglo." *Transactions of the Jewish Historical Society of England* 23 (1971): 11–22.

Ryder, N. B. "The Cohort as a Concept in the Study of Social Change." *American Sociological Review* 30 (1965): 843–61.

Sagarin, Edward. "The Research Setting and the Right Not to Be Researched." *Social Problems* 21 (1) (1973): 52–64.

Said, Edward. "Israel-Palestine: A Third Way." *Le Monde Diplomatique*, September 7, 1998, 6.

Schroeter, Daniel. "Anglo-Jewry and Essaouira (Mogador): 1860–1900. The Social

Implications of Philanthropy." *Transactions of the Jewish Historical Society of England* 28 (1984): 60–88.

———. "La découverte des juifs berbères." In *Relations judéo-musulmanes au Maroc: Perceptions et réalités*, ed. Michel Abitbol, 169–87. Paris: Editions Stavit, 1997.

———. "A Different Road to Modernity: Jewish Identity in the Arab World." In *Diasporas and Exiles: Varieties of Jewish Identity*, ed. Howard Wettstein, 150–63. Berkeley: University of California Press, 2002.

———. "In Search of Jewish Farmers: Jews, Agriculture, and the Land in Rural Morocco." In *The Divergence of Judaism and Islam*, ed. Michael M. Laskier and Yaacov Lev, 143–59. Gainesville: University Press of Florida, 2011.

———. "Jewish Communities of Morocco: History and Identity." In *Morocco: Jews and Art in a Muslim Land*, ed. Vivian B. Mann, 27–54. London: Merrill Publishers Limited, 2000.

———. "The Jewish Quarter and the Moroccan City." In *New Horizons in Sephardic Studies*, ed. George K. Zucker and Yedida K. Stillman, 67–81. Albany: State University of New York Press, 1993.

———. "The Jews of Essaouira (Mogador) and the Trade of Southern Morocco." In *Communautés juives des marges sahariennes du Maghreb*, ed. Michel Abitbol, 365–90. Jerusalem: Institut Ben-Zvi pour la recherche sur les communautés juives d'Orient, 1982.

———. *Merchants of Essaouira: Urban Society and Imperialism in Southwestern Morocco, 1844–1886*. Cambridge: Cambridge University Press, 1988.

———. "Morocco, England, and the End of the Sephardic World Order." In *From Iberia to Diaspora: Studies in Sephardic History and Culture*, ed. Yedida K. Stillman and A. Stillman Norman, 86–101. Leiden: Brill, 1999.

———. "Orientalism and the Jews of the Mediterranean." *Journal of Mediterranean Studies* 4 (2) (1994): 183–96.

———. "Royal Power and the Economy in Pre-colonial Morocco: Jews and the Legitimation of Foreign Trade." In *The Shadow of the Sultan: Culture, Power and Politics in Morocco*, ed. Rahma Bourqia and Susan G. Miller, 74–102. Cambridge, Mass.: Harvard University Press, 1999.

———. *The Sultan's Jew: Morocco and the Sephardi World*. Stanford, Calif.: Stanford University Press, 2002.

———. "Trade as a Mediator in Muslim-Jewish Relations: Southwestern Morocco in the Nineteenth Century." In *Jews Among Arabs: Contacts and Boundaries*, ed. Mark R. Cohen and Abraham L. Udovitch, 113–40. Princeton, N.J.: Darwin Press, 1989.

Schroeter, Daniel, and Joseph Chetrit. "Emancipation and Its Discontents: Jews at the Formative Period of Colonial Rule in Morocco." *Jewish Social Studies* 13 (1) (2006): 170–206.

Scott, James C. *Weapons of the Weak: Everyday Forms of Resistance*. New Haven, Conn.: Yale University Press, 1985.

Sémach, Y. D. "Charles de Foucauld et les juifs marocains." *Bulletin de l'Institut des Hautes Etudes Marocaines* (1936): 264–84.

———. "Un rabbin voyageur marocain Mardochée Aby Serour." *Hésperis* 8 (1928): 385–99.

Serfaty, Abraham. *Dans les prisons du roi, écrits de Kenitra sur le Maroc*. Paris: Messidor Editions Sociales, 1992.

———. *Écrits de prison sur la Palestine*. Paris: Arcantère, 1992.

———. *Lutte antisioniste et révolution arabe*. Paris: Quatre Vents, 1997.

———. *Le Maroc, du noir au gris*. Paris: Syllepse, 1998.

Serfaty, Abraham, and Mikhaël El Baz. *L'insoumis: Juifs, marocains et rebelles*. Paris: Desclée de Brouwer, 2001.

Shannon, J. H. "Performing al-Andalus, Remembering al-Andalus: Mediterranean Soundings from Mashriq and Maghrib." *Journal of American Folklore* 120 (2007): 308–34.

Shatzmiller, Maya. *Nationalism and Minority Identities in Islamic Societies*. Montreal: McGill-Queen's University Press, 2005.

Shokeid, Moshe. "Jewish Existence in a Berber Environment." In *Jewish Society in the Middle East: Community, Culture, and Authority*, ed. Deshen Schlomo and Walter P. Zenner, 105–22. Washington, D.C.: University Press of America, 1978.

Silverstein, Paul. "Masquerade Politics: Race, Islam and the Scale of Amazigh Activism in Southeastern Morocco." *Nations and Nationalism* 17 (1) (2011): 65–84.

Skinner, William. "Mobility Strategy in Late Imperial China: A Regional Systems Analysis." In *Regional Economic Analysis*, vol. 1, ed. Carol Smith, 327–64. New York: Academic Press, 1976.

Slouschz, N. "La colonie des maghrabim en Palestine ses origins et son état actuel." *Archives Marocaines* 2 (1905): 239–56.

———. *Travels in North Africa*. Philadelphia: Jewish Publication Society of America, 1927.

Smith, Carol. "How Marketing Systems Affect Economic Opportunity in Agrarian Societies." In *Peasant Livelihoods: Studies in Economic Anthropology and Cultural Ecology*, ed. Rhoda Halperin and James Dow, 117–46. New York: St. Martin's Press, 1977.

Soifer, M. "Beyond Convivencia: Critical Reflections on the Historiography of Interfaith Relations in Christian Spain." *Journal of Medieval Iberian Studies* 1 (2009): 19–35.

Stein, Sarah. *Plumes: Ostrich Feathers, Jews, and a Lost World of Global Commerce*. New Haven, Conn.: Yale University Press, 2008.

Stillman, Norman. *The Jews of the Arab Lands: A History and Source Book*. Philadelphia: Jewish Publication Society of America, 1979.

Tawfiq, Ahmad. *Al-Mujtama' al-maghribi fi al-qarn al-tasi' 'Ashar (Inultan, 1850–1912)*. Casablanca: Matba'at al-Najah al-Jadida, 1983.

Tessler, Mark. "Alienation and Urban Youth." In *Polity and Society in Contemporary North Africa*, ed. William Zartman and William Habeeb, 71–101. Boulder, Colo.: Westview Press, 1993.

Tonkin, Elizabeth. *Narrating Our Pasts: The Social Construction of Oral History*. New York: Cambridge University Press, 1992.

Trevisan Semi, Emanuela, and Hanane Sekkat Hatimi. *Mémoire et representations des Juifs au Maroc: Les voisins absents de Meknès*. Paris: Publisud, 2011.

Tsur, Yaron. "The Religious Factor in the Encounter Between Zionism and the Rural Atlas Jews." In *Zionism and Religion*, ed. S. Almog, J. Reinharz, and A. Shapira, 312–29. Hanover, N.H.: Brandeis University Press, 1998.

Turner, Victor. *Celebration: Studies in Festivity and Ritual*. Washington, D.C.: Smithsonian Institution Press, 1982.

Udovitch, Abraham L. "At the Origins of the Western Commenda: Islam, Israel, Byzantium?" *Speculum* 37 (2) (1962): 198–207.

———. *Partnership and Profit in Medieval Islam*. Princeton, N.J.: Princeton University Press, 1970.

Udovitch, Abraham, and Lucette Valensi. *The Last Arab Jews: The Communities of Jerba Tunisia*. New York: Harwood, 1984.

Van Leeuwen, Richard. "The Lost Heritage: Generation Conflicts in Four Arabic Novels." In *Alienation or Integration of Arab Between Family, State and Street*, ed. Roel Meijer, 189–206. Richmond, Surrey: Curzon, 2000.

Van Paassen, Pierre. *Days of Our Years*. New York: Dial Press, 1940.

———. *The Forgotten Ally*. New York: Dial Press, 1943.

———. *Jerusalem Calling!* New York: Dial Press, 1950.

———. *Palestine: Land of Israel*. Chicago: Ziff-Davis, 1948.

Weinreich, Uriel, William Labov, and Marvin Herzog. "Empirical Foundations for a Theory of Language Change." In *Directions for Historical Linguistics*, ed. Winfred P. Lehmann and Yakov Malkiel, 95–188. Austin: University of Texas Press, 1968.

Westermarck, Edward. *Ritual and Belief in Morocco*. 2 vols. London: Macmillan, 1968.

Wettstein, H., ed. *Diasporas and Exiles: Varieties of Jewish Identity*. Berkeley: University of California Press, 2002.

Williams, J. J. *Hebrewisms of West Africa: From the Nile to Niger with the Jews*. New York: Dial Press, 1930.

Wilson, Stephen. *Ideology and Experience: Antisemitism in France at the Time of the Dreyfus Affair*. Rutherford, N.J.: Fairleigh Dickinson University Press, 1982.

Wolf, K. B. "Convivencia in Medieval Spain: A Brief History of an Idea." *Religion Compass* 3 (2009): 72–85.

Yassine, Abdessalam. *Winning the Modern World for Islam*, trans. Martin Jenni. Iowa City, Iowa: Justice and Spirituality Publishing, 2000.

Yehuda, Z. "The Place of Aliyah in Moroccan Jewry's Conception of Zionism." *Studies in Zionism* 6 (2) (1985): 199–210.

———. "Zionist Activity in Southern Morocco: 1919–1923." *Revue des Études Juives* 119 (4) (1985): 363–68.

Zafrani, Haïm. Deux *mille ans de vie juive au Maroc: Histoire et culture, religion et maggie.* Casablanca: Eddif, 1998.

———. *Pédagogie juive en terre d'Islam. L'enseignement traditionnel de l'Hébreu et du Judaïsme au Maroc.* Paris: Adrien Maisonneuve, 1969.

Index